"A fascinating and very poignant story of professionalism, dedication, and survival! I understand Joanie Schirm's efforts to preserve the details of her father's saga."

—LEE R. HILTZIK, PhD, assistant director and head of donor relations and collection development at the Rockefeller Archive Center, New York

---

"Out of the emotional landscape of her father's experiences comes an extraordinary story of hope, passionately written. . . . At the heart of this book is the message in one letter that changed the way Dr. Holzer lived his life. This book is a labor of love for a daughter who tells a compelling story of a father who lived an exemplary life."

—BILL NELSON, U.S. senator, Florida

"Schirm's power as a writer lies in her gift of crystalline focus. Her family story is one of grace in the face of universal struggle: full of awe, dappled synchronicities, and complicated life 'happenings' that touch one's core. It is a gift for the next generation and the next."

—PAT WILLIAMS, senior vice president of the Orlando Magic and author of *Coach Wooden's Forgotten Teams*

"I sometimes wonder what I would have done. . . . Would I have seen that the only real choice for survival was to leave the people I loved and everything I knew? Or would I have stayed, confident (wrongly so) that things would get better? Thank you for touching my heart and moving me to think about questions like that."

—LAURIE LEE, former deputy director of Just Read, Florida! Florida Department of Education

"Through her books and the meticulous research that supports them, Joanie has brought to light the remarkable Holocaust story of her father, Oswald Holzer, and his friends as they fled occupied Czechoslovakia."

—MITCHELL BLOOMER, resource teacher at the Holocaust Memorial Resource and Education Center of Florida

---

"The Oswald A. Holzer archival collection is one of the most substantive and comprehensive collections I've reviewed about a particular individual's experience during the time period relating to the Nazi occupation of Czechoslovakia. From this rich information, author Joanie Schirm has created a story that brings this tumultuous past to life again and today echoes loudly as a warning we must heed."

—ALLAN J. STYPECK, accredited senior appraiser, American Society of Appraisers

---

"*My Dear Boy*, which shares an incredible story through voices of seventy-year-old letters, including a father's timeless message, will bring our world more peace and tolerance."

—DR. NAVID VAHIDI, member of the Orlando Baha'i community

MY DEAR BOY

MY DEAR BOY

A World War II Story of Escape, Exile, and Revelation

JOANIE HOLZER SCHIRM

Potomac Books

An imprint of the University of Nebraska Press

Epigraph illustration: Chinese man on donkey, 1940. Caricature by Oswald "Valdik" Holzer.

Library of Congress Cataloging-in-Publication Data
Names: Schirm, Joanie Holzer, author.
Title: My dear boy: a World War II story of escape, exile, and revelation / Joanie Holzer Schrim.
Description: Lincoln: Potomac Books, an imprint of the University of Nebraska Press, [2019] | Includes index.
Identifiers: LCCN 2018028078
ISBN 9781640120723 (cloth: alk. paper)
ISBN 9781640121713 (epub)
ISBN 9781640121720 (mobi)
ISBN 9781640121737 (pdf)
Subjects: LCSH: Holzer, Oswald A., 1911–2000. | Jews—Czech Republic—Benešov (Okres)—Biography. | Jewish refugees—China—Shanghai—Biography. | Jews, Czech—China—Shanghai—Biography. | Benešov (Czech Republic: Okres)—Biography.
Classification: LCC DS135.C97 H657 2019 | DDC 940.53/18092 [B]—dc23 LC record available at https://lccn.loc.gov/2018028078

Set in Adobe Caslon by Mikala R. Kolander.
Designed by Roger Buchholz.

One day I will write a book about people and places I've seen.
I might begin with a story about real pirates, a sea-dog from Shantung,
and an undercover photographer for *Life* magazine. I'll continue with a
quizzical tale about a farting missionary, a charming Grandpa who spoke
Chinese to me, to which I responded in Czech in order to call attention
to his oversight. I'll describe missionary ladies over the age of sixty
who with their constricted lips look like industrial teachers and about the
Chinese and Japanese cruel warfare with travel in blacked out trains. All
these things I went through in the past two months. It was
life so colorful I could never imagine it could be so.

—Oswald "Valdik" Holzer, md, Pingting Hsien,
Shansi (Shanxi) Province in North China, to his cousin Hana
Winternitz in Great Britain—Refugees from their Nazi-occupied
Czech homeland, March 8, 1940

CONTENTS

ILLUSTRATIONS

INTRODUCTION

How Emptying Boxes Filled My Life

Hopefully, education and knowledge of history linked together
with pure compassion and humanity will let us recognize the origins of
old-new dangers and tie down the demons of hatred and evil
before they grow to overcome us again.

—VÁCLAV HAVEL, Czechoslovakia's first postcommunist president
and the first president of the Czech Republic

T hey met in Peking (Beijing), China, in 1940.[1] She was a
vivacious young American teacher returning to the Christian mission where she'd been born. He was a Czech Jewish doctor who'd fled the Nazis and taken refuge in China. They
fell in love and married five weeks later, near the steps of Peking's
Temple of Heaven, where the Taoists believe heaven and earth
intersect.

They were Ruth and Oswald "Valdik" Holzer; they were my
parents.

The culmination of their story was as romantic as the beginning. They shared their love, their lives, and their obituary. After
nearly sixty years together, they died within forty-eight hours of
each other—two wings of the same rare bird. Ruth went first, one
hour after midnight at the turn of the twenty-first century, and
Valdik followed on January 3, 2000.

1. Chinese lacquer box with letters from Valdik Holzer's collection.

I thought I knew everything about them, especially my father—his Bohemian past transformed into an American dream.[2] That was, until I discovered the contents of two red lacquered Chinese boxes.

A week or so after my parents' joint memorial service, my siblings, Tom and Pat, and I walked into their Florida beachside condo. It looked as if they had stepped out to visit a friend—water glasses half-full in the sink, bills in the mailbox, the refrigerator filled with my father's collection of specialty mustards and some prime stinky Limburger cheese. The odor brought to mind being in a restaurant with my dad years earlier. When a fly landed on some beer cheese and we kids reacted in disgust, my father had grinned and announced, "It's ready." As I closed the refrigerator, I pictured his gray eyes twinkling and his knowing smile.

Despite the evidence of two lives ended mid-gesture, the house, steeped in memories of travel to exotic places, was orderly, except for my father's study. That room had remained a mess for many years, a rare sore spot between our parents. It was crammed with collections untouched for the two decades my parents lived in the condo: canes, wooden pipes, magazines, coins, stamps, books, and heaps of papers. Tom, Pat, and I agreed to tackle that room first.

We gathered at the rosewood dining room table, clearing space amid unread mail to be able to put down our glasses of iced tea. So many memories had begun here—Thanksgiving and Christmas dinners reciting our family traditional Chinese prayer, birthday parties. It was strange to be there without our parents, but I swear the bouquet of jasmine and lily of my mother's Chanel No. 5 lingered. My siblings and I reminisced about the memorial service, agreeing the joyful ceremony had exceeded our expectations. Our parents would have approved.

Then we fell silent until Pat brought us back to the task at hand, asking, "Where do we start?"

"With the Chinese red lacquered boxes." Tom laughed.

Pat and I joined in. My brother had piqued our curiosity for what had always been just out of reach. Those two boxes, decorated with scenes of a sword fight against a backdrop of trees and mountains, had been on the periphery of our lives since we were children. They had been kept for decades in our parents' bedroom in our family home on the Indian River, always positioned beyond a child's grasp. Although they were constants in our memories, we had never looked inside.

Climbing on a footstool, Tom retrieved the first box from a bookshelf. He carried it to the dining room table as if it were the golden chalice. As he unhooked the latch, we gasped in unison. Inside, slightly curved to fit the container, was a huge collection of old letters. Some were on yellowed onionskin, others on heavy linen paper; all appeared as if they might crumble if we were careless. Tom lifted the bundle and placed it on the table. The first letter was typewritten in English on four five-by-seven-inch pages in Courier font.

Tom handed me the first letter. As if left there for the three of us to find precisely at that moment, it was the original version of my parents' "meeting story" sent in 1940 from our mother in China to her former missionary parents, Horace and Emma Lequear, in Pennsylvania.

College of Chinese Studies . . . Sept. 28 . . .

Dearest family . . .

By the time that you receive this letter it will be old news . . .
for things are happening so fast around here that I have
hardly had time to breathe . . . This time next month I will be
Mrs. Holzer . . . the wife of a former Czechoslovakian army
surgeon . . . and to think that when I see you again I may
present you with a family . . . Now don't faint or be afraid that
I am doing things too fast . . . You know what I told you, Mom,
that when I got married it would be fast . . . well . . . it is true.

We have known each other for eight days to be exact . . .
He is dark, has black hair and gray eyes . . . has a winning
personality . . . five-feet eleven tall . . . weighs about 186

pounds . . . or maybe less . . . he isn't sure . . . anyway it is distributed well . . . ha ha. He is 29 years old and more fun than a barrel of monkeys . . . which you knew would be true . . . and the rest of it is that I cannot believe that it is true.

We will be married on the 19th of October . . . at eleven o'clock in the morning . . . and listen to this . . . it is my idea and I am asking for advice from everyone so that it will be thought of all right . . . and that is that we be married on the steps of the Temple of Heaven here in Peking . . . Everyone that I have asked so far has thought it the most unique idea that they had ever heard . . . and think what fun it will be for our children to say that we were married at a place like that.

When I'd finished reading the letter aloud, my brother, sister, and I sat motionless. Raw with grief, we'd been transported in time to before we even existed: "and think what fun it will be for our children to say that we were married at a place like that." Tears streamed down our faces as our mother's heart was spelled out with red highlights. I had no doubt that these words of hope and passion were stored in the Chinese lacquered boxes on purpose.

That was the first of many surprises we received following our parents' deaths. In that red box were about fifty more letters dated 1939 to 1943, mostly handwritten in Czech on onionskin paper. I would have lingered over each mysterious word on each fragile page, but none of us spoke or read Czech, our father's native tongue. We had too much to do to settle the estate. Reluctantly, Tom, Pat, and I turned our attention to Dad's study and its cabinets full of papers, books, records, pipes and tobacco, slide albums, and old magazines. At first we didn't find anything of significance, so we rushed through it, hoping to get some trash out the door.

While sorting through papers, I came across an old Czech menu covered with a patina of dust. The picture on the cover was the beautiful Prague Castle, one of my favorite places in the world. I smiled as I admired how the menu had earned a place of honor there on a shelf, where it had sat for a decade without being disturbed. Opening it, I found two dark pieces of paper with fancy white Gothic lettering. They appeared as official documents—and they were. On one page were the words *Oddací list,* followed by the names and birthdates of my grandparents Arnošt and Olga. Another page had the date, "27. června 1909," and the words *Praha Hotel Bristol* in script on one line. It must have been my Czech grandparents' marriage certificate. Two other records had *Rodný list* printed at the top—they looked like birth certificates for my grandparents and their parents.

By the time Tom, Pat, and I finished going through every room in the condo, we had gathered nearly 400 letters written between 1939 and 1946, plus another 130 documents dating all the way back into the 1800s. Most were in Czech, including carbon copies of letters written by our father when he was young, signed with his Czech nickname, Valdik.

We also uncovered a box of old 8 mm film reels dating back to 1940 and hundreds of pictures from the dozens of countries my parents had visited. Many were accompanied by matching three-ring binders containing elaborate slide collections. Among his accomplishments my father was an award-winning photographer, so we knew it was not going to be easy to throw out over sixty years' worth of pictures. I offered to take these items home as part of my inheritance.

Our findings seemed endless. I chose old books about the Kingdom of Bohemia, a historic province of the Czech Lands, and Czechoslovakia and from my parents' days in China. I picked an aging paperback titled *The Yellow Book,* stamped with the mark of the French embassy in Peking, and photo albums filled with pictures, starting with my father's arrival in Shanghai in 1939. There were two artfully compiled albums from the year of my parents' marriage that contained the receipt from the Peking Union Church, congratulatory note cards, and photographs from their honeymoon in the Western Hills, outside Peking, which meant that I now had images to illustrate the meeting story.

I was drawn to an array of personal items, like my physician father's two leather bags, still containing his stethoscopes and blood pressure cuff, and his Chinese hand-carved chop, the seal bearing his name that he used to mark his many books. We also turned up my mother's white leather Bible, gold-embossed on the front with RUTH A. HOLZER, a surprise from my father for her fortieth birthday. On the inside, under "Presented to: Mummy Chick," were our childish signatures—Tommy, Patty, and Joan.

The three of us continued poking into the crevices of our parents' lives, alternately laughing and gasping at what we found. As weepy sentimentalists and cold-blooded liquidators, we identified items to be donated, stored, sold, or tossed. Tom and Pat leaned toward artwork and the furniture and mementos they had most identified with. I'm not sure why I was more drawn to the letters, perhaps because I'm the youngest and came along at a different point in my parents' lives. I know I inherited my father's curiosity and tenacity, which made me suited for the work and obligations the letters conveyed. My dad had preserved the last echoes of family and friends from his stolen land. Some had died in the Holocaust, also referred to as the "Shoah." They were my father's people, which meant they were mine. I had to know what they were saying.

I traveled a twisting emotional path for over a decade as I untangled my father's story. Fortunately, Dad was an excellent correspondent and a dedicated packrat. I gleaned myriad details from his well-annotated scrapbooks, train tickets, luggage stickers, business cards, postcards, stamps, menus, posters, brochures, travel itineraries, shipping orders, and of course, the letters.

As a modern-day Nancy Drew, I approached each clue as a piece of a puzzle to be solved. I knew that I might find the answer to how and when, after unspeakable loss, my father had reignited his healing force of deep compassion. I enlisted a small army of translators and historians to help me navigate. My investigative travels didn't equal my father's, but I visited a good deal of Europe and the United States, tracking down sources to confirm and amplify Dad's anecdotes. I couldn't visit China but spent months in the virtual world looking for clues. I mapped my global queries using Google, YouTube, Twitter, LinkedIn, Skype, ancestry websites, and more.

In what I consider the biggest blessing, I discovered a letter hidden away for five decades that charted the course for my father's life after World War II. As you'll see in this book, what I call "The Letter That Changed Everything" provided the answer to why my father left a legacy of uncommon compassion toward others. This powerful letter, which began "My dear boy," changed the narrative of my life.

Dad left hints throughout his papers about his intention to write his story—an adventure-filled travelogue illuminating his search for meaning in the life he lost and the one he built. Although he never had a chance to fulfill his writing dream because of his dedication to heal and help others, he left no doubt that it was paramount to him—clues were everywhere. For example, in 1940, from his post at an American Brethren mission hospital, he wrote to his friend Franta Schoenbaum in Prague. After thoroughly describing a trip from Shanghai to Peking to Pingting Hsien (Pingding County), he declared his intent to write a book "on Japanese paper, numbered with the author's signature":

> I am the head physician of a provincial hospital. On Sundays, I go to sing in church. I am learning Chinese. I live such a strange existence, an adventurer against my will . . . For amusement, I will write a similar book of novellas like the one you are writing and I will probably christen it the same way. I even wrote several stories already, naturally with illustrations, how else? The first story about a "farting missionary" is about a Grandpa who welcomed me in the last promontory of civilization, which was at that time being starved by the Japanese, by a months-lasting blockade . . . I will write a story about Trebitsch Lincoln, who issues warnings to warring powers and corresponds with the Dalai Lama, who is eight months old.

My father never shared his vision of a book with me, but for most of my life, as I listened to his tapestry of tales, I thought that one day I'd write a few down. So, in the spring of 1989 I drove from Orlando, where I lived, to Florida's east coast with my cassette recorder and my five-year-old son. I wanted Derick to experience the magic of my father's stories as I had when I was a child. I'd begged Dad to open his window into that fantastic world: "Tell me about the mean Japanese soldier interrogating you as if you were a spy—the one with the Russian guy there." I thought of Dad's whole life as a highlight reel.

He held me spellbound by speaking carefully and methodically, with pauses for deep breaths as he recalled vivid details—describing the shade of a wood grain desktop, someone's white-suit attire with bow tie and straw hat on a muggy day on the docks of Hong Kong, or the history of a place like Shanghai, with its kaleidoscopic cultural scene. He brought his broad hands up and forward as he made points, sometimes joining them together; as the surgeon he was, his hands were never at rest. He often had a white handkerchief to wipe his brow of perspiration. Sometimes when he spoke, he would mash his lips together, bit by bit delivering the tale.

The conversations I recorded provide the reference points and the chronology of this book. Dad was in his late seventies then and had grown slower in his movements and speech, but when I listen to his voice on those tapes, I still picture him as he was in my youth, dignified but jovial, his silver-streaked hair fluttering out from beneath his houndstooth check racing cap as I sat beside him while we sped along Florida's sand-strewn beach roads in his agile sky-blue Alfa Romeo Spider. His aging mind retained the power to travel back in time, swimming in an icy Bohemian fishpond or photographing swaying Bactrian camels tromping on muddy clay beside the massive stone walls of Peking.

I was satisfied that I'd taped the whole story and promised myself that one day I'd write a book about my remarkable father and his adventures. One day tumbled into the next, and soon it was all a blur as the busyness of midlife got in the way. When that time came, it was too late to ask more questions.

And so, what you're about to read is Valdik's story—in his voice, as I heard and discovered it, partially through those recordings, which frankly, didn't contain the whole multilayered account of his struggles. To fill in the gaps, I mined the letters, journals, and photographs and interviewed people across five continents. Valdik unfolds his sweeping story chronologically, with the knowledge he held at the time I interviewed him. On occasion his voice offers historical context to what he was aware of from word of mouth, newspaper, or radio reports. Dealing with what is one of history's most exhausted subjects, as a writer I decided to accept this complicated time on its own terms rather than judge and analyze it by present-day standards.

I've taken the liberties of narrative nonfiction biography—like a posthumous memoir—to faithfully represent what could have been uttered during actual events. To this myriad dialogue I make no representation as to its veracity. Much of the dialogue is drawn from my father's carbon-copied letters and the taped interview. Or from my blurry childhood memories of conversations long ago—like Dad's comment about performing a kind of open-heart surgery on himself: "We can't choose what haunts us. The choice that matters is how we deal with the outcome."

What follows is Valdik's voice, along with others', caught in the vortex of wartime. It might help to sip a big mug of foamed Pilsner as you read—things are about to get hot.

Notes

1. When my father was in China during 1939–41, the Wade-Giles system of transliteration was in use; thus, his old letters are filled with Chinese place names not seen today. The modern Pinyin system (literally "spelled-out sounds") approximates the pronunciation of standard Chinese—for example, *Beijing* rather than *Peking*. In an attempt to stay true to my father's voice in both his taped interviews and his letters, I have stayed with the Wade-Giles system. Within "Valdik's Story," at the first use of the word, I place the more modern Pinyin version in parentheses to clarify for the reader. To add an additional twist, over the years the capital city of Beijing has had various versions of its name. In this story you will periodically encounter the name *Peiping*, the Wade-Giles romanization of the Mandarin pronunciation of the Chinese Nationalist name for Peking.

2. Somewhere in history the word *bohemian* was hijacked to mean "unconventional." My father never liked the word adaptation as he thought a native Bohemian from Central Europe ingrained by long tradition rarely deviated from the norm of "being Bohemian." The French believe that the Roma originated in Bohemia, so the term also is coined to refer to a "vagabond life." In that regard the word might work here.

MY FLIGHT

VALDIK HOLZER

Late March 1939

A t any other time I would have enjoyed a hike through the bucolic Moravian countryside of golden barley glistening with the early shoots of spring, but on this occasion, as I'd just escaped the cutthroat Nazis, I wasn't dressed appropriately. My boots were sturdy enough for a long march, but along with most of my attire, they marked me as an enemy soldier of our now-occupied nation. I began my self-liberation thinking not about Hitler or even my worried parents but about how I could alter my appearance to keep from being shot as a deserter if I crossed paths with the Wehrmacht and their vicious dogs. I figured I could get by with my gray riding britches, which would suit any well-tailored equestrian fellow, but my jacket and high-collared shirt were military issue. I needed to swap them for civilian clothes. So, with head down and hands deep in my pockets, I set out on foot, traveling west along a little-traveled dusty road. I walked twelve miles to the nearby city of Brno to see an old acquaintance named Mr. Levy. A textile manufacturer, he was the father of a former girlfriend, and I knew he'd be glad to see me.

I was wrong. An old servant woman barely muffled a shriek when she opened the Levys' door and saw my uniform. I started to explain who I was, but with lips stretched back to her ears, she tried to close the door in my face. I pushed hard enough to keep it open while trying not to topple the old lady, but she managed to shut the latch, leaving me outside. I had no choice but to knock once more. When the door opened this time, I was delighted to see Mr. Levy. Before I could explain myself, he yanked me inside and shut the door. With eyes wide open, he pulled out a small silver cigarette case and offered me one, but I declined as he waved his hand for the maid to leave the room.

"We're alone," he said. "You can say whatever the hell you want. Be honest with me. I know you aren't sightseeing. What are you doing here? You know we could be in a hell of a mess if the Germans find you."

That was the shocking start of my adventurous escape, and many harrowing events followed.

MY DEAR BOY

You know, when one gets out into the world, only then is one able to see what a conceited simpleton he has been. I realize more and more how unworldly, and in a way provincial we are. And so, Adolf provided us with at least this profit, albeit we dearly paid for it.

—VALDIK HOLZER, from China, to cousin Hana Winternitz in Great Britain, March 8, 1940

1

Valdik's Story

A Gifted Life

What makes a life? It's not a series of events but memories embedded with emotion transformed into stories told around tables. And so I, Valdik Holzer, must decide, from my seven decades, what stories am I going to tell? If I'm fortunate, a few will enlighten and leave a worthwhile echo behind.

It's difficult to know where to begin. My migration early in life across five continents was filled with daring adventure and the pursuit of love and acceptance. I was hunted and displaced. I encountered shady characters, experienced tremendous peril, frustration, and guilt, while I faced painful choices. Sometimes there were no "best" alternatives. I learned that an action sometimes can cause a consequence greater than inaction. I suffered my darkest days as a refugee, but I encountered compassion and courage as well. I did not sour on life or abandon my humor. I didn't allow the world to write my story. I became the author of my life.

Wherever I've traveled, no matter what language I've spoken or clothing I've worn, I've led a gifted life. "Gifted" because my time on Earth was not supposed to be long and fulfilled. According to Hitler's psychotic plan, I—Valdik Holzer—was meant to be terminated in 1942 by gas, starvation, beating, or gunshot.

It should have ended in that way, that year, at the hands of the Nazis, as it did for forty-four of my relatives, but instead, at twenty-seven, I embarked on a trek that covered much of the world—Europe, Africa, Asia, North America, and South America. Because I dared to break from the past and brave the dangers and loneliness in a strange land, I survived to now share my Homeric tale. My memories are embedded with the emotion of every wrong move and miscalculation that, when recalled, sting anew. After all these years I still can't answer if my survival was because of fate, chance, or something higher. You get to decide.

As an old man looking at my diminishing future, my greatest wish is to finish well. I can achieve this and help humanity at the same time by sharing the last letter my father wrote to me before he perished. In this 1942 letter he made a timeless, universal wish that ties us together as humankind. I've done my best to follow his advice.

But first I need you to comprehend the historical context in which his request was made. We're all products of our histories, events layered one upon another, with the present carrying the past within it. So, to paint the picture of the genesis of my father's wish, I should start my tale where it all began—with my Bohemian roots and my grand entrance into my gifted life.

2

Bohemian Recollections

Pre-1914

My delivery on July 23, 1911, as the only child of Arnošt and Olga (née Orlík) Holzer, took place in the town of Benešov in a corner room on the second floor of the three-story townhouse my parents shared with my grandmother, Marie Holzer. With over two centuries of solid Bohemian background, my grandfather Alois Holzer, who'd bought the entire city block, had built the Holzer house and store in 1897. It faced the little town square on the northeast corner, with Butcher Alley running along the north side to the main square.

Until his death some seven years before my birth, Alois operated a wholesale high-end grocery business (in Czech, a "koloniální zboží") on the first floor, importing dry goods from the European colonies. Tea arrived from Ceylon, now called Sri Lanka, and coffee, sugar, and exotic spices from Africa. In our small town Alois also sold chocolates. At his death my paternal grandfather, Alois Holzer, left his grocery store to my father, his oldest son, and his name to me— Osvald *Alois* Holzer. My Czech first name, English spelling *Oswald*, derived from a cousin my father admired. Thus, following the Czech tradition, I became known by the diminutive nickname "Valdik."

My maternal grandparents, Jakub and Teresia Orlík, had lived in a large house near Alois and Marie. Grandfather Jakub was a horse trader, importing animals from Hungary, Algeria, Morocco, and Tunisia. He supplied fine steeds for the wealthy, including nearby nobility like Archduke Franz Ferdinand d'Este.

Grandfather Jakub arranged my parents' marriage, and as things turned out, he was a superb matchmaker. Olga was the youngest of his six children, which included four daughters. Short, with an hourglass figure, Mother had an artistic temperament with a broad range of emotions. At the same time, she was gentle, kind, and generous. Her round face with the warm glow of green eyes and heart-shaped lips were set off by her flawless peaches-and-cream complexion. She had flowing glossy brown hair that my father loved to move his hands through and leave tousled. It wasn't long after their 1908 wedding that my mom became pregnant. Sadly, she suffered a miscarriage, which, as my father told it, made my arrival two years later "even more celebratory."

When I was old enough to hear it, one night when we sat down for a dinner of roast pork, steamed and sliced dumplings, and red cabbage, Dad described how our diet interacted with my birthright: "You had the good fortune to be born into a prosperous middle-class Jewish family that owned a grocery store in a town that has seen its share of luck along with the misery of conflict. That we aren't Orthodox is a benefit so you can eat a lot of tasty pork."

We all share a past that provides the forces that affect our lives.

Located twenty-five miles southeast of Prague, the first official mention of Benešov was in the eleventh century, when it was owned by the lords of Beneschau. As it still is, the cultivated countryside surrounding Benešov is typical of Central Bohemia—a mosaic of lush forests, flower-filled meadows, farms, and small, mostly man-made ponds filled with carp—a misleading picture of tranquility. From its start Benešov endured repeated invasions and turmoil.

"This makes us who we are," my dad—*táta* in Czech—would say. "But don't forget—Bohemia is not just the charming countryside. It's a living backcloth to our ancestor's emotions that create the topography of your heart. If you study the social dynamics of time and place, my son, you will learn how the world works. *You'll foresee what is coming.*"

Even though for me that last sentence hasn't always held right, I've followed my father's reason as to why everyone should be a

2. Tennis club, Benešov, Czechoslovakia, ca. 1920. Arnošt Holzer (*back row, fifth from left*) and Valdik Holzer (*sitting child, front row left*).

student of history: "If you know what went before, you will come to understand the present with a knowing mind and heart."

With no guile or hidden motives, Dad's heart was the purest of anyone I knew.

The closest Bohemia came to realizing a prophecy of national unity was in the fourteenth century. Charles IV, a fellow as skilled at making allies as he was at vanquishing enemies, was crowned king of Bohemia in 1346. As emperor of the Holy Roman Empire, he united the Czechs and Germans and made Prague the capital and a seat of culture and education. The first major university in Central Europe still bears Charles's name; it is my alma mater. He hired Italian and French architects to build palaces and churches and ordered the construction of a bridge across the Vltava River, which was named in his honor.

I wish I could say the spirit of King Charles lived on and that unity and prosperity continued for generations. During the Thirty

Years' War (1618–48) Benešov was plundered and endured more disastrous fires. Even the Swedish army torched half our town as it traveled on the famous trade route from Linz, Germany, to Prague. The best-known occupiers established the Austro-Hungarian Empire, which over time encompassed Austrian Germans, the Magyars of Hungary, Slovenes, Slovaks, Romanians, Poles, Ruthenians, Serbs, Croats, and my people, the Czechs. Nothing much held us together except the constantly changing lines drawn on a map. "It took compromise," my dad would say when describing the mess.

The earliest documentation of Jews living in the area was in 1570—five people were registered as the heads of Jewish families. By 1893, living in twenty-seven surrounding villages, the Jewish community was officially recorded at around eight hundred. My father, born in 1885, and my mom, in 1888, would have appeared on the registers, although neither came from religious families.

As was true throughout Europe, restrictions were often placed on Jews, including how they could earn a living, whether they could marry, where Jews could live, and with whom they could associate. On occasion they were thrown out of their homes and villages altogether.

The Czech Lands became overwhelmingly non-Catholic from the fifteenth-century influence of Jan Hus, the great Reformist leader who, one hundred years before Germany's Luther, challenged how the Catholic faith operated. The Protestants prevailed at first until the Catholic Austrian Habsburgs came to power in the sixteenth century.

This is where the story gets personal and, as my father reflected, "made you who you are." Determined to convert the Czechs by force, in 1620 the Habsburgs under the Holy Roman Imperial forces of Ferdinand II and Catholic League German troops defeated the mostly Protestant Bohemian army at the Battle of White Mountain.

The immediate consequence of the defeat was the plunder of the Bohemian crown properties and a significant forfeiture of lives. The Orlíks, my mother's family, were on the losing side. The Hapsburgs declared non-Catholic worship and book ownership "heretical," and people were severely punished. As a member of some degree of low-level Bohemian nobility, the Protestant Orlíks were given an ultimatum to convert to Catholicism or emigrate—leave their ancestral land.

Rubbing a hand against his heart, Dad described their choice, according to family legend: "Exhibiting a shrewd but stubborn streak that would be passed down to their descendants, including your mother and you, the Orlíks refused both choices and instead selected a third option—converting to the Jewish faith. Jews at the time were minor players in the Catholics versus Protestants scene. Therefore this seemed a safer choice."

The Orlíks lost their supposed castle, but the conversion allowed them to stay in the Bohemian land they loved. Thousands of other leading Protestant families were exiled, their property confiscated and given to those who helped the Habsburgs in their conquest and push for re-Catholicization of Bohemia. The White Mountain defeat began three hundred years of Catholic-driven persecution of the mostly Protestant population. For the small enclave of Jews, some new, some old, scattered throughout the lands, let's say they had their ups and big downs in how they were treated.

My paternal family side also may have found its identity shaped by religion and politics. As the legend goes, sometime around the mid-1760s, during Empress Maria Theresa's reign over the Austro-Hungarian Empire, a freeman named Vršecký lived in a little Bohemian village. The Czech word *Vršek* means "the top of something," like a hill. Freemen, who ranked above serfs but below nobles in the feudal system, knew it was smart politics to adopt a German-sounding name as a show of loyalty to the empress.

This was during a period when Maria Theresa was "Germanizing," seeking to transform her empire by unifying laws, ideologies, and language. It was a time when most Ashkenazic Jews from Central and Eastern Europe didn't have hereditary family surnames, except in a few rare places in Europe. One of those exceptions was Prague, the capital of Bohemia, where it was documented during the sixteenth to eighteenth centuries that Jews regularly used surnames.

So, Vršecký went looking for a German bride and found a woman named Holzer. She happened to be Jewish, and he took her surname. In a romantic ending to his often-told tale, Dad would add, "I'm sure it was true love."

That was how my father's family "happened" to be Jewish, at least according to family lore. I'm not sure of all the facts or the exact dates, but there is an old Italian phrase that here serves my storytelling well: *Even if it isn't true, it is well made.*

In the early 1800s Benešov developed as a center of national rebirth for Czech-speaking Bohemians. It grew alongside the resistance movement to the predominance of the German language and other cultural aspects of the Habsburg rule, which lasted unhappily for three hundred years. When the town was connected by rail in 1871, many people with business in Prague lived in this hamlet.

The whole place was developed around the Benešov Royal Estate and the Castle Konopiště, a French-type Gothic castle that was home to a variety of nobles since the Habsburgs took over. The castle's occupant at the time of my birth was the second most prestigious Habsburg of all—Archduke Franz Ferdinand d'Este—the heir apparent to Emperor Franz Joseph. That Franz Ferdinand would become the emperor was a big deal for Benešov.

When I was a boy, automobiles were new and uncommon in Central Europe. Our neighbor Franz Ferdinand had the first car in town. My father bought the second car, and occasionally in the summer we would pass the archduke on the dusty roads. That was his one connection to our family until the archduke took off in his car for an official visit to far-off Bosnia.

3

A World at War

1914

I was three years old when our noble neighbor and his wife were assassinated by a young Serbian nationalist, Gavrilo Princip, while riding through Bosnia, Sarajevo. It was the match strike that helped spark World War I and guaranteed Benešov at least a short line in the history books. Although a defining moment of the twentieth century, of more importance to me, my father was called into service in 1914 into the Austro-Hungarian army as a second lieutenant in an all-Czech Bohemian infantry regiment, #102, stationed in our garrison town of Benešov. Until his untimely demise, Franz Ferdinand served as regiment commander.

Before the war the Realist Party took root in this fertile ground for disaffection caused by a constant flow of threats, broken promises, persecution, and nationalistic ferment. At the time intellectuals across Europe questioned the old monarchical order and advocated the development of popular nationalism. Some men in Benešov were active in the Realist Party, a group of increasingly nationalist liberals who tried to overthrow Austrian rule or at least push for significant political change in the monarchy. My father was among them. The party leader was a Prague University professor, Tomáš Garrigue Masaryk, who considered anti-Semitism a blight upon society.

When the war broke out, my father had no more choice about serving in the Austro-Hungarian army than he had about living under its government. There was no love lost between the Czechs and the German Austrians, who were allied with their German cousins. Our Slavic soulful identity set us apart from the German subjects of the empire. The Austro-Hungarian army's high command got nervous about keeping an all-Czech regiment full of potential separatists in Czech territory, so the men were transferred to Hungary and then to the Russian front to "fight the mad Russians," as the Austrians described it.

When my father went off to war, at age twenty-nine, my mother, twenty-seven, took over the family line of work. Typical of women at that time, she had the equivalent of a middle school education. Being from a family of means, she had studied foreign languages and embroidery and had gained an appreciation for music, art, and cooking while at finishing school. She was a talented painter, and I inherited my artistic gifts from her. Mom's specialty was making needlepoints of flower arrangements or colorful fruit with the lifelike look of Renaissance-era artwork. I later drew caricatures and embraced photography, recalling her attention to details of color, line, texture, shading, and motion.

She never received any business training, but with her husband gone, she had no choice but to manage while caring for little me. A high-end grocery business was hard to maintain when the war was raging. Most products became scarce as trade routes to the countries producing the raw materials were interrupted.

There were enormous food shortages in Bohemia, so everything was rationed. There was no tea or coffee. People stood in line for meats, flour, and potatoes. Paying exorbitant sums on the black market was often the only way to obtain necessities. Because of our grocery business, my mother was able to give food to the hungry people on the Benešov streets. When I was a small boy, she took me with her. In sometimes freezing weather, we stood in the small square handing out fresh warm bread, salt, and potatoes. I had an excellent role model for charity and compassion and a mother who made me feel secure enough to explore new environments.

For my father at war in Russia, the eastern front offensive didn't go as the Austrians had planned, probably because the Czechs weren't as enthusiastic as they were. With bands playing Czech patriotic music, the Czech soldiers—including Dad—marched out of the trenches and surrendered to their Russian Slavic brethren. The Russians didn't know what to do with several thousand Czech deserters, so they shipped them to a prison camp in Siberia. For the six months that my dad was a Russian prisoner of war, my mother did not receive a single letter from him. Busy with her responsibilities to sustain our economic health, which meant support for my grandmother, me, and the store, my mother shielded me from her constant worry. Nightly, after she tucked me into bed, with my rapt attention on her, Mom would review our circumstance.

"Your father is off on a great adventure with other soldiers from our village. When he returns, he'll tell you of grand Russian places and the people he met." As her fingertip traveled with cautious hope across a world map to where she thought he might be at any given time, with a determination to make the best of the situation, she held Dad's photograph up for me to gaze at. With his bright smile emerging from under a dapper military mustache, I never doubted he'd return. After our nightly tour, Mom and I would clasp our hands together. Before she left the room, with the scent of floral perfume trailing behind, she liked to exude confidence, but on occasion, as I lay in my featherbed, I could hear her sob in the next room.

I don't know the details, but in 1917 my father ended up in Vladivostok, a seaport in the far east of Russia on the Sea of Japan at the rail line's eastern terminus. When Dad arrived, he wrote my mother a letter that came through the United States and let her know he was safe. By the time the war was finished on the western front, the army had transported my father and his cohorts around India and through the Suez Canal to Trieste, Italy. From there he made it home.

My father returned to Benešov four years after he had left, his muscular body much thinner. Had it not been for the photograph my mother showed me each night at bedtime, I might not have recognized his gaunt face. I was nearly seven years old.

4

A House of Many Rooms

1918

I can't recall my father describing the worst of what he saw as a soldier after the ancient monarchies of Austria, Russia, and Germany chose to engulf Europe in the First World War. I wanted to know more detail, but he wouldn't say much. Or couldn't. What he shared with me from this bloody conflict was philosophical, such as: "Even when the skies got rough, I knew every storm runs out of rain."

Or when he told humorous anecdotes about his "trip" and incarceration in a Russian prisoner of war camp in Siberia with a bunch of German officers. "Most were aristocrats. Each day, when the Russians held roll call, all the Germans would step forward, click their heels militarily and say, 'Von Hoffmann' or 'Von So-and-So.' I felt inferior because I was just Officer Holzer, so I'd step forward and say loudly, 'Von Holzer from Benešov.'"

Dad resumed store management in the little square near Butcher Alley. Each morning around ten, after sharing a breakfast of dark rye bread, cheese, and salami with Mom and me, he would appear in front of his shop and wait for a neighbor to show up so they could discuss the daily politics. By then the nearby retailers were standing on the square, all having read *Prager Tagblatt*, the widely read liberal-democratic German-language newspaper in Bohemia, whose journalists were mostly Jewish. Although they may have been separated by political ideas, they all received their news from the same source.

Peace celebrations after World War I came early for us. Before the armistice between the Allied powers and Germany was signed on November 11, 1918, the Austro-Hungarian Empire, which had ruled the land into which my parents and I were born, collapsed, on October 28, 1918. As the victorious Allies set to work on a redrawn map of Europe, we Czechs—slightly prematurely—were already toasting the birth of our new country. We weren't sure what the borders would be.

When the new national map was settled under the Treaty of Saint-Germain, my father lay a hand over his heart and whispered that it looked "more or less like a carp." Pieced together like patchwork from territories we know today as the Czech Republic, Slovakia, and Carpathian Ruthenia, the new fish-shaped country of Czechoslovakia held some of the most industrialized regions of the former Austria-Hungary. The country's diverse population of around fifteen million included Czechs, Germans, Slovaks, Hungarians, Poles, Ruthenia-Ukrainians, and Jews. Most spoke languages other than Czech, which was curious since Czech nationalism was birthed of a desire for freedom to use our own language. Among the country's population there were too many religious affiliations to count—Catholic, Orthodox, and Protestant Christians and more than 350,000 Jews. Three million ethnic Sudeten Germans, mostly Catholic, lived within the new Czechoslovak boundary amid the Sudeten Mountains.

"Without Books, History Is Silent"

1919–1929

At the republic's formation, postwar economic challenges and relations between the respective nationalities were tense. Slovakia and the Sudeten area had to be incorporated into the republic with the use of military force. Gradually, the rationing system was abolished, and things began to change. This period became a grand time for my family and for our new republic—an exemplary democracy flourished even as surrounding states sank back into authoritarian regimes. My father's general goods store provided a robust lifestyle for a middle-income family, including our 1929 French Buchet automobile and enjoyable visits to cosmopolitan Prague and Adriatic seaport towns like Trieste in northeast Italy. After the war Dad expanded the business, so he took a partner, and together they founded a button factory. They made buttons out of artificial material—a precursor of plastic.

Professor Tomáš Garrigue Masaryk was now President Masaryk, and the great humanist faced the challenge of forging a unified nation from the disparate ethnic and religious groups. A democrat to the core, he tried to create a model of mutual respect and assimilation with complete separation of church and state. "By tolerance we shall make our way from Habsburg theocracy to democracy," Masaryk proclaimed. Dad described the transitory procedure as "de-Austrianized."

For us this was a pleasant prospect. Like most Jews in Europe,

Jews in the Bohemian Lands had struggled against acts of anti-Semitism. During my youth in the First Republic, Jews had sought to live peacefully as integrated Czechoslovak citizens. Most of the Holzer and Orlík families visited synagogues only on High Holidays. There were a few relatives who were more devout, but most of the small group of Orthodox Jews in Bohemia were immigrants from Sub-Carpathian Rus or Galicia and not related to us.

Bohemia was a more secularized region of Europe—not just for Jews but for Czech Gentiles. My father, a loyal citizen, identified himself as Czech, not Jewish, and he wasn't alone. Although the option to claim "Jewish" as a nationality was guaranteed in the 1920 Czechoslovak constitution, nearly half the Jewish population in the 1921 census registered their nationality as Czechoslovak. This ethnonationalism was a complicated issue of differentiation that involved understanding that nationalism and patriotism were parts of a common whole. Recognizing that civil and human rights had a place in Czechoslovak society—for all the freedom the republic offered and the other for religious and cultural unity—one got a chance to choose.

Although Dad's choice was a sign of our family's enduring support of an independent Czech country, over the years he had observed an undercurrent of long-standing anti-Semitism, especially in Prague, when he attended the German Business Academy. Although he needed no reminder, with the establishment of the republic, violent anti-Semitic riots broke out in Prague upon the triumphant return of Masaryk from abroad. Verbalizing the pro after the con, Dad often told me, "What brings pain to one generation builds insight for the next." Feeling a jolt to my body, I wondered where my insight would come from.

During my childhood in Benešov, the Jewish population dwindled to around 350 Jews, likely all distantly related. Over time about half the marriages were intermarriage (Jew with non-Jew), or "mixed" as some referred to it. By my father's description the Jewish population in my hometown was made up of three main groups. One self-described as "fine Jews" and would have nothing to do with the others. A few of its members were the "manufacturers"—owners of a skin tannery, a grain wholesaler, and the like. Then there were the middle-class Jews—the businesspeople who had retail stores on the square. Those were "our Jews"—the Holzers, Orlíks, Ohrenstein, Furths, and Schoenbaums. Dad looked up to Uncle Ohrenstein and Uncle Furth for their business acumen and was friends with the Schoenbaum brothers, who owned the hardware store on another corner of the square. Lastly, there was a "poor group of Jews," like the glazer who installed windows. Even if they spoke German, they were loyal Czechs, although they weren't involved in town government.

I never thought of myself as Jewish. I felt being Jewish, like being Protestant or Catholic, meant belonging to a religious community and going to services, which my family rarely did. Like others in Bohemia who mixed Jewish and Czech Protestant traditions and culture, we celebrated Christmas and Easter in a non-religious way that today we might describe as commercial.

I don't know how devoted the earliest Holzers were to practicing Judaism, but I do know that Bohemian life was mostly secular. At the beginning of his education, my dad studied in a Jewish school. He later attended the neo-Renaissance-style Benešov Gymnasium, the Czech equivalent of high school, where Catholic monks taught. I followed in his footsteps. The Piarist Order Gymnasium teachers used strict discipline. German was the primary language.

Dad was a sensitive and attentive father who never made me feel that our creative sides had to be discarded. He had a wicked tennis serve and loved to debate politics. After winning a low-stakes poker game, he'd often invite me on a long hike through the woods. Tuned into the world abroad and those around him, in our town he founded the chamber of commerce and was active in the tourist club—always taking its members on an annual trip. His interests were broad, with a few favorites. He wanted that for me.

As a teenager, Dad introduced me to Jaroslav Hašek's satirical sketches about an eternal "dummkopf," Good Soldier Švejk, who in literature represented the Czechs' passive resistance to their bureaucratic Austrian and German overlords. Farcical patriotic sermons and preposterous superior officer pep talks to Kingdom of Bohemia civilian soldiers introduced me to what I envisioned would be my future conflict with army discipline. The bumbling yet compassionate main character, loyalist Švejk, offered me ideas on how to circumvent any stupid superiors I might encounter in my looming compulsory service.

Music was a recurring theme in our lives. When my father returned to Benešov from the war, he expanded the grocery business, but he was never happy as a businessman. He was an artist, a musician at heart. He played viola with a string quartet and belonged to an a cappella singing group called Ozvěna, or Echo. They performed twice each year in the Benešov Concert Hall and collaborated with the Catholic Church choir for major Christmas and Easter productions. My father encouraged my appreciation of music. "If you love music, you will love life," Dad liked to say. If only it were that simple.

In our home bookshelves in each room were filled, along with an overflow of books stored under the bed. Dad appreciated stories that took him somewhere he'd never been to—like the Far East or America. My favorite evenings included his retelling of the books he'd read when he'd urge me to learn more on my own. "Without books, history is silent," he'd say.

Books like those by Czech author Karel Čapek led to my interest in medicine. Čapek's writings stimulated an interest in humanity's fate and the role of science and technology in human life. His surrealistic humor mixed with serious science fiction always involved finding hope and the way out of bad situations. That interested me.

A friendship with Benešov doctor Karel Teuner fueled my interests. Dr. Teuner was the head physician at the district hospital. His oldest son, Francis, my age, was the godchild of Franz Ferdinand and his wife, Sofie. His father was a prominent man in town and served as Franz Ferdinand's physician until the archduke's untimely demise in Sarajevo.

One day my father set up a meeting for me with Dr. Teuner. World War I provided a stimulus to medical processes with new approaches from the battlefield, so the calamity my father had endured had some merit. I glanced at all the thick, leather-bound books on the shelves behind him and admired the doctor's thick mustache and handsome gray three-piece suit. He made intense eye contact as he spoke to me about advances in medical technology providing new ways to treat severe cases of tissue damage and burns. X-ray equipment was newly being used to locate shrapnel during operations. In his deep voice he described how as a doctor he "shared in people's darkest and happiest moments."

He watched carefully to witness my encouraging reaction and then continued: "By the time the war ended, twenty million people in Europe died of the flu. Scientists are looking for advances in medicines to be ready for the next epidemic. You can be one of those, Valdik."

I liked the sound of that.

6

Proud Czechs First

1931–1937

nd so, thanks in part to Dr. Teuner, throughout my
boyhood I dreamed of attending Charles University in
Prague. Established in 1348 by the king of Bohemia and
emperor of the Holy Roman Empire, Charles the Fourth, it was
the first university of its kind in the whole of Central Europe.
Over centuries it weathered the politics, including an 1882 decree
issued by Emperor Franz Joseph that divided the university into
two independent institutions, with Czech and German as their
respective instruction languages. In 1911, the year of my birth,
Albert Einstein served as a professor of theoretical physics in the
German university. By the time I arrived, Charles University was
recognized among the world's finest institutions of higher learning. Graduates of Charles University included doctors of philosophy, law, natural science, and medicine.

After I graduated from Benešov's gymnasium in 1930, I didn't
have to leave home to attend university because home came with
me. As the Great Depression seeped into and strained the Czechoslovak economy with a credit crisis in the summer of 1931, my parents decided to close, at least temporarily, their Benešov wholesale
business. Although I was ready for independence, the choice to
relocate as a family to Prague was a practical one. I needed a place
to live, and my dad needed to find more opportunities to support
our family. I was comfortable with this arrangement as my parents
never hovered so long as my grades were satisfactorily maintained.

3. Small square reconstruction; Holzer house and store just beyond tree, Benešov, Czechoslovakia, 1931. Used with permission of Czech Republic–State Regional Archives, Prague, State District Archives Benešov, Collection of Photographic Documentation, i.n. 6164.

Dad became a Prague *velkoobchodník* (wholesale merchant), offering more than buttons for export. We settled in a spacious two-bedroom apartment in the Žižkov neighborhood with large windows overlooking the busy street below.

Even with this challenging time of growing unemployment and uncertainty, with its mix of modern and medieval art and architecture and music of all kinds, Prague was an exciting place to be. Splendid palaces and stately churches were intermingled with a lively café scene and an immense sense of possibility that charmed commoners and kings over centuries and made believers of us all.

The cultural depth and beauty that had inspired and nurtured the talents of Wolfgang Amadeus Mozart and Franz Kafka began to inspire me. Feeling as if I'd moved a few centuries back in time, I imagined Mozart holding a half-liter mug of beer in a pub and conceiving the prelude to his best-known opera *Don Giovanni*.

Where Gothic architecture had previously prevailed, cubist and art nouveau buildings made Prague an international center of innovative art and architecture. Not long before I arrived, the city designers had embraced modernism, signaling a break from the imperial past and a renewed faith in life, our national identity now tied to democracy. Famous for composers such as Smetana, Dvořák, and Mozart, during the 1920s, Prague, like New York City and Paris, was enveloped in jazz music, which remained popular in the 1930s.

The ambiance around our apartment was "Bohemian" in the sense that Americans know the word—it was a working-class neighborhood favored by artists, writers, and musicians. The outside had elements of art nouveau balustrade, stucco ornaments on the walls and ceilings and a courtyard-facing balcony. For its day it was a hip place to be, with a pervading communal spirit even as times turned desperate for those who faced unemployment. With our wood floors adorned with four Persian rugs, bronze chandeliers, and art deco furniture relocated from Benešov, it was an elegant home away from home. Mom enjoyed her kitchen and chair for knitting, and Dad settled in with his onyx writing set placed proudly on his oak desk.

The Winternitzes were frequent guests. My cousin Hana Winternitz became a great friend. Her mother, Dad's sister Olga Winternitz, was an arts supporter and a vocal Zionist. Although her position seemed odd coming from our lukewarm religious family, with minimal visits to synagogues, my parents listened. I'm not sure what they felt, but they were sympathetic to her case for the resumption of Jewish sovereignty in what is now Israel.

Uncle Rudolf Winternitz, Olga's husband, had a prosperous design and construction business in Prague, which had begun to feel the pain of the Depression. The company's portfolio included Prague's central train station and a number of art nouveau villas, many of which housed Prague's affluent Jewish families—lawyers, physicians, factory owners, and artists.

The city's Jewish population was at about thirty-five thousand at this point. The beautiful Gothic Old-New Synagogue from the

4. Charles University professor operating in Prague, 1935.
Caricature by Valdik Holzer (Prague and China), 1935.

late thirteenth century aroused my curiosity to know more about the atrocities and anti-Semitism intermittently thrust upon the Jewish community. I worried if a time might come when violent intolerance would resurface.

Defined by its music, poetry, and legend, Prague's unique topography, graced by a grand castle on a route called "Royal Way" and cathedrals overlooking the Vltava River, provided its famous literary landscape. The Charles Bridge bound it all together. Even in the cold evening gray mist on my way from a pub along a warren of narrow, dark alleys, I enjoyed walking across the stone bridge with tall statues of saints and kings. Even with my impaired eyesight, I saw our radiant past as long shadows stretched from glowing lanterns.

Fulfilling my childhood dream, I entered the medical school. There was no such thing as premed; our medical studies were incorporated into other courses in one six-year degree program. The focus was to train doctors with a broad medical education, able to communicate well about scientific matters. Simultaneous with my studies, I worked in the university's Medical and Neurological Clinic and in the Institute of Histology and Microscopical Anatomy as an anatomical draftsman.

Because the medical school was part of the university, I had friends with varied interests, including several law students as well as talented artists and architects. There was no distinction between Christians and Jews because no one in my circle dwelled on religion. In official registries, such as our university papers, it was common to indicate "no religious preference." We were proud Czechs first, believing our assimilation and patriotism demonstrated loyalty and acceptance in an enlightened society. The Café Mánes reflected this spirit.

7

As if Stopped Mid-Gesture—Café Mánes

1930s

hat I loved best as a young man was how one's imagination thrived amid Prague's maze of cobblestone streets and in its parks and cafés. The stimulating environment that produced my favorite satirical book, Jaroslav Hašek's *Good Soldier Švejk*—about a boob in passive resistance to army discipline—was now my inspiration. I spent hours enveloped in a tobacco smoke haze at the fashionable Café Mánes on the right bank of the Vltava River. Mánes became the domain of the university students, and they in turn attracted other young people.

Next to the café, the functionalist styled Mánes Exhibition Hall was built on concrete pillars spanning the river's narrow part onto where the old Štítkovský Mill was located. Developed by an influential group of artists, the Mánes Union of Fine Arts members included Emil Filla and brothers Josef and Karel Čapek but drew from beyond Prague's borders, exhibiting Pablo Picasso, Joan Miró, and Salvador Dalí. The intent was to expose Prague to the latest in European art while showcasing Czech creative life and our position at the forefront of the international avant-garde. Even Tomáš Masaryk was a Mánes financial supporter of this pillar of Czechoslovak art.

Beyond Mánes Hall, on a bridge between the riverbank and Slovanský Island, was a garden restaurant with terraces. The blue-walled French restaurant on the lower level featured a mural by Czech artist Emil Filla, and the room was crowded with wooden

5. Café Mánes postcard, 1939.

tables covered with white tablecloths. Large windows framed a view of white mute swans floating past on the river. Beyond the restaurant was our smoky café and bar.

The creative Mánes environment was perfect for a budding thinker. I relished the company of sculptors, architects, animators, and painters. Even French writer and poet André Breton, the founder of surrealism, lectured in the gallery. On the sunlit garden terrace I drew caricatures of various medical school professors and showed them off to my artistic allies, sculptor friend Julius Lankáš and well-known caricaturist, writer, and lawyer Adolf Hoffmeister. The attention my drawings got was the right kind: the university displayed them on its walls.

For a few cents I could get a glass of *pivo*—that's Czech beer—or Turkish coffee. I'd light my pipe and settle in for a game of chess and a rousing discussion of politics or sports or the latest theatrical production. Much like the contemporary gilded youth of the same class elsewhere in Europe and North America, we were well educated and comparatively well-off. My companions included close friends from medical school Vláďa Wagner and Pavel Körper; childhood friends and brothers Franta and Karel Schoenbaum;

and lawyer Karel Ballenberger, whom we called "Bála." Serving as the public reading room and information exchange of our time, newspapers and magazines were at our disposal. I felt much at home. The conversations unified us, despite our differing positions about politics, of which my laid-back attitude was unique among the group.

These warm coffeehouse get-togethers had many advantages over gatherings at home, not the least of which was central heating. We were young men and women hopeful and excited to start our adult lives. Thus, half our time at Café Mánes was spent ruminating aloud over our beers, planning more fun, like going bowling or making visits to wine cellars or taking ski trips to the Krkonoše Mountains on the Polish border. We were a friends-in-folly close group. A few were married, some in mixed marriages—Jews with non-Jews. The rest of us prowled the café scene for companionship.

I often gravitated to my friend Vláďa Wagner's table. His dream in medicine was to become a hematologist; mine was to enter private practice as a surgeon. Many "study" hours were filled with discussion of our ambitions. Like me, Vláďa devoured books. Through political literature Vláďa explored the works of Lenin and Engels but found Marx "too dry to read." After a period of teenage fascism, Vláďa had become attracted to the right wing of communism, which was in many ways the left end of social democracy at the time. "My father calls it 'Salon Komunismus,' or communism by the well-to-do, and he doesn't take my interest seriously," Vláďa lamented.

In many ways Vláďa was the exception. What most of us had in common at Mánes was our lack of well-defined political opinions. With Czechoslovakia approaching its position as the last surviving democracy in our region, we were still forming our judgments on what political party we would follow. I considered both extremes a threat to our parliamentary democracy. It occurred to me that much of humanity seemed to have already taken diametrically right or left turns. What united us was the emerging threat of Hitlerian fascism, and as it loomed larger, our position against it began to form. By the end of 1932 every one of us knew that there was a threat, even from a distance, in the inhumanity of Hitler's ideas, although how they'd catch on was not yet known.

Our intellectually engaged group often immersed ourselves in deliberation about solving the world's social and political problems, which were increasing too swiftly for us to keep up with, even though we tried harder than many. As Czechs, we were keenly aware that history had a way of beating a path to our door and sometimes knocked it down. Tyrants who built dark empires that confiscated property endowed us with our black humor tempered with gentle irony.

After one alcohol-fueled debate, his foot tapping beneath the table, the always clear-sighted Karel Schoenbaum described our unpromising circumstance: "For Hitler, Czechoslovakia is his chief enemy. While we offer refuge to a growing number of antifascists and Jews fleeing Germany, we are the country that constantly criticizes his totalitarian practices. He would do best to see us gone."

Germany's massive unemployment, spurred on by onerous reparations, a depressed global economy, and lingering humiliation over its defeat in the war, seeded fertile ground for hate. In the 1932 election Adolf Hitler and his virulently anti-Semitic Nazis won about a third of the seats in the Reichstag, or parliament. It wasn't a majority, but it was larger than any other party. Hitler was appointed chancellor in January 1933 as part of a coalition government, but the coalition was short-lived. At Mánes our optimism was shattered with the elections that brought Hitler to power. Germany left the League of Nations and began intensive rearmament.

For a while the most naive people, me included, believed that a government of law limited Hitler's power. That assumption lasted until the moment when an awkwardly organized but highly effective event occurred. When Berlin's Reichstag building exploded in flames less than a month after the election, the Nazis blamed the Communists and used the accusation as a pretext for eliminating all opposition. Remember, Berlin is about 175 miles from

Prague, so imagine if you lived in Orlando and this was happening in Palm Beach, Florida.

The Nazis didn't try to hide their brutality. Germany opened its first concentration camp at Dachau less than two months after Hitler took office. A few weeks later the Nazis initiated a boycott of Jewish businesses. Soon Jewish government employees, including teachers, were fired. As the waves of Nazi intimidation surged, refugees streamed over the border into Czechoslovakia. The majority were Jews, and the situation inflamed those people who were already leery of assimilation. Many ethnic Germans who lived in the most economically depressed parts of Czechoslovakia responded enthusiastically when Hitler urged them to blame their government for their troubles.

With no reaction from Britain or France, Hitler made a stunning denouncement in March 1935. He ignored the Versailles Treaty disarmament clauses and brought forward compulsory military training. After hearing this news, my father became visibly shaken. Blowing out a series of short breaths to regain control as he paced the floor, I listened, realizing the old soldier had a good point about defending our country. He said: "The simple hollow pillboxes we're building on the German border had better turn into something much more massive to stall a sudden attack. If we have any hope of our allies mounting a defensive countermeasure once the Germans start coming over the border, we need a lot more reinforced concrete."

My Café Mánes friends and I disagreed about politics as easily and often as we disagreed about girls or movies, but all of us—Jews and non-Jews—were united in our loathing for Hitler and all he stood for. One cold evening the bullnecked Bála Ballenberger, who as a labor attorney was intensely political, talked me into contributing some of my drawings to a popular left-leaning Social Democratic Party newspaper. "For a modest sum," Bála told me, "you can make a difference showing Hitler, this offspring of an illegitimate-born Austrian, as the buffoon he is." Nursing an ever-colder cup of coffee, I agreed and sent them several caricatures of an odd little man with a cropped mustache and a funny head. As the drawings left my hand, a foreboding overtook me. I wished I'd never agreed to the commission.

The situation in the country next door grew more troubling and for me more personal. In 1935 the Nazi regime adopted the Nuremberg Race Laws, which formed the legal basis for the systematic persecution of Jewish people it deemed of lesser value. Even though the law just affected Germans, I saw it as Hitler's attempt to define Jews everywhere in this manner and target us for some malfeasance. Among other effects the laws stripped Jewish Germans of citizenship and made it illegal for them to marry non-Jews. Intermarriage subjected violators to a jail term. The laws defined Jews by lineage rather than religious affiliation, putting even more of us in danger.

Having spent time in Italy after he graduated from college, my father took particular interest when Italy launched an attack on Abyssinia (now Ethiopia) from Italian Somalia. He was glad when the League of Nations, with Edvard Beneš, foreign minister of Czechoslovakia, serving as president, voted to impose minor economic sanctions on Italy. Then Dad became disappointed as he watched nothing being enforced. "If the League can't enforce the obvious," he said, "then it will soon be finished and of no help." When I asked what would happen next, he started talking to himself under his breath and, with some hyperventilation, left the room.

Hitler launched his campaign for territory in March 1936. His first target was the Rhineland, which the Allies after World War I had forced Germany to demilitarize as a buffer zone between Germany and France. Hitler ordered his invading generals to turn back if the French tried to stop them, but France did nothing, and Hitler's success caused his maniacal confidence to swell.

The same year, one year before we were to graduate from medical school together, my friend Pavel Körper visited Nuremberg, Germany. Fluent in German, Pavel was a Jew with blonde hair from a mixed background. His father owned a liquor store in Prague. As I did, after two years of entering "Israelit" (Izraelský) under the question of religion on his Charles University papers, Pavel wrote "without religion" (bez vyznani).

Reporting on his visit, with his spine straight as a pencil, Pavel sat at a white-clothed Mánes table as the crowd hung on his words. Moments earlier the space had been filled with the sound of laughter and jazz, but a silence overtook the room as Pavel reported what he had seen: "Hundreds of men dressed in brown uniforms were marching in massive rows while Hitler, with dramatic hand gestures and a voice like a foghorn, lectured fanatically about racial superiority. The roaring salute of the bewitched German crowd was frightening. The sound was reflected in a sea of swastika pennants waved back and forth by a group of men, women, and children. When Hitler walked near us, a stout man broke into tears and shouted he could die now as he had seen the Führer's face . . . I became sick to my stomach."

After Pavel finished, it felt as if the smoky air had been sucked out and we were left with the smell of peeled onions. All listeners were acutely aware that Germany had declared an official boycott of Jewish doctors, lawyers, and civil servants shortly after coming to power in 1933 and that life had grown desperate for many not so unlike us in the room. We'd seen the first refugees show up on Prague streets, and the local welcome was not always evident.

For a while not a word was spoken, each man filled with anxiety about his compulsory service with the Czechoslovak army. Squirming in our chairs, Vláďa and I exchanged looks. We knew after graduation, if things didn't go well, we might face this not-so-cartoonish führer's face in a tide of blood. Yet in Hitler's eyes I was a Jew and Vláďa was not.

In a voice pitched high and loud with urgency, Pavel ended the silence as he spoke of what most of us had on our minds: "These massive spectacles are bringing the German nation into unity around Hitler's policies of hate, including his ideas of racism, especially anti-Semitism."

With an uncharacteristic fixed from-under stare like an approaching bull, Pavel attempted to assuage our fears. "But let's remember," he said, "our modernized army has reorganized, and we're building massive permanent fortifications along the border with Germany. Our mobile units will be able to destroy the enemy advancing through gaps, and we'll wear them down with our combat activity. Surely this will protect us all by delaying a German advance by several days, allowing for French or English allies to arrive."

I don't know why it came to mind, but a French phrase that my father taught me by Hector Berlioz slid off my lips. "Ah, the French. *Le temps est un grand maître, dit-on, le malheur est qu'il tue ses élèves.* It means: We say that time is a great teacher. The misfortune is that it kills all its students."

No one laughed. Most people muttered excuses and left the café.

In the weeks that followed, Germany signed a treaty with Japan pledging to cooperate in fighting the spread of communism. Italy, another fascist state, joined them. The agreement formed the basis of the Axis powers, an alliance that threatened the entire civilized world, but regrettably, not enough people realized this in time.

It was against this backdrop of looming international bedlam that my parents gathered with a large and admiring group of uncles, aunts, cousins, and friends to see me receive my Doctor of Medicine degree with honors on March 6, 1937.

8

In Service of a Doomed Country

1937–1939

That summer, as I turned twenty-six and prepared to leave home for the first time, Germany's new Asian ally, Japan, launched an all-out invasion of China as it prepared for further conquests in the Pacific. My student deferment from the military lasted long enough for me to serve a six-month medical internship at Bulovka Hospital, a private institution associated with the university. I was able to evaluate patients, make decisions about diagnosis and therapy, and perform some procedures and treatments. We were supervised by attending physicians but allowed considerable clinical independence. It was a good way to start my transformation into a mature doctor.

On October 1, 1937, I put on an off-the-rack army uniform—baggy even on my stocky five-foot, ten-inch frame—and was transformed from Dr. Holzer, Bulovka Hospital intern, to Private Holzer, Twenty-Eighth Infantry Regiment.

In the mid-1930s our able war ministry had begun grand-scale investments to modernize and keep pace with worldwide military development. The effort included tanks, antitank guns, and machine guns. This buildup was being matched with vast numbers of men in uniform. As a new soldier, I was told that if you compared our military expenses to national income, we ranked sixth in the world, even ahead of Great Britain and the United States. Now what was needed was manpower, and that mobilization was well under way. We needed to train for combat.

Doctors in our country weren't inducted as officers, so we had to swallow a healthy dose of humility while bellowing sergeants herded us through basic training in all the essential military skills, such as spit-shining our boots and saluting as we marched around the parade grounds.

After a month of intense drills with no furlough, we were roused well before dawn on October 28 to participate in the celebration of the nineteenth Czechoslovak Independence Day. Uniforms brushed and rifles gleaming, we marched through the streets of Prague to be reviewed by President Edvard Beneš, who had succeeded the elderly President Masaryk when he resigned in 1935 because of ill health. A few weeks before the celebration, after suffering a stroke, the revered Masaryk had died on September 14, 1937.

At the parade we were ordered to turn our heads slightly toward President Beneš as he stood on his platform returning our salute. As a multitude of bands played, my proud parents and Uncle Rudi, Aunt Olga, and their daughter, Hana Winternitz, watched all this pomp and ceremony. A slew of friends from Café Mánes who had nothing better to do came to cheer me on. Although I tend, as a Czech, to favor a small dance over an ostentatious show, the pride of representing my country in a parade in front of those I loved was significant.

After the celebration we soldiers were given our first evening off, so I joined my companions at Mánes. Most of my friends had graduated from university and started their professional careers; some had completed their compulsory military service, while others were under way. The length of service had originally been fourteen months, but due to the security threats to the republic, it had grown to twenty-four.

Following this first night out, army life improved. We were all promoted to private first-class, with permission to leave camp two to three times a week. Not only could I resume my social activities, but I could do so in style. I exchanged the baggy uniform for a tailored one more suited to a doctor on temporary army duty.

Rather than being trained as a combat soldier, I received cavalry instruction because the army followed the old Austrian tradition of requiring medical officers to be on horseback. So, each day we marched to the stables, saddled up, and proceeded to the exercise grounds to put the horses through their paces. Sometimes I'd get a docile old mare, other times a wild pony. Equestrian training turned out to be my favorite part of training. I grew attached to my army special-order gray riding britches with balloon legs and custom-made buttons that held the pant bottoms tightly under my boots.

The other big priority was teaching us how to shoot. As a doctor, I expected to be treating bullet wounds, not causing them, but we were required to practice with all sorts of weapons, including rifles and light and heavy machine guns. In between riding and shooting we practiced wearing gas masks and crammed in some classroom time on tactics and strategy. After two months we were promoted to corporal.

By Christmas everyone in our unit had made sergeant. That's where half my fellow medical recruits topped out, but I finished my training with high marks and a rank of second lieutenant. To me the distinction was as rewarding as graduating from medical school with honors. Now I could get on with life as a doctor and an officer. When we were given the chance to request our next assignment, many picked army hospitals where they could get further medical training. I figured I was going to spend the rest of my career in hospitals, so I requested an assignment to the Third Mountaineering Regiment in the Tatra Mountains—an impressive landscape for cross-country skiing.

The Tatras are a beautiful snowcapped range along the Polish border, resembling the Alps but not as tall. The other doctors weren't interested, so I got my request. I had to work in the army's venereal disease clinic in Košice for six weeks while I waited for my transfer, but I received another promotion for my trouble so that I arrived in the Tatras as chief battalion medical officer. I discovered the mountaineering center was a retreat for senior officers and that the rest of us were expected to cater to them. I had little to do except sit in the swimming pool and once in a while

In Service of a Doomed Country

take part in a search for lost hikers. When I wasn't tending to the headaches and hemorrhoids of my superiors, I even got the chance to take off on the occasional ski trip.

Skiing provided adrenalin-fueled adventure as I challenged the Tatras' steeps, recapturing the virgin rush of my first day on skis. At eighteen my wild skiing had led to breaking both my tibia bones, but I wasn't going to let that stop me. Racing down the side of a cliff, I recalled Franta Schoenbaum's instructions on an earlier excursion to Sněžka, the highest peak of the Krkonoše Mountains: "Ignore your instincts! Turn your body down the hill. If you point your arms over the side of the cliff and get low, you can look over the edge."

The Tatras' skiing was exhilarating, but the edge was sometimes hard to spot. I skied alone, so no one would see me fall. Fear was inevitable, but I tried to avoid it. Up there one thing was clear—if I went over a sheer edge, I'd be sleeping on the frozen mountain under the ridge with my later-to-be-discovered body in a ravine. All the yodeling in the world wouldn't save me.

Zipping about the mountains would have been a marvelous way to pass my entire tour of duty, but it was impossible to ignore the war when listening to radio news of the Japanese assault on major Chinese cities. The Japanese occupation of Manchuria was ratified by Germany in February 1938, which inched the Nazis toward a more pro-Japan position. I also followed the war news of muddy clashes in Spain between Gen. Francisco Franco's Nationalist rebels and Republican Loyalists.

Other events nearer to our mountain retreat were drawing us closer to conflict. In March 1938 the Nazis marched into Austria without firing a shot. Hitler, the man I'd portrayed in cartoons, the son of an Austrian customs official, paraded through the streets of Vienna as the howling crowd of a half-million Austrians cheered the *Anschluss*—the "connection" between the two countries. Germany had been banned from uniting with the state in the Treaty of Versailles, but that meant nothing to Hitler as he wanted the land and about six million more Germans. This was an alarming development as it allowed the German army to move to our south, where our defenses were weakest. For several years Czechoslovakia fortified the line of bunkers and artillery emplacements along the German border, manned by individual regiments, but the annexation of Austria offered the Nazis a much broader line of assault.

All the while Adolf Hitler was working on a pretense that would justify more aggression. Konrad Henlein, the Sudeten German Peoples Party leader in Czechoslovakia, made visits to Berlin, causing political disorder when he returned. While the Prague government was offering some concessions to counteract the Sudeten Germans' demands for autonomy, the Czechoslovak war ministry reacted in May to the heightened threat by calling up some three hundred thousand reserves. Many people joined even without being summoned. Gas masks were distributed throughout the Czechoslovak populace, even in schools.

The summer 1938 was one of social unrest among the sympathetic ethnic Germans living in Czechoslovakia as Hitler and fellow Nazi Hermann Göring called for reunification with Germany. Hitler demanded the Sudeten border region gain self-determination and vowed military assistance. Encouraged, the Sudeten Germans began to arm themselves and adopt the Nazi slogan "One nation, one country, one leader."

The French declared they would come to the Czechoslovaks' aid if we were attacked, and my cushy assignment in the mountains ended as my troop was mobilized as border guards to the fortifications along the German border. I was intrigued by what we might find in the concrete turrets and system of defensive bunkers but also nervous. We traveled in a swarm of tanks.

At first the advice my father gave me when I began my military training came in handy: "The first step into danger might be the hardest. Remember downhill skiing and leave your apprehension behind." But my situation got worse faster than expected. We could see the ss [Schutzstaffel] forces goose-stepping on the border's other side. Seeing German soldiers with ferocious German shepherds standing beside them made me realize our plight.

We were a small nation facing the most ruthless warlord we'd met in our history, one who'd sworn to destroy Czech freedom and our very existence. Czechs had a long history, but our nation had a short one. Our army was outnumbered. I started thinking crazy thoughts: *A man can only die once. We are at the mercy of what Europe will do.* Although no shots were fired, it was the first feeling of confrontation I'd experienced since joining the army.

Hitler began the massive bombardment necessary to destroy our defenses before his army marched in—his weapons were words instead of artillery. Each day the German-language newspapers and radio became more vicious in inventing some new outrage by the Czechoslovaks against the German Sudeten population, on the western border of Germany, south of the Sudeten Mountains. The Nazis vowed to defend the Sudeten ethnic Germans against Czechoslovak oppression and warned of grave consequences if things weren't resolved. The German population responded as Hitler hoped, crying for the sort of "liberation" that Austria had experienced. On September 13, 1938, agitators took over the train stations and control of many police stations, post offices, and Jewish shops. The Sudeten leadership refused to negotiate with the Czechoslovakian government because the breakdown of law and order made the internal situation impossible to resolve. Martial law was declared.

Unfortunately for Europe, the Sudeten Germans found an audience in Neville Chamberlain, Britain's prime minister. Chamberlain had already caused his foreign secretary, Anthony Eden, to resign in protest when the prime minister attempted to appease Italy's fascist dictator, Benito Mussolini. Now Chamberlain began pressuring Czechoslovakia to allow the Sudeten districts (referred to now as "Sudetenland") to secede. When our government refused, Chamberlain flew to Munich to join French and Italian representatives as they listened to the crazed little man threaten to take the territory by force. Hitler was hoping Britain and France would step aside so he wouldn't have to carry through with his threat, and they agreed to do exactly that.

Without even consulting the Czechoslovak government, which wasn't invited to the conference, the English and French agreed on September 29 to let Germany occupy the Sudetenland. Also ceded from Czechoslovakia were smaller parts of southern Slovakia and southern Ruthenia to Hungary. Poland received Těšín and two minor border areas in northern Slovakia in return for Hitler's promise not to invade the rest of Czechoslovakia. Naive and spineless, Chamberlain flew back to Britain with the now-infamous Munich Agreement (or "Munich Dictate," as we Czechs referred to it, as we had no say in its terms) in one hand and his umbrella in the other. He assured the world that Germany would be satisfied with this one last bit of territory and waved a single sheet of paper signed by Chamberlain and Hitler. That pact, named the "Anglo-German Naval Agreement," was, as Chamberlain described it in the newspaper, "symbolic of the desire of our two peoples never to go to war with one another again." The German occupation of the Sudeten districts began the next day.

All of us who cared about the future of Czechoslovakia felt betrayed, depressed, and vulnerable. Over twenty years we had developed a considerable military, but our army and air force were about a tenth of the size of Germany's. Until the Munich Agreement, Britain and France had pledged to protect our republic. Now we stood alone, and I had no illusions about what that meant. Czechoslovakia, born of the last war, was in danger of disappearing if another war broke out.

I already knew the struggle between the Slavs and Germans had deep roots. Like the Jews, Czechs and other Slavic peoples stood in the way of the German drive for Lebensraum, "living space," in the east. Hitler viewed the rich expanses of land to the east of Germany to be its natural sphere of influence and the heart of a future greater German empire. My father often told me what he'd heard from his German friends about Hitler's racial ideas recorded in his 1925 book *Mein Kampf*, "My Struggle." Dad described it as lunacy and shared why we couldn't ignore it: "What Hitler wants most is to enslave our Slavic peoples to Germans and to remove us Jews."

But it wasn't one man's plan to cull the non-Aryan Slavs and Jews. While I was in medical school in 1933, the German legislators of the Nazi state enacted the Law to Prevent Hereditarily Diseased Offspring. This law kept "undesirables" from having children, through sterilization by German physicians of certain mentally or physically impaired individuals. Among their targets were also the ethnic minority Roma, known as "Gypsies." Did their physicians have no hearts?

At night, as I lay stewing in my bed along with the other not-quite-ready-to-do-battle soldiers, I thought about the world leaders who'd signed the Munich Dictate. They knew who and what they were dealing with. Years before Adolf Hitler became the German chancellor, in countless speeches he'd espoused his belief of racial "purity" in what he called an Aryan "master race." Even while I'd drawn my Adolf-like caricature as he was, not particularly tall with brown hair, he let the world know the "superior" Aryan physical traits, or Nordic type, and "inferior" traits of non-white and Slavic peoples. The nature of this man's character should have been a warning to the world. In the meantime our small regiment received new orders.

We were ordered to retreat and surrender the Sudetenland to the Germans while helping to supervise our evacuation. It took less than three weeks for the occupation forces to assume their positions and incorporate the region into Germany. It was a strange and sickening feeling to arrive in Sudetenland and realize the land I was standing on—land we'd been sworn to defend—had become German soil because of a paper signed by the leaders of other countries. It was even more disturbing to discover we had no leader of our own. Five days after the betrayal at Munich, President Beneš resigned and fled, accepting an invitation to lecture at the University of Chicago. Middle Europe was once again in flux and Czech sovereignty again in danger. The vultures were circling. As a Slavic man fitting the Nuremberg definition of "Jew," I saw myself as a double target.

With orders to observe the turnover of our land to the Germans, our troops watched German soldiers cross the old Czecho-slovak border near Grulich (today's Králíky). The Germans arrived as motorized infantry and cyclists, celebrated by what appeared to be all three million or so ethnic Germans living there. Cheering, the locals were already waving the German flag. I knew the loss of our defenses and industries in that area was a brutal blow to our nation's security.

In ominous silence we packed our gear and watched the Germans move into our bunkers. What remained from the dictate of our truncated country was cobbled into the Czecho-Slovak Republic. Known as the "Second Republic," it consisted essentially of Moravia and Bohemia in the west, Slovakia at the center, and Subcarpathian Ruthenia bordering the Ukraine to the east. As the turmoil unfolded, a Slovak autonomous government formed, as did two factions in Subcarpathian Ruthenia.

The peaceful transfer proved to be a cruel fiction as the Nazis set off a wave of violence against anyone who opposed their plan to Germanize the entire territory. As my fellow demoralized soldiers and I retreated, we observed many Czechoslovak citizens become homeless refugees. Through the bitter cold, along windswept roads, they traveled with a few belongings on their carts.

I barely had time to absorb this disturbing scene before I received orders to return to the Tatra Mountains, where there was nothing to do but resume hiking and skiing. When I arrived, the contrast between the mountains and what I'd just left seemed surreal and unfair. But there was nothing any Czech could do to save the Sudetenland. In a chess game played by others, we were a forfeited pawn.

My post remained tranquil until I took the wrong day off to go skiing. While I was gone, a drunk general fell into an empty swimming pool and suffered a small bruise and laceration on his head. "Where did Holzer go?" echoed through the camp.

I should have been there to stitch him up, but a doctor from another regiment had to be called in. When I returned from the slopes, one of our most arrogant officers, a big noise in the organization, grilled me: "Where have you been, Holzer? What were you thinking? Don't you understand your responsibility?" My ears buzzed, while my eyes fixed on his inward-facing bushy eyebrows.

In the spirit of the moment, as my muse Švejk would have done, I launched into a long ramble about how anyone can make mistakes. For several minutes, with sweat dripping from my brow, I described many unrelated examples of errors I'd observed while on assignment in the mountains. In the end, unlike Švejk, I recovered my better self, but it was too late—from the officer's eye roll, I knew I was in trouble.

As punishment, I was transferred to the hinterland of Subcarpathian Ruthenia as head surgeon of the Forty-Fifth Infantry, a tank battalion made up of nearly all men of both Russian and Ukrainian ethnicities. Ruthenia was the small eastern tail of our country that rested on the eastern Carpathian Mountains' southern slopes, bordered on the east and west by rivers. The Austro-Hungarian Empire used the term *Ruthenian* for "Ukrainian." Before becoming part of the new Czechoslovak Republic after World War I, Ruthenia was under Hungarian rule for many years and then was briefly under Russian occupation. The region was destitute, the inhabitants mostly peasants and woodcutters. But under Czechoslovak rule they were the recipients of improved infrastructure and more liberal education inclusive of the various ethnic groups. Their language, made up of several dialects more akin to Ukrainian than Russian, wasn't suppressed, and they managed to escape the famine that took place in Ukraine in the early 1930s. Since the Czechoslovak unit was made up of primarily Russian speakers, I was forced to learn Russian to add to my Czech and German.

A densely tree-covered, hilly region interspersed with picturesque rolling hayfields supported a rural population. The towns were about 80 percent Jewish, and bearded Hasidic Jews could be seen walking around in their long black coats, their sidelocks of curly hair dangling from fur-trimmed hats on Saturdays. The Sabbath, Shabbat, was their day of rest and spiritual contemplation. The non-Hasidic Jews had neater haircuts, were sometimes clean-shaven, and sported more fashionable hats. Newspapers published in Hebrew, Yiddish, and Hungarian reported the news.

The Ukrainians who lived there were Orthodox Christians and the Hungarians Catholic and Lutheran. I enjoyed this variety because all the holy days were honored by our troops, sometimes providing several three-day weekends.

The infantry traveled on half-tracks—trucks with regular wheels in the front and caterpillar wheels on the back. Our unit was equipped with some light Czechoslovak-made Škoda tanks and motorcycles. As a military officer, I had five ambulances for my own use and was assigned a small Tatra car—the equivalent of a jeep. For guidance I was given a map of our reworked nation, which proclaimed, "Small but ours." How long it would remain ours remained a mystery.

At the beginning of my new assignment, all was peaceful. But as a reminder of the ever-evolving tumultuous world beyond, someone had put up a poster in our living quarters reading, "We'll all be soldiers at time of need," to which someone else had added, "The enemy did not defeat us—the friend betrayed us."

Around mid-November a local Jewish newspaper account reported that Germany had rounded up thousands of Polish Jews living in Germany and deported them. The paper disclosed that the Germans had transported them by train, then "dumped them across the Polish border." The Poles didn't want them either, so for weeks thousands of desperate people were stranded in a small border town with little food or water. Then the paper reported about the madness in Germany after a young Jewish man shot a German diplomat in Paris. Turned out he was a member of one of those families and had taken action.

On my radio I heard the desperate teenager's emotional statement from Paris. With maturity beyond his years, the young man articulated the situation: "I was not motivated by hatred but by love for my father and my people, who've endured unbearable suffering. To be Jewish is not a crime—we are not animals. The Jewish people have a right to live."

By then Nazi Germany had determined that being Jewish was indeed a crime. Nazi Party propagandists saw this incident as a good way to incite people against German Jewry. Newspaper reports from Prague, which reached us a few days late, revealed these attacks. Nazi storm troopers took revenge by burning hundreds of synagogues and temples, thousands of Jewish businesses, and dozens of Jewish communal buildings. Even old folks' homes were attacked. Thirty thousand Jews were rounded up and sent to concentration camps. The Nazis beat up countless Jews who were protecting their homes or businesses, killing about one hundred that night. So many store windows were shattered that the rampage became known as "Kristallnacht," the night of broken glass.

It was now obvious what the Nazis were capable of carrying out. The news didn't stop there. Over the next two weeks reports of brutal beatings and persecution in Germany were so depressing that there was no celebration this time when our diminished country received a new president.

Emil Hácha, president of the Supreme Administrative Court in Czechoslovakia, was chosen by the national assembly on November 30, 1938, to lead our country. With no previous role in the governments involved in the dismemberment of the country thus far, he faced new demands from Hitler and his allies to give up more territory. Rather than waiting for a reply, ill-trained and poorly equipped German-allied Hungarians poured over the borders to seize parts of Ruthenia. My unit traveled between the borders, in frigid subzero weather, trying to plug all the holes in the Czech defense, which resembled Swiss cheese. With a crack of his knuckles, our commanding officer warned us, "If we attack the Hungarians, the Germans will invade." Our orders were strict on how to proceed so our clashes didn't launch an actual war. I was committed to that approach, but it was not so easy to carry out. As the single Jewish soldier in our small enclave, I was most aware of the looming danger.

While we were holding the line between Berehovo and Mukačevo, my regiment captured about three hundred Hungarian insurgents in civilian clothes who had been trying to blow up bridges and sabotage railroads. They were insurgent nationalists, but from the Czech point of view, they were terrorists. They did their dirty work at night while hiding in haystacks by the day. If we suspected someone was in a stack, my team set it on fire so the wide-eyed Hungarians would run out as fast as they could. As I waited, unsure if anyone was in the smoldering hay, my heart raced so fast I felt as if I'd pass out, but I never did. Our orders were to fire shots into the air. I suspected there was a reciprocal order on the Hungarian side. But even without a declared war, we heard that five Czechoslovaks were killed and six wounded in border clashes. The Hungarians' commanding officer was Count Esterházy, from a well-known aristocratic family, and we took him captive.

We held our prisoners in an old castle ruin in Mukačevo. One day my commanding officer called me to his office. "I want you to go up to the castle to see Count Esterházy as he is complaining of pain and discomfort," he told me. "He's announced to the guards that he is on a hunger strike. He may be bluffing, but either way, report back."

His order meant a beautiful drive in the old Austro-Hungarian town, nestled at the foot of the Carpathian Mountains. The centuries-old castle, with its massive stone walls and turrets, was famous. Known as Palanok Castle, the fortress became a prison sometime in the 1800s. When I arrived, a scowling guard escorted me to Count Esterházy.

As I entered his cell, he lay on a straw mattress, his feet stretched beyond it because of his height. Esterházy turned his thin face with its prominent nose toward me, raised his mustached upper lip, and demanded to know my commission. As I didn't speak any Hungarian and he didn't offer any Czech, we conversed in German.

"I'm a second lieutenant."

"Then you should be standing at attention as I am a colonel in the Hungarian army," he bellowed.

That struck me as silly, and I started laughing before I stated the obvious: "Now wait a minute! You are my prisoner, and besides that,

In Service of a Doomed Country

I am a doctor. I don't see any reason why we should play soldier. You tell me what's your trouble, and I will see what I can do for you."

With that the count mellowed and with nose wrinkled started complaining that the food he had been given was army-issue bread and water and he was constipated. I examined him, confirmed his diagnosis, and gave him a laxative. Although we represented opposite sides, I felt a bond with him in the wish for an improved diet. I ordered him some better food, but his improved rations merely lasted about three more days because the government in Prague instructed us to chase the prisoners back into Hungary. I always suspected they turned around and came back to do more mischief as sometimes a face on an escapee from a burning haystack looked familiar.

While I was concerned with haystacks, it wasn't lost on me from brief exposure to radio broadcasts that instability was not confined to our new borders. On January 26, 1939, Barcelona, the heart of the Republican resistance, fell to General Franco's Nationalists. After a bloody civil war, a dictator controlled another powerful European country. The fall from freedom reminded me of many debates my friends and I had held in Café Mánes, speculating on the outcome in Spain. Studious Karel Schoenbaum would always end our deliberations with a question: "Fascism or antifascism? When the resolution occurs, what will it mean to us?" I knew the answer. Franco prevailed with the help of Nazi Germany and Fascist Italy. With no ally Czechoslovakia was likely the next pawn to be moved in Europe's ever-growing totalitarian chess game.

Our Czech psyche continued to deteriorate as Hitler demanded we surrender what remained of our independence and accept Germany's "protection." Our history, full of uprisings, occupations, reversals, and betrayals, was a constant reminder of life's uncertainties. If we were to accept this guy as our safeguard, we were headed for an all-time low. My father felt the same way, and I thought how, if he'd been marching beside me, he would have reminded me: "We must persevere and be patient. Remember, the word for 'patience' has the same root as the verb 'to suffer.'"

I never was sure why he liked to tell me that last part.

As I lay on my lumpy mattress one frosty evening, trying to forget the latest haystack that scorched my eyebrows as it burst into flames, I had no idea that Hitler had summoned President Hácha to Berlin on March 14, 1939. He informed Hácha that German troops would enter Prague the next day and warned that any resistance would result in severe punishment inflicted on the civilian population. The next day, true to his word, the German army marched into snow-swept Prague. My country ceased to exist, and my anticipated September 1939 army discharge vanished. As an icy wind howled, I watched my breath float above me, forming white steam. With a shiver I imagined Hitler's hand around the throat of my country.

The next day Hitler stood beneath fluttering swastika flags at Prague Castle. He was flanked by two of his top thugs, Heinrich Himmler, commander of German Police, and Reinhard Heydrich, chief of the Reich Security Service, which included the Gestapo. The Germans formed the Protectorate of Bohemia and Moravia out of the western provinces. Slovakia became independent, with a Slovak Catholic-Fascist government led by priest Jozef Tiso, under the protection of Germany, intensifying already-in-place anti-Semitic policies. Poland and Hungary seized areas farther to the east that they had long felt belonged to them. Subcarpathian Ruthenia, which was in turmoil, was left to Hungary. In the middle of this mess in Ruthenia were two fully armed Czechoslovak army divisions—including mine.

Sometime around the nineteenth of March, after consultation with the unit commanders, our commanding general retreated to Slovakia. Before our groups started moving, the general offered to allow anybody who wanted to go to Romania, a non-occupied German territory on the border of the eastern part of Ruthenia, to do so. A few soldiers, most of them Jews from Slovakia and some from Bohemia and Moravia, accepted the offer and were given transportation. (After the war I met up with one fellow in New York who told me they sailed from Romania to Palestine and ended up in the Czechoslovak exile army in Britain.)

I chose to stay with my unit. Technically, the Czechoslovak army no longer existed, so we scattered to different army installations when we arrived in the town of Prešov. I ended up in barracks downtown. The Slovaks wanted to disarm us and take our heavy equipment, tanks, artillery, and everything else—they considered us prisoners of war—but nothing happened. The Slovaks posted guards at the gates of the downtown barracks—untrained men in civilian clothes with armbands and all kinds of odd weapons like hunting rifles, much tamer than our puška vz. 33 bolt-action rifles. My unit learned that Czech engineers were still operating the railway in Prešov and in most of Slovakia. The officers made an agreement with the Czech railroad man still in charge of his station to assemble several trains at the Prešov station. At about two in the morning on March 22, we started marching out of the barracks with the tanks in front of us to the train station. Out-manned, the Slovak national guardsmen looked the other way. At the station my unit placed its tanks on flat cars and boarded the train for the Moravian border.

When we arrived in Moravia, we met a group of German soldiers, perhaps twenty or thirty, who did not know what to do with us. Now amid them were two armed divisions of the defunct Czechoslovak army. All kinds of negotiations followed, and then a German armored train arrived with a horde of well-dressed German generals. With dirty faces, long messy hair, and foul body odor, we resembled a bunch of bums because we'd been in the field for about four weeks. I wore the same shirt for five days. The generals sat down with the Czech staff officers and decided to incorporate us into the German army. And so we were installed in the order of the German high command with the Wehrmacht emblem, a straight-armed *Balkenkreuz*, a stylized version of the Iron Cross. The flag for the commander was red and black with an arrow cross—a swastika—at its center. Both symbols blanketed my homeland on public buildings, railway stations, parks, and museums—emblems of how life would change for the Czechs.

The regiment continued to the outskirts of Brno, Moravia's capital, where our soldiers were scattered throughout different barracks. With nothing to do, we still got up at 6:00 a.m. for daily exercises, gymnastics, and soccer. I went to an office each morning and sat there as usual, taking care of soldiers' runny noses and diarrhea, but I became restless, trapped in an army within an invading army.

I recalled our afternoons at smoke-filled Mánes and Pavel Körper's description of the maniacal dedication the German people had for the Führer and his henchmen. I thought about the newspaper images after Kristallnacht, when Nazis ransacked Jewish homes, hospitals, and schools and arrested thousands. Sometimes there is no time to duck before history punches you in the face. I'd taken a left hook at full force. All I wanted was to return home, so after about ten days, I decided I would. *But how?*

In the Czechoslovak army the medical officer was also the hygienist and veterinarian, responsible for the quality of the unit's meat supply. Betting the Germans I'd deal with would never be able to read Czech, I wrote myself an order to go to the slaughterhouse to inspect the meat. Knowing how much Germans love official stamps; I covered the letter with rubber stamps and signed it with an illegible name. Then I asked my orderly, Václav, if he wanted to return to his home in the nearby town of Slavkov (Austerlitz in German), where Napoleon had once defeated the Austrian and Russian emperors. With a glimmer in his eye and an obvious yearning to return home, he agreed, and I told him to come along with me. We got into a military car and started toward the secured gate, where we were met by a burly, square-jawed German guard who greeted us with a stern "Where are you going?" As a single drop of sweat slid down my forehead, I handed him my papers. The German asked me if I could translate. "Of course," I answered in German, and the guard returned the order to me. I could have translated the order without looking since I wrote it, but I stared at the paper and read back to him in German. After a glance at the official stamps, the guard clicked his heels and responded, "Alles ist in Ordnung [Everything is in order]."

6. Valdik Holzer, Czechoslovak army, 1938.

With trembling hands gripping the steering wheel, Václav drove us through the gate, down a gently sloping road, meandering until we were about four blocks away from the barracks. My pulse raced as I fixated on the constant twitching of Václav's ashy pale cheek. At first not a word was spoken as we contemplated our individual fates. As I fidgeted with the mock order, I imagined a rifle shot to my head, a sadistic beating so brutal my liver burst, and a German shepherd jaw ripping my arm from my body. As Václav turned to face me in the back seat, he jolted me back to the present. With a cockeyed smile he bellowed, "You did it!"

"It wasn't only me. Together we outsmarted those bastards! You're the best driver ever!"

Our celebration was short. We knew the bastards would be coming after us.

"I have no interest to die young, do you? To be less conspicuous, we should separate."

Václav's foot slipped off the gas pedal as he turned onto a side street, where we parked the military car and shook hands. Without a long goodbye, I watched him stride briskly down a street toward the outskirts of town on his way to surprise his parents. He turned around once, allowing himself a small tight smile. I stood frozen and listened to his boots click on the cobblestones. The sound grew fainter, then silence, like a scene from a film in which I wished I'd played no part.

9

Compassionate Strangers

March 31–May 22, 1939

The pleasure of my springtime hike to Brno was diminished by my urgency to escape the Nazis. After what seemed an eternity but was a moment of hesitation, my old girl-friend's father, Mr. Levy, invited me into his home. His demeanor was cold and panic-stricken as he paced up and down the room.

I nodded, holding my breath until Mr. Levy cracked a thin-lipped half-smile to let me know I was safe, at least for the moment. I apologized for imposing and explained my clothing situation. "Normally I would be proud to wear my uniform," I told him, "but I need to blend in with the surroundings." Without a word Mr. Levy left and returned moments later with one of his shirts, a tie, and a handsome tweed jacket and knit vest. Luckily, we were about the same size. Mr. Levy then inquired how I was fixed for cash, and I confessed to being flat broke. He graciously gave me enough money for a train ticket to Prague, with some left over for a salami sandwich and coffee along the way. I thanked him and shook his hand before I headed for the station.

Brno was a relatively major city, so the hundred-year-old railway depot was large and ornate in the European fashion. It was formal, too, with arched entries and broad staircases. I strolled in, looking like a businessman on holiday, but froze as the train platform came into view. Uniformed German guards were checking everyone getting on or off the trains for identification papers. I had no documents of any kind—certainly not an army discharge—so I

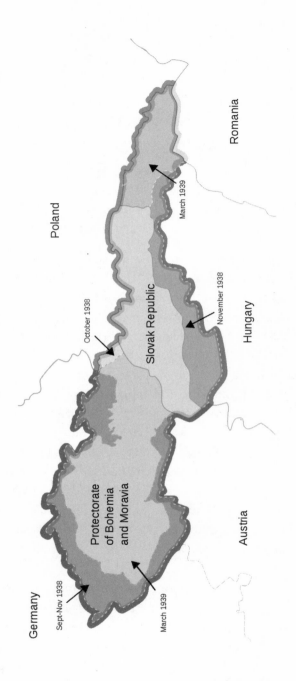

7. Partition of Czechoslovakia, 1938–39. Used with permission by U.S. Holocaust Memorial Museum.

wasn't sure what to do. I bought a ticket to Prague and stopped to get a German newspaper while I thought about my next move. I stood on the platform with the paper open and pretended to read, peering over it at the guards. I noticed there weren't enough of them to question each passenger, so they were shuffling between platforms, making random checks. I waited until I saw one guard leave his post and begin marching to another. I tucked the newspaper into the crook of my arm and aimed for the now unguarded train door. I still can't believe I got away with it.

I took a seat and congratulated myself for getting that far without incident. Seeing no immediate danger, I started to read the paper. The big news that day was once again about Neville Chamberlain, who had been awakened from his pipe dreams of appeasement. Chamberlain and the French were promising to fight if Germany invaded Poland. Next to the story was a photo of Hitler. I wondered if this new pledge could have much effect on the German führer after the British and French had proven themselves to be so weak. They'd allowed our once valiant little democracy to be devoured.

A quiet but stern voice interrupted my musings. I looked up to see the conductor leaning over me. I was fortunate he was a good Czech still operating the rail.

"The Germans won't fail to notice those army boots of yours," he said as he glanced around the car.

My pant legs had risen as I sat down. I pulled the material over the tops of my boots.

"That won't help," he urged. "You have to keep moving. There are Gestapo on the train, and they march through asking for discharge papers."

"How do I stay away from them?"

The conductor explained that they were systematic.

"They start at the front of the train and then get off at the next station, and on the next train they start at the front again. Seldom do they make it all the way through the train to the last car. As long as you keep ahead of them as they walk through the cars, you will be all right."

I thanked my new friend and started for the rear of the car, still clutching the newspaper. The photo of Hitler had shaken me as much as the conductor's warning. I thought about my caricatures, which were printed in a newspaper published by the Social Democrats, opponents of Nazism. Even if I made my way to Prague, would anyone there remember those drawings and connect them to me? The fear of the consequences of my innocent cartoons burned in my mind until the train had neared its destination, and I was startled by the conductor's voice once again. With his lips tightened, he warned me the main railroad terminal in Prague was full of German military police. "Before we get to the terminal, we will stop at a station where they are assembling the freight trains going east of Prague. The name of the station is Vysočany. The Gestapo patrol always gets out there on the train's left side. I will open the door on the right side so you can get out. You should crawl under the freight trains and get out of the station fast. Good luck."

I quietly thanked him and tried to tip him with the money I had received from Mr. Levy, but the brave patriot refused. With a dodge, duck, and a dive under freight cars, I followed the conductor's directions and slinked away from the well-armed Gestapo-infested station. In full view my knit vest served well as camouflage. When I left the train station, I climbed on a Prague tram.

My parents were now living in a modern district called "Vinohrady," southeast of Prague's New Town. It had been more than three weeks since I'd corresponded with them. I'd had no way to let them know my whereabouts because mail service was suspended in the chaos of the occupation. My mother was thrilled by my arrival. As she closed the door and jumped up and down, crying and laughing, she whispered in my ear, "If I'd lost you, it would've been unbearable."

The seismic changes that had happened at home along with the agony of my disappearance showed as new lines in her fifty-one-year-old face. She hugged me long and hard while my obviously relieved father waited his turn. He proceeded to give me a detailed and depressing description of the German army's entry into Prague.

"It's as if a light turned on a half-darkened stage with a series of new shadowy characters arriving in Prague with the spectacle of a German military parade," my father huffed. "The rhythmic click-stomp of German boot heels slapping down through the snow on the old stone streets was drowned out by the endless roar of big tanks and hundreds of motorized vehicles rolling up to St. Wenceslas Square. Behind the army were Gestapo with the face of boxers in high boots and black Mercedes with megaphones and submachine guns. Streams of German planes flew overhead, to make their presence known. Our resident Germans yelled out "Sieg Heil!" (Hail victory!), while many long-faced Czechs stood by in silence. As always, we show such a baffling willingness to comply. The radio advised everyone to remain calm, as if referring to a modest rainstorm. Once again we buckled while the Germans effortlessly entered our land and suffocated its life."

He continued, pausing to suggest we sit. "The happiest are the street vendors selling sausage. They've never seen such a lucky break with the number of soldiers, ten times our military, all at once on the streets of Prague." He stood and walked to the window and gazed at the scene below. "The worst part is before the proclamation of our dissolution; this German führer soiled the sheets of our castle, the former home to the kings of Bohemia. But this Hitler is an ordinary man. He would be nothing without the people. Don't worry, my boy. When things don't go well for them, they will come to their senses."

Standing, then sitting, then standing again, my father compared us to a nation of Švejks. "You know, son, Švejk tended to outsmart everyone by playing stupid. When Švejk amused himself, he turned the world around him into an enormous joke. I fear that some Czechs might believe our famous ironic sense of humor would be enough to overcome the German oppressors. I witnessed some people wearing badges with 'We will not surrender' and 'Beneš is not asleep.'"

My father's descriptions of stiff-arm salutes and fanatical shouts from the pro-Nazi rabble that had come out of the shadows in the days since the occupation affected my mood. To cope, Dad and I discussed the merits of alcohol under these powerless circumstances and wondered if any good wine cellars were still open to us.

Mother insisted on feeding me hearty roast pork with white cabbage and potato dumplings, and I insisted on eating every last bite. She told me there was already a scarcity of eggs and certain meats because the Germans were raiding our warehouses. To serve her traditional Bohemian buffet, she got out antique plates along with her finest crystal water glasses and arranged it all on a white tablecloth.

Not wanting to be outdone, my father brought out Becherovka, a potent herbal liqueur, and we toasted, "To togetherness." Nothing else seemed toast worthy. As we ate, our conversation was filled with family member updates. Grandmother suffered from gout; Uncle Rudi feared his construction business would collapse, and Aunt Válda and Uncle Jaroslav were worried about their sawmill and if sons Jiří and Pavel would be able to continue their schooling. My parents described how, two days after the occupation, a radio broadcast announced that special commissars were put in charge of Jewish shops, prompting their concern over my mother's sister Karolina losing her retail store and livelihood.

With Nazis patrolling Prague and Benešov streets, the Jews all had great apprehension about leaving home, even for the most mundane tasks. If they did, it was in ones or twos. With downcast eyes Dad declared the musical scene had almost died out. I held back from describing what I'd observed during my Nazi encounters. As the Becherovka took hold, our conversation turned light, with me telling stories from the field, like the incident when the officer dove into a waterless pool and I was nowhere to be found. My father couldn't quit laughing as he cited my many "good soldier" characteristics. He made me chuckle when he said, "Flattery will get you anywhere."

When I finished eating, I set out to find my old friends and see how Prague was faring. Venturing into the streets, I discovered that my city had become Hitler's city. The German army had replaced the Castle Guard at Prague Castle, where Hitler had issued the decree establishing the Reich Protectorate of Bohemia and Moravia. The title described the relationship of "protective" Germans to their "protected" territory, which included the two historic Czech Lands, Bohemia being the westernmost area. My stomach turned from their euphemistic designation, which suggested they were shielding us with its fiction of an autonomous Czech regime.

German soldiers patrolled everywhere, and red, black, and white swastika banners—some several stories tall—hung from prominent buildings, defacing the City of One Hundred Spires and the mélange of architecture that fostered such pride among all Czechs. The occupation force had declared German the official language, and official documents and signs were now bilingual—in German and Czech. Further confusing the situation in Prague, the Germans mandated a right-hand traffic system, forcing the end of Czechoslovak left-lane driving and creating temporary chaos in the streets.

Charles University still functioned, but it was in a state of flux, like most everything in Prague, including my old college haunt, Mánes Café. I found hardly anyone I knew there, which came as no surprise. It was obvious most people weren't venturing out if they could avoid it. What I saw of our city under siege fit all too well with what I'd observed in the Sudetenland. I wanted nothing to do with the situation in the so-called protectorate. I could see that the freedom of my heart and mind was disallowed and it was worth risking my life to escape from the domination.

When I got home, I told my parents that I planned to leave and would devote myself to figuring out how best to do that and where to go. They sat on the sofa as I paced anxiously across the wood floor. "I didn't want to tell you about how the Germans treated the Czechs fleeing from Sudetenland," I said, "but I must inform you their use of dogs was bloody brutal, with jackboot tactics. I've heard enough of their rock crushing as they goose-step on our pavement." Mother and Dad appeared unfazed by my abridged stories; I assume they were trying to throw me off my track during my spiel.

To say something about World War I that would resonate with my dad, I described the arrogant gaze of one German general, Von So-and-So, when they incorporated my army unit into theirs: "With well-polished boots, the general noticed my not-so-well-shined boots after us soldiers had roamed aimlessly on dusty roads for weeks after their occupation. He spit on my boot and mocked me in German, saying, 'You're the perfect example of why Czechs can never win a war with your so-called superior army. You don't fight back, you cower with dirty shoes.'"

Unable to read my dad's expression, I stated my proposal: "It is most important, I stress, for you both to come with me. We must leave together." My doleful mother, sitting like a statue with a white handkerchief in her hand partially covering her face, looked at my father rather than me. Without hesitation he answered for them both.

"If you feel you must go, we'll support you," he said. "But you must not worry about us because there is nothing to worry about." His eyes drifted down. "We have been through much worse than this, and so has this country. Even President Hácha's speech the day after occupation described the invasion as 'a short episode in our national history.' Just another one in a long line of tyrants, I tell you. You go make a life for yourself, and who knows? Maybe when you're a great doctor somewhere in the world, you'll send for us and we'll be glad to join you."

My father's easy smile, usually so reassuring, made me wonder if he understood what was happening around us. Gesturing to drive home my point, I started to tell longer stories about goose-stepping invasion troops with smug faces driving out desperate refugees and uniformed guards at train depots with swastika armbands pompously giving orders, but my father's expression never changed. When he'd heard enough, with piercing eyes and upturned chin, he shook his head to cut me off. The palm of his hand fell heavily onto the table.

"You seem to forget that I endured my own war—a smelly trench war with cigar smoke mixed with gunpowder and the stench of death. The bloodshed, chaos, and senseless cruelty around me as people lost limbs or lives have not been erased from my mind. Four empires, millions of lives lost in a conflict on a scale never seen before. We were introduced to new horrors such as chemical weapons and shell shock. War is madness! You don't have to provide me with new images of Germans who view us as imbecilic!"

In a few sentences Dad blurted out more description than I'd ever heard from him about World War I. Then, as if to boost his own morale, his tone changed: "That war swept away most of those old dynasties. You must remember our families lived under the Habsburgs for centuries, and we made out all right. I don't think this Hitler will last nearly as long." Smoothing his shirt, he glanced at Mom, whose face had gone blank. "I know the Germans better than you do, better than most. They love to parade around and make noise, but in the end they'll be gone, and we'll still be here. Son, you must take my word. Our history has shown surprising powers of endurance."

His speech put a stake through my mother's heart. Before he finished, she'd left the room, and I could hear the tea kettle at full boil. She tried to pour me a cup, but her hand shook wildly. With the handkerchief at her eyes, she sobbed as she choked out, "You will have to pour your own tea."

I made several more attempts to change my parents' decision over the next two months, but I failed to persuade them. It surprised me, although I suppose it ought not to have. They didn't want to leave their home, livelihood, family and friends. I told them I would continue to think things through and leave when the time was right.

One evening my dad gazed at me with a look in his eyes I'd never seen before. His somber words held the final tone of a good-bye: "I hope I've been a worthy tutor for you on how to live your life with independence and self-sufficiency. As our only child, my dear boy, I gave you my undivided attention. Now what I wish for you is a decent and fulfilled life."

It was one of those rare moments when the past was asking something of the future. At first I couldn't get words past my lips. My weak response, "I hope I've been a good apprentice," was followed by a strong embrace. As I leaned in and let go in the circle of my dad's arms, I felt a healing balm.

Above all, my parents did not want to be a burden to me. I know they wished I could stay with them, but we all understood that was impossible as I had no army discharge papers and would be arrested. My circumstance placed them in danger of detention or worse.

I managed to contact several of my friends and even had a couple of informal reunions at Mánes, although the carefree atmosphere had changed at any café that still allowed Jews. As was true all over in Prague, patrons now spoke softly and looked around for unfamiliar faces before saying anything that could be interpreted as a complaint about the Germans. My old crowd shared my apprehension, but the degree of concern for their safety varied. Most Jews assumed they would always have the option of surrendering their valuables in return for an exit visa. "The Nazis mostly are thieves," they would say.

Some friends and relatives were in what the Nazis had proclaimed "mixed marriages"—unions of Jew with non-Jew—like Franta and Andula Schoenbaum and my father's sister Valerie (Aunt Válda) and her husband, Jaroslav Mařík. Once a rarity, mixed marriages had grown in the country by the time of occupation to the highest proportion existing in Europe. My father thought the trend was nurtured by our republic's separation of church and state and free choice of religious denomination, along with the legalization of civil marriage. He often said with an easy smile that all the intermarriages helped "grow indifference to religion while extending goodwill as most people living in Prague are becoming related to Jews."

Initially, there was a degree of leniency toward Jews in such marriages, so many didn't rush to leave the country. The roundup and arrest of Social Democrats and other anti-Nazis was under way. Some planned to emigrate if they could get exit permits. Alarmed at widespread arrests, the British Legation became active in securing these permits. Karel "Bála" Ballenberger left for London just before the occupation, as did Karel Schoenbaum and his wife, Katka, rumored to have been warned at Karel's workplace that the invasion was coming. As Jews, they predicted that they would be unwanted—or worse—in the protectorate.

Bála, the Social Democrat activist who had persuaded me to submit those now-incendiary caricatures to the party paper, seemed confident he was at risk of arrest. Encouraged by her father, Leopold Langer, a prestigious Jewish lawyer in Prague, Bála's wife, Milena, stayed behind with their two children. She gave German lessons to earn money with the hope she could join Bála in London.

My cousin Risa Porges was lucky. I ran into him on a rainy street in Old Town Square after he'd heard the news he'd been cleared to emigrate to Palestine. Near us were several ss officers strutting around, one a captain with a black collar patch with three pips. In a hushed, nervous tone, as we ate spicy sausage dogs tamed by bitter sauerkraut, Risa explained how his escape was to unfold: "The priority is given to groups of Czech antifascists and émigrés from Germany who found temporary asylum in Czechoslovakia and are in the most danger. From the transporting agency, we've received confidential information that we'll travel by boat on the Danube River to Romania to the estuary of the Black Sea. To reach the Danube River, we'll take a train from Prague to Vienna. Once there, we'll sail to Palestine, where we'll enter illegally and at our own risk. We need passports and ten reichsmarks each. Our luggage has to be under forty pounds."

Risa paused for an excruciating moment, tears filling his worried eyes. "I'm anxious now as I need to say goodbye to my family," he said. "We leave within a few days."

Nearby the skeleton on the medieval astronomical clock mounted on the Old Town City Hall struck the hour. I thought of what might become of us all. Risa and I shook hands, and as he turned to walk away, his lips curved into a wistful smile. I smiled back. I tried to avoid all the dark possibilities. My local circle of friends was becoming a worldwide circle, and I was helpless to change it.

By mid-April even subdued discussions at Mánes became impossible. I arrived one day to find a sign on the door: NO JEWS ALLOWED. A passing stranger joined me. "That Pácal is a bastard," the man imparted as he turned away in disgust, referring to the café's manager by name. "He was happy to take the Jews' money all these years, but now he shows his true colors."

How many other bastards had been smiling at me as they waited for the day they could put up such a sign? I decided to hurry up with my exit plan before I found out the hard way.

The first thing I had to do was get a passport. I was required to surrender my old one when I entered the army. I went to the passport division of the state police in Prague, where I encountered a long line. After about three hours of waiting, I spoke with a friendly Czech policeman. Except for my army discharge papers, which I did not have, I presented the policeman with all the required documents. He overlooked the discharge paper requirement and issued passport number 7783 right on the spot. Staring deep into my eyes, the Czech policeman apologized: "I'm terribly sorry; it won't be a good old Czechoslovakian passport anymore. I have to put this little label on it." Out of his drawer he pulled a tan-colored sticker, licked it, and stuck it on the front page. It read: "Deutsches Reich, Protektorat Böhmen und Mähren" (German Reich, Protectorate of Bohemia and Moravia). Then he turned to me and whispered, "Now you see, Dr. Holzer, I didn't stick it on too tight, so when you get across the border out of Germany, you take it off and you have a real Czechoslovak passport again."

I started to thank him for his kindness, but he interrupted: "Another thing, I'm not allowed to make the passport for more than ninety days. It says 'exit only—no return.' So, when you get to Paris or London, go straight to the old Czechoslovakian embassy if it is still functioning. They will change it so you can return to Czechoslovakia when the time is right."

I had to leave the Czech Lands within ninety days, but I still needed permission from the secret police—the Gestapo—who were now headquartered at Petschek Palace. The Petschek (Pečeks) were German-speaking Jewish bankers, in the vein of the Rothschilds. At one time they had branches all over Austria-Hungary. After World War I they built a large, somber, gray stone building near Prague's Woodrow Wilson Railroad Station that housed their bank offices and some apartments on the top floor. In 1938, as the Nazi threat loomed in Europe, the Petschek family departed for the United States. When I arrived at the palace, the line outside reached several blocks. People stayed for days waiting with their passports to get an exit permit. Visas, landing permits, and passports were tangled in a complicated bureaucracy. Some families took turns and brought along chairs and even folding cots so that they could keep their spots in the slow-moving line. This wasn't a matter of waiting for tickets to a concert or even for bread; they were waiting in line for survival.

I decided there must be a quicker way to get into the palace but failed to find one until several days later, when I ran into Dr. Veselý, my old acquaintance from Benešov. He was related to our neighbor but not a lawyer, a physician. I worked under him on my first army assignment at the venereal disease clinic. Intense with a cautious voice, he told me he was secretly negotiating with the British to take a group of doctors and nurses to Rhodesia, and he asked if I wanted to join them. I told him I would love to go. "There are things you have to do on your own to make this happen," his directions came out in one nervous burst. "You need to get an exit permit from the Gestapo. Then take it to the British embassy and get the necessary visa." I knew it sounded easier than it was. Then Dr. Veselý added a suggestion that made a big difference in my quest and perhaps my life: "You can get a Gestapo exit permit if you go to Zlín in Moravia."

I knew Zlín well as Bata Shoe Company's headquarters, founded by Tomáš Baťa, so I set out immediately. Although famous for being one of the world's first shoe manufacturers, ubiquitous Bata was much more. It produced aircraft, bicycles, tires, and other machinery. At that time the company employed around sixty thousand people worldwide in some thirty countries, and more than forty thousand workers were Czechs and Slovaks. More important to me, Bata had an active medical department, where I had worked during medical school. For their employees the company had built housing, schools, and hospitals, for which they'd assembled quite a medical staff. I spent one summer in Zlín when Bata was making protective chemical weapons gas masks for the Czechoslovak army. I did research so the masks would fit properly. My job included drawing and measuring face profiles of Bata company employees. In my army basic training I practiced with those masks that I had helped refine, and fortunately, I still knew people at Bata.

On my arrival in Zlín, I contacted a couple of doctors in the medical department, and they told me the Bata company usually got permits for its employees in Uherské Hradiště, the county seat, nineteen miles away. One doctor described people who were refused permits heading to northern Moravia, where an underground tunnel connected coal mines to Polish mines on the other side of the border. "The coal miners take people down and escort them to the other side."

I hoped not to become that desperate. Before I left Zlín, one of my Bata acquaintances gave me a letter of recommendation indicating I was to become an employee in the Bata office in Singapore. Although no longer on their payroll, I sensed I was part of an effort to send workers and equipment from Nazi-occupied lands for purposes other than ensuring durable footwear.

Upon my arrival in Uherské Hradiště, I went to the Gestapo office, where, much to my surprise, the fellow in charge was a former skiing partner from my Tatra Mountains army assignment. He was part of the German minority population living in Slovakia at the time, and since we'd last seen each other, he'd gone to

Germany and become an s s member. He recognized me but pretended he didn't. I wasn't sure if he knew how I had left the army, but I appreciated that he didn't expose me.

The s s officer behind the counter told me he'd give me my required authorization but that I was obliged to go to the nearby Internal Revenue Department to get a certificate showing that all my taxes were paid. I had never paid any taxes as I had gone from medical school into the army, so I worried about what would happen next. With a weary sigh, the official at the revenue office asked me what I wanted the certificate for.

"It's for the Gestapo."

"Why sure," he replied in Czech with a smirk. He typed a letter stating my taxes were paid. "Now, here you have that Gestapo shit. Have a good trip," he murmured as he handed me the form. I nodded appreciation and was on my way.

I returned to the Gestapo with the required paperwork and received a stamp in my passport indicating that I had to leave the country by June 17, 1939. It was May, so this was less than half the ninety days the Czechoslovak policeman had thought I would have—the Nazis wanted Jews gone. With my limited passport and little time before my exit visa expired, I needed to work fast. I returned to Prague and searched for Dr. Veselý but couldn't find him. The Rhodesia plan had fallen apart.

I now had to change some money into foreign currency so that I could buy tickets once I left the country. The Czechoslovak crown was not worth much by then because of the German occupation. After the Munich Agreement a group of English people who disapproved of how Czechoslovakia had been sold out by Chamberlain established a fund of about one-third of a million pounds. This fund, administered by the lord mayor of London, provided foreign currency to those who left Czechoslovakia for political reasons. The Quakers in Prague managed the money, and I was eligible to buy up to two hundred British pounds at the official exchange, at that time amounting to about a thousand dollars. The fund paid for transportation to any place on earth, but to receive the money, I had to present the administrators with a visa to my country of destination.

At that moment the United States was not a possibility. The U.S. Congress had passed the first immigration restriction laws in 1921 and 1924, and the number of Eastern European immigrants were limited through a system of quotas for different countries. The entry of persons they thought would become a public charge was prohibited. The decision on who came to the country fell on American consulates abroad. A friend told me the yearly quota for the United States had been filled.

Acquiring the necessary documentation had grown even more complicated after the July 1938 Evian Conference held on the shore of Lake Geneva in France. It took place two weeks after Hitler annexed Austria, giving the Nazis control along the southwestern borders of Czechoslovakia. Of the thirty-two countries that met to discuss the problem of European Jewish refugees, only one—the tiny Dominican Republic—expanded its immigration policies to allow for more asylum seekers for agricultural work. France described being "at the extreme point of saturation." This decision meant that thirty-one nations, including the United States, had closed their borders and rebuffed the desperate Jews seeking sanctuary.

The conference sent the clear message that most of the world's countries would not stand up to the Nazis and their so-called master race. I'd been taught not to do to your neighbor what you find hateful. To me this was more than a casual snub at a time of crisis for German Jews. Now, short of a year later, it mattered to this one Czech identified by the Nazis as a Jew.

China, although already at war with Japan and torn by internal conflict with the Communists, was one semi-bright spot for Jewish refugees. China did not participate in the Evian Conference, and its embassy in Prague was still functioning, but I'd heard it was no longer receiving any money from its government. I learned there was a man named Mr. Tung at the embassy who was willing to sell a Chinese visa for around twenty-five hundred Czech crowns. In 1939 the exchange rate was twenty-five Czech crowns to one U.S. dollar, so the visa would have cost me around one hundred dollars, an exorbitant price at the time.

Mr. Tung had no qualms about issuing a visa even though the Imperial Japanese Army occupied the Chinese coast. Although I didn't realize at the time how it all worked, the Japanese required no paperwork for entry because the Chinese had no authority there. This made Shanghai the single port in the world at that time with unrestricted entry, where one could gain access without a visa or a landing fee. I knew that getting an entry visa to Shanghai, along with other required documents, would allow me to obtain an exit visa from the Nazis. A visa was also required to book passage on a ship.

There was more going on. Mr. Tung took the occasion to make a dishonorable profit by selling visas to Shanghai. (Austrian authorities later found him to have been smuggling goods as well. In contrast, the Chinese consul general in Vienna, Feng Shan Ho, saved lives by producing thousands of visas for desperate Jews, helping families leave Nazi-occupied territories after the Anschluss and Kristallnacht. The difference was Ho didn't sell visas; he issued them at his own expense.)

Lots of people, mostly Jews from Germany, were fleeing to Shanghai. Hundreds arrived after Hitler's rise to power. I'd been told the local Jewish community in Shanghai, which included wealthy Persian Jews, had set up dorms and soup kitchens for the refugees. From one of my old Charles University professors, I heard the community appreciated the skills these refugees brought to Shanghai, especially physicians. For me China was not the end goal; it was a means of gaining passage out of Nazi-occupied territory to other countries, such as France. It also fulfilled the requirement for the Lord Mayor's Fund. (Years later I learned I was one of only twenty-six thousand Czechs who legally emigrated from Nazi-occupied Bohemia and Moravia before the end of 1941.)

I put my life in a suitcase and prepared to leave behind everyone and everything I knew. I packed a few articles of clothing, an English-Czech dictionary and a copy of Pearl S. Buck's *The Patriot*, my Kodak Retina II camera, a typewriter, my diploma from Charles

University, some medical equipment, an address book, and a small brown leather notebook containing four tiny pictures from home.

Under ordinary circumstances, at the end of my two years of compulsory military service, I'd have been looking forward to building my private practice, perhaps as a cosmetic and plastic surgeon; socializing with my friends at Mánes; enjoying an occasional dinner with my parents at their apartment; and wooing a potential bride. Instead, I was listening to accounts of arrests by the Gestapo of politically active Jews and anti-Nazi German refugees. Old jails, long out of commission, were reopened for operation.

Before I left, I headed to my aunt Karolina's perfume store to say goodbye. As I meandered down the narrow streets noticing placards with ARYAN SHOP in some windows, I heard the melancholic tones of Dvořák. In contrast to my somber mood, the warm springtime illuminated the blossoming cherry trees, making me second-guess my imminent exodus. I was leaving all that was dear to me for the complete unknown.

Aunt Karla greeted me with a long embrace as if she knew why I'd come. As I slid from her arms, I stood back to muster my farewell. But first, she started a conversation that surprised me. "Did you hear about the recent Prague Orchestra's rendition at the National Theater of Smetana's patriotic performance of 'Ma Vlast' [My Country]?" she asked me. I thought it odd she wanted to talk of music, but I let her continue. "Their performance was followed by an ovation that lasted fifteen minutes, ending with the conductor kissing the score. We bravely showed our solidarity." As I started to tell her my plans, two German soldiers sauntered in, looking to buy something, probably for their new girlfriends. My aunt was polite as she spoke to them in German. Luckily, they hadn't heard what I'd been saying, and I don't think they realized she was Jewish.

On Sunday, May 21, 1939, my uncles and aunts joined my parents to bid me farewell at Prague's art nouveau Woodrow Wilson Railroad Station. A bronze statue of the U.S. president stood beside our farewell point. The sculpture, by Czech American artist Albin Polášek, represented our two nations' mutual value of

8. Arnošt and Olga Holzer, Prague, Bohemia, ca. 1941.

democracy. The rights of Czechs were nonexistent as we shared our tender goodbyes.

We fell silent in the way people do who are unsure they will meet again.

With heaviness in my chest as I boarded the Prague-Paris express, I called out to my parents, "I'll see you again soon." My heart ached in a much different way than when I'd left for the army to defend our borders. At that time I knew the dates of my military service and was confident I'd pursue my medical career when my service was over. Now I was leaving without a return date in mind. From the train window I studied my family's sorrowful faces for clues to what they were thinking. Tears streamed down my mother's face. My father stood, wearing his favorite gray suit, looking more solemn than I'd ever seen him, his proud shoulders slumped. The engine hissed and white steam encircled Dad, yet he never moved.

I wrote in my journal: "I once set out for the world; God knows that aimlessly I didn't even know where I was going and what I was going to do. At home it was looking murky; no one knew what tomorrow would bring. And so, I collected a piece of luggage, threw some underwear in it, clothes, and a few of my medical instruments, took all my little savings and hooray into the world. Well, it was not really such a hooray, Dad grit his teeth, Mom's eyes turned moist, and I myself, at the railway station, did not yet know whether I actually would leave."

I lingered as long as I could, then made my way to a cramped compartment, where I ended up with five other Jews, all somber and quiet. We did not know each other, but our faces and small suitcases told our shared story. For some reason they'd left me a window seat. What I heard was the train puffing away and the echo of a haunting horn. What I felt was the Prague blues. I gazed through the glass, hazy with dirt, at the passing Czech countryside with peaceful villages and ponds filled with carp and geese and offered a mumbled goodbye to my homeland, uncertain when I might return. Amid that melancholy I was excited by the prospect of seeing much of a world I had read about. I was two months shy of my twenty-eighth birthday, typically a time of great promise.

When we reached the German border, where there was still some formal passport control, a Czech inspector with a nose similar to the curved beak of an eagle and stubbly jaw walked through the train and stamped passports but didn't question anyone. With empty stomach and legs cramped from lack of motion, my thoughts drifted to the dreams of the First Republic—the unity the nation had wanted for its people. I felt wistful for my youth. I wondered if I'd ever use my dance skills while courting some talkative, tall, blonde Czech beauty on an open-air dance floor on a boat ride down the Vltava River. Or if I'd see my good friend Franta again for a long, fast ride down a powdery mountain slope on our way to grab a dark lager. As my eyelids grew tired and I glanced at my reflection in the train window, I was surprised to see glistening on the glass, the tears running down my cheeks.

Early in the morning on May 22, with the clatter of wheels grinding to a halt, the train reached the French border in Kehl on the Rhine River. The dreaded ss, wearing black uniforms with the skull and bones emblem on their hats, had replaced the regular border guards. The sticky slime from the ss slugs trailed everywhere. They stood thuggishly in sight near the customs officers, and I must admit I was trembling. The customs inspection was brutally thorough, and I had to strip completely. My pockets and entire luggage were examined, but nothing they deemed objectionable was removed. I assume if I'd had anything of value, they'd have stolen it, but medical equipment was not yet high on their list. When we returned to our travel compartment, I learned that a Moravian woman had concealed her diamond engagement ring in her vagina. The ring was found and confiscated.

Once the train had crossed into France near Strasbourg, I removed the little tan sticker from my passport and placed it in my bag for safe keeping. As the policeman in Prague had promised, I was once again the proud owner of an original Czechoslovak passport.

10

The Long Route to China

May 22–July 7, 1939

The train ride from Prague to Paris took around fourteen hours, maybe more. It was supposed to be nonstop, but that didn't account for a few stubborn cows on the tracks or equally stubborn Germans. I tried to sleep, but that was impossible. I was too excited by the thrill and the anxiety of what awaited me.

I held no apprehension about the safety of my worldly funds because I had nothing in my pocket. Of the two hundred British pounds I'd been credited in exchange for my Czech currency, I received two in cash. The remaining money would be available to me on my arrival in Shanghai. The mayor's fund contributed sixty-one pounds and ten shillings for ship's passage from Marseille. That ticket was now my most valuable possession. At least this was a good time of year to be crammed into a train compartment with strangers—it wasn't too hot inside to breathe, and it wasn't too cold outside to open the windows. I tried to relax while inhaling a rush of flower-scented air mixed with coal dust and smoke that seemed to billow straight from the train's stack into my nose.

I disembarked in Paris, groggy but energized by the feeling that I'd already accomplished something imperative. I had left the country of my birth twice before, once when I traveled as a child to Trieste with my father and again as a university student in 1934, when I went to the seaside resort Varna, Bulgaria, on the Black Sea, with a side trip to Istanbul. I was about six years old when we traveled to Trieste, and I had suffered a severe bout of

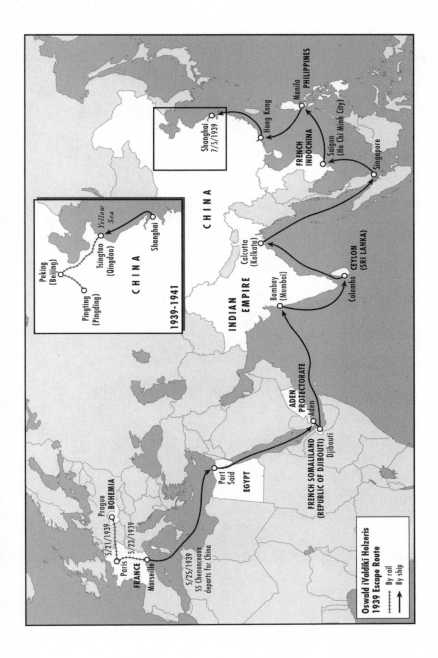

9. Valdik Holzer's escape route, 1939. Map by Erin Greb Cartography.

10. Valdik Holzer, passport photo, 1939.

seasickness on the Adriatic. Now I made my way to one of the world's great cities—the City of Light! More important, I was beyond the Nazi reach, whom I'd come to despise. My father had arranged with a business associate to secure a hotel room for me. For three nights I slept soundly at the Paris-Lyon Palace Hotel, an edifice as impressive as it sounds. The place was a little younger than I was, but it had the grand look that suited its location. The design was from the period of European history that started in the 1880s and ended when World War I began—literally the "Beautiful Age," or as the French started to call it, the "Belle Époque." Before I left Prague, my dad described the period to me: "This was a stable time for the French, one where they experienced the joy of living before the war engulfed us all."

From the hotel at 11 Rue de Lyon, it was a short stroll to the River Seine and Notre Dame Cathedral, a walk I enjoyed on my first day. Looking up at the famous gargoyles, I could feel the presence of Victor Hugo and sense the inspiration that he and so many other writers and artists had drawn from the beauty all around me. Everyone called Paris the "City of Light," but to me it was the City of Sights, and I wanted to see them all.

My father had told me that I could depend on his associate for further help, but I refused to impose, as I supposed my parents were reimbursing the fellow. I did treat myself to a gift so I could remember my short stay in Paris—a London-made Digby pipe. The carved brierwood bowl was dark brown with a silver ring around the stem. I figured the pipe would be the calming companion I needed for my trip. Traveling light allowed me to cover a lot of ground. I even took in a breathtaking view of the city's fabled rooftops from the top of the Eiffel Tower. The scene would have been even more impressive if it hadn't been a hazy morning, but after I climbed down, I shot a picture of the tower shrouded in the gathering mist. A few years later I entered that photograph in a competition and won a prize!

The clearest image of Paris remains the somber and imposing Arc de Triomphe, which stands astride the Avenue des Champs-

Élysées as a monument to all who fought for France. Beneath it is the tomb of a nameless soldier from the First World War. I thought of my father's role in that war as a combatant, of his capture and internment as a prisoner of war and the long journey home. It was supposed to be the war that ended them all, a lasting lesson to Germany and the world that aggression would not be rewarded. Yet here I was, over six hundred miles from my family and home, uncertain when I'd be able to see them again because the world hadn't gotten the message. The day I arrived in Paris, the foreign ministers of Italy and Germany signed a treaty called the "Pact of Steel." The two fascist regimes agreed to fight along-side each other "in the event of war"—in other words, if Europe found the backbone to stand up to Hitler. I wondered when that would happen and how many more monuments to fallen heroes would have to be built as a result.

I was ready to join the fight, but the French weren't. Paris had such appeal for me that I made inquiries about work all over the city, but nothing turned up, so I made a gesture of loyalty to France by filling out the documents to enlist in the French Foreign Legion. I was turned down and told noncitizens weren't allowed to join in peacetime. This was shortsighted, but there was nothing I could do. Perhaps they did not want more commissioned officers. So, at the end of my third day, I boarded a train for the port city of Marseille. I stayed there for forty-eight hours, long enough to wire my uncle Rudi Winternitz's brother-in-law in Hong Kong—a man named Leo Lilling. I told him to expect my arrival on the Messageries Maritimes Company steamship *Chenonceaux*.

The single-chimney, 172-meter *Chenonceaux* was a relatively small boat, no rival to the *Queen Mary* but nicely finished in the classic French style. I stored my suitcase in my couchette compartment, berth number 214, and set out to explore the decks. My Kodak Retina II and I found our way to the wheelhouse, where the captain agreed to step aside as a crew member snapped a picture of me dressed in something that resembled sailor attire steering the ship. All on board survived my brief time at the helm. Back on deck my ears picked up the familiar sounds of Czech, which led me to several Bata company employees who were also headed for Singapore or Shanghai. My fellow wanderers, a group of women and men in their thirties, befriended me, and the hours flew by as we played cards and dined in the Infusions Café on French rump steak Bercy and bouillabaisse phocéenne. The passenger population proved interesting. The Bata employees were from Bohemia and Slovakia, and none had been in any foreign country before. The young men had been schooled in Bata schools and were immensely loyal to the Bata system. Exhibiting a kind of religious fervor, they were sent halfway around the world to sell shoes. None spoke Chinese.

Besides the Bata workers, there was a unit of French Foreign Legionnaires being shipped to what was then French Indochina (now Vietnam). A group of French nuns was on their way there to teach and spread Christianity, and a company of primarily half-German, half-Chinese actors were returning to China after performing in an opera in Germany. We were on our way to a land Hitler's boots hadn't yet trampled.

On May 26 the ten thousand–ton *Chenonceaux* sailed into the Mediterranean Sea, and I left Europe for the first time in my life—forced to encounter the unexpected. Since I didn't have an actual final destination in mind, I figured I couldn't get lost. As I stood at the railing, I decided to embrace what lay ahead. I decided to take the opportunity to snap as many images as I could with my camera. Comparable to a hunter on safari seeing the whole lot as photographic prey, my goal was to capture people of all ages and backgrounds. Unlike in my homeland, where persecution raged, I longed to find different peoples—Malay, Chinese, Indian, and Eurasian—living in harmony.

I had my first glimpse of the Orient when we docked at Port Said, Egypt, gateway to the Suez Canal, the traditional passage between the West and the East. My father had traversed this route in the opposite direction on his World War I return from Vladivostok. Destiny and war had taken us on the same voyage—one returning home, one fleeing.

After refueling, the *Chenonceaux* sailed through the Suez into the Red Sea to Aden, an ancient city in Yemen with a natural harbor in the crater of an extinct volcano. We did our sightseeing from the steamy deck, as passengers weren't allowed to disembark during our time in the busy port. On June 5 we arrived in Djibouti, French Somaliland (now Republic of Djibouti), where the ship remained for a day, long enough to allow an excursion in the Horn of Africa. We arrived as Mussolini's invasion of Abyssinia (now Ethiopia) was under way. Several groups of Abyssinian refugees were camped in Djibouti at the point where the railroad connected to the capital city, Addis Ababa. The Italian fascist dictator, Mussolini, was trying to create a new Roman Empire in North Africa and had made progress as Italy now controlled Libya and Albania.

My newfound Bata friends and I chatted loudly in Czech as we walked the crowded Djibouti streets wearing our newly acquired pith helmets made from an Indian swamp plant. Somebody ran out of shop and began speaking Czech. A middle-aged gentleman named Mr. Vacek explained to us that he used to be the director of the Abyssinian National Bank, but when the invasion started, he left Addis Ababa and moved to Djibouti, where he opened an ice cream parlor. It was a profitable undertaking. After he had fed us free ice cream while prying out of us information from home, he went back to the harbor with us and helped us board the barge for our ship.

The *Chenonceaux* sailed east to Bombay (Mumbai), Ceylon (Sri Lanka), and Calcutta (Kolkata), where I found the coalescence of British and Indian culture intriguing but did not enjoy the intense tropical heat and crowds. In Colombo, the capital city in the British Crown colony of Ceylon, I took a trip to Mount Lavinia. An excellent restaurant sat on the beautiful rocky beach with stunning water views. It was sweltering, even with wooden ceiling fans spinning lazily, and not a soul was inside. I was served hot tea, much like the tea I assume my grandfather Alois had imported from Ceylon a half-century earlier for his grocery. The white-coated staff could tell I was a foreigner, and the director of the establishment, quite an inquisitive gentleman, thought he could place me by my accent. He wound up the gramophone and played Tchaikovsky's 1812 Overture; as often happened, he mistook Czech for Russian.

The ship went on to Singapore, the crossroads of the East, where some Bata employees disembarked for good. We had become friends, and when I arose in the morning, I thought about putting my letter of Bata engagement for Singapore into motion. Bata representatives met the ship, and I toured the city with them, staying overnight at the famous colonial-era Raffles Hotel and drinking Singapore Slings. At the Bata office I overheard the familiar notes of "Towards a New Life," a festive march by Czech composer Josef Suk, who lived his last years in Benešov. I ran to the gramophone in its oak cabinet as if it were an old acquaintance, thinking of my father's string quartet concerts. I yearned for one note from his viola, yet I was curious about what lay ahead on my journey to the unknown, so I returned to the ship. (Following World War II, I learned the Japanese bombed the Bata Singapore factory, and there was a massacre at the Alexandra Military Hospital in which patients and staff were bayoneted to death. Had I stayed, this may have been my assigned post.)

From Singapore we went to Saigon, where most passengers disembarked. The city was not well-known to Europeans at that time beyond the French colonists, who I was told were more in control than ever. Large sampans, flat-bottomed wooden boats, some with shelters, were under way in the harbor, mixed with large cargo freighters tied at the pier. Natives in oxcarts and cycle rickshaws, "cyclos," invented by a Frenchman maneuvered the streets while directed by arm-waving traffic police in the center guiding traffic.

Using money that my dad's friend in Paris insisted I take on the trip, I stayed three days in the Hotel Majestic Saigon. Built in 1925 by a local Chinese businessman in a classical French Riviera and Colonial style, columns and arches glorified the golden age of this architecture. From my private balcony I could see the hurried street life and striking views of the Saigon River. The group of actors I'd sailed with invited me to visit a Chinese neighborhood with them, and there I ate my first Chinese meal with chopsticks. Into my pant pocket I slipped an extra pair of these unique eating utensils, imagining the day I'd challenge my dad to try them on a pile of potato dumplings.

I'd read with great interest about the 1860 rediscovery of the twelfth-century Angkor Wat temple complex, which was built by King Suryavarman II to honor the Hindu God Vishnu. The French explorer Henri Mouhot brought attention to the strange ancient city lost in the jungle. I arranged with a French travel agent to take a quick ride through the wilderness to visit it, and the amazing site of temples and canals was worth the side trip.

I enjoyed touring Saigon but couldn't picture myself living there. Medical care for the French colonists was well organized, but there were only two physicians for every 100,000 Vietnamese. As I assumed the French might soon be in a precarious position with the Germans and thus wouldn't focus on this place, I didn't envision a future for the services of a Czech Jewish physician.

From Saigon the ship proceeded to Manila, where we spent a few hours in port to unload cargo. I made good use of this time by taking photos of locals engaged in daily tasks—shoppers wandering through markets filled with local delicacies, seamstresses at work, and unskilled sweating laborers known as "coolies" clad in loincloth of cotton and straw sandals pulling loaded carts.

By the time we were ready to set sail, I had developed a fever. I spent the next day and night shivering and sweating in my bunk. I'd fallen victim to my first tropical disease, malaria, which could have been devastating but wasn't. When the misery passed, I was thankful for having acquired a mild case. My strength returned when we reached Hong Kong a few days later, one month after leaving Marseille.

Hong Kong's harbor was among the busiest in the world and the most chaotic. Large steamer ships and small junks competed for each inch of space. As we sailed in, Chinese men wearing large round hats and rowing small wooden boats swarmed in, like birds to a handful of seeds, from all directions. The scene on land was equally manic, as peddlers and porters and passengers all rushed about, each trying to shout louder than the next. Fortunately, I didn't have to try to make sense of this chaos. Leo Lilling had received my telegram and met me at the dock. Leo looked every bit the prosperous European businessman, smartly dressed in a banded straw hat to cover his mostly bald head and a white jacket, with a handkerchief peeking out of the breast pocket. His dark, bushy mustache matched the bow tie that was pulled high and snug in defiance of the stifling humidity.

"Welcome to summer in Hong Kong," he yelled out, offering a firm but friendly right hand while gesturing with his left for a porter to carry my bag. A willow-thin Chinese man materialized, attaching himself with equal insistence to my suitcase and my side as he flashed me a look of complete servitude. I had no need for a porter but no wish to offend Leo, which turned out to be the right instinct. I was fortunate in my passage out of Europe to meet strangers who helped me when they could have left me to the mercy of the Gestapo. Leo, related to me by marriage but not by blood, started offering ideas for what my time in Hong Kong might include, from sightseeing to thoughts about jobs I might be able to obtain. As we left the docks, Leo told me that three months earlier, during a bombing raid on Shenzhen, the Japanese had accidentally dropped a few bombs in the Hong Kong territory, destroying a train station and a bridge. Leo tried to provide an objective historical perspective.

"You are now squarely positioned amid our seesaw struggle. You know, the whole situation could have been averted. In World War I Japan fought on the side of Britain, France, and the United States, despite its simmering competition for influence in the Pacific, especially China. When the peace treaty was drawn up, Japan didn't like how it wasn't rewarded with more territory. This led to these fanatical nationalists in the government allied with the army. Now we see the result of that folly after the war, as you saw in the mess of the Sudeten crisis."

Leo had immigrated to China in the late 1920s to start a business importing Czech linen (which was as prized as Irish or Swedish linen) and exporting embroidered tablecloths and napkins to the United States and Europe. He'd done well. At age forty-eight he had an office in Shanghai and another in Hong Kong, where he kept an apartment.

Leo's friend Franta "Frank" Urbánek joined us on the dock. President of Czechoslovakia's Škoda Works Company for the Far East, he was a short, muscular man with a barrel chest and dark wavy hair. He had been in Asia since the end of World War I, after serving as an officer in the Czechoslovak Legion in Siberia. His claim to fame upon the establishment of the first Czechoslovak Republic was that he'd been charged with being the "supreme auditor of the legion's finances in Russia." This led to a position with Škoda Works, and in the early 1920s he opened offices in Vladivostok, Charbin, and Dairen in southern Manchuria. Škoda Works exported the makings for sugar factories, power stations, railway bridges, ships, locomotives, transformers, and more. By the mid-1930s he managed commercial representations in Shanghai, Tientsin, Canton (Guangzhou), and Hong Kong with the export of weapons made in Škoda Works in Pilsen. These included guns, tanks, ammunition, planes, and light automatic weapons from the Brno, Moravia, factory for the army of China. With the Japanese imperialist army now in the mix along with two Chinese armies (Communists and Nationalists), the plot was thickening, approximating a spiced-up pot of goulash. I wondered how he could keep it all straight.

Like two middle-aged lions pacing back and forth, they were good friends who were comfortable with their surroundings. But Frank, his eyes tight with worry, wanted to apprise me of the region's tense situation. "Seven months ago Japanese forces occupied Canton, a nearby city on the China mainland," he told me. "Following that, the British began to fear Japanese attacks and built fortifications along the land frontier with Kwangtung [Guangdong] Province. It's a shame you didn't arrive a year earlier, when the air wasn't filled with uncertainty."

Despite the unease, Leo and Frank invited me to stay for two weeks in Hong Kong at their expense. I moved into the Peninsula Hotel, known as "The Pen," in an industrial area known as Kowloon, meaning "Nine Dragons." To my already extensive collection of ephemera, I added a swank Peninsula luggage sticker, commemorating one of the last colonial hotels built during the turmoil in China that ultimately destroyed the British Empire. Leo arranged a bond with the Hong Kong government and a temporary visa to allow for my stay.

Frank Urbánek and his wife, Vera, befriended me. Vera was playful, with a coquettish smile, short hair, and fine legs. She was the only Russian I met who spoke Czech without a Russian accent and the daughter of a White Russian general. Having nothing to do with skin color, the term *White Russian* came from the "White Guard," who fought against the Bolsheviks, or "Red Guard," in the Russian Revolution.

As a now-stateless young man, I appreciated their company and the chance to converse in my native language. Leo proved to be an excellent companion, often inviting me to his apartment, located eighteen hundred feet up Victoria Peak in the saddle of Hong Kong's central range of hills. The elevation delivered temperate weather compared to the subtropical climate in the rest of Hong Kong. Many foreigners left the city during the summer to escape the oppressive heat. On a bright day Leo's balcony afforded a spectacular panoramic view of the entire colony, giving me my first introduction to Far East luxury and a perfect perch for taking photos of the city below. Leo's vintage brandy went down smoothly as I admired jade carvings and a series of paintings that he'd acquired in Shanghai by an artist named Chang Dai-chien. From a folder he handed me my first gift from the journey, some Dai-chien sketches that he'd not yet framed.

When I inquired why he chose China for his business, Leo's mustache rose. "There are around five hundred million people consuming and producing all kinds of goods," he said. "I buy goods from different countries and sell them in the Far East and then sell Chinese products such as silk purses and tea overseas. The merchant partners I work with are reliable, and I have many pleasurable relationships with my business partners. Where else in the world could one find such an opportunity?"

As I gazed at the sunset across the harbor, I could see the lights of the city come on one by one. The reflections in the water reminded me of Prague's Vltava River, sans castle. I wondered if I could become as sure as Leo was about making China even my temporary residence.

As I settled in, I received news of events back home. I'd been pretty much cut off from the world as I journeyed from place to place, and anxiety about my family and friends had begun to dampen my enthusiasm for travel. Two events reported in the newspaper captured my imagination as to worsening conditions caused by internal and external forces.

On June 17 a time bomb exploded in Riva's, a Prague café popular mainly with Jews. Believed to have been set by Czech fascists, it injured thirty-nine people. I'd never known my parents or friends to go there, so I hoped all were safe. Three days before I arrived in Hong Kong, the Nazis had begun to enforce anti-Semitic laws in Bohemia and Moravia. Jews and children of mixed marriages were officially declared inferior citizens without full rights. I thought of my friends Franta and Andula and their young son, Honza, now an innocent in the maelstrom. Many non-Jewish Czechs fared little better under their new masters. Police armed with machine guns had begun raiding houses and businesses, rounding up thousands of suspected "troublemakers," meaning anyone who showed the slightest resistance to their brutal occupation. I knew it was good that my friends who were active Social Democrats had left for London. Even though my parents wouldn't intentionally do anything foolish to insult the Nazis, I worried about their safety.

With great excitement I began to receive correspondence from Europe. The first letter arrived from my friend Bála Ballenberger in London. He was safe and employed by the British Committee for Refugees from Czechoslovak, but he was pessimistic about his prospects and those of other émigrés. He wondered if he should join me in the Orient, and I resolved to be vigilant for any opportunity that might suit him. Also safe in Britain was my lawyer friend Franta's brother Karel Schoenbaum, who had fled Prague with his wife, Katka, just as the Nazis arrived. His letter ended with a question that struck hard: "What news do you have from your parents?"

I had no news from my parents, and concerns about their well-being weighed on me. When I thought of my father telling me they wouldn't leave Prague, I felt my nerves bundle as I had when the words left his mouth. I may not have been right about many things, but about the Nazis I wasn't often wrong. The best thing I could do for my parents was to establish myself somewhere and then send for them to join me.

Leo, who had agreed to help me find work, spoke with a Hungarian friend named Hora, who operated an import-export business and had contacts with the Anglican archbishop in Hong Kong. Although the Japanese occupied the China coast, the English still had hospitals in the interior in "free" China that could be reached through the proper channels.

Being adventurous and with no other options, I accepted an offer at a British mission hospital. I packed a small suitcase and left the rest of my meager belongings with Leo. From Hong Kong to Canton I traveled by ferry and contacted the Chinese Anglican missionaries responsible for sending personnel to the mission. They were to smuggle me into the hospital in the interior.

The missionaries arranged for the trip in conjunction with providing supplies to the hospital, starting with a midnight rendezvous on Canton Canal. With Leo's help I arrived at my appointment in a chauffeured car and boarded the small boat. The leap from the old, shaky dock wasn't as difficult as the leap of faith involved in the hour-long trip across Japanese lines. Soldiers could be seen along the canal banks during the day, but they mostly retreated to camp at night, when they were vulnerable to ambush by the natives. We made it through safely.

At six o'clock in the morning the missionaries and I disembarked and began walking through rice paddies. Unfamiliar with this kind of agriculture, I did not realize there were paths, so I fell into the water a few times. Eventually, the team reached the primitive mission hospital, which consisted of several one-story buildings, some with collapsed walls and broken windows. A few had whirling metal fans, but most did not. Over the past two years there had been fighting going on in that colony, and the Japanese had burned some of the buildings, leaving the site in disarray. As I spoke neither Mandarin nor Cantonese and my English was limited to reading, my best contact at the hospital was a sixty-five-year-old German nurse named Etta. Before and during the First World War, she had worked in a German hospital in Tsingtao (Qingdao), north of Hong Kong. With such limited communication I was unable to do much work, and I didn't know how to occupy myself. In addition to boredom, the weather was terrible, numbingly hot. Sauna-like heat seeped from the floorboards and through slatted shutters as trickles of sweat crept down my arms. After a week's trial I returned to Hong Kong. I reversed the trip, traveling first by foot back through the rice fields and then by the midnight boat ride.

Much of what I saw in Hong Kong was intriguing, but I learned that graduating with honors from Charles University did not suffice to gain employment as a doctor. Without a British degree I would be unable to work. I applied to the University of Hong Kong for a position as an assistant professor of medicine and surgery. My application was acknowledged but not accepted.

I attempted to enroll in the British military, but they were only slightly more welcoming than the French. I could wait for a reply but had no idea how long that would take. Accepting that I wasn't likely to earn a livelihood in Hong Kong, I departed on the next French ship for Shanghai, with no concept of what I would find there.

11

China Pulls Me In

July–September 1939

The seven-hundred-mile sea voyage from Hong Kong to Shanghai took much longer than the train ride from Prague to Paris. As we threaded our way between the mainland and Taiwan, I used the time to snap more photographs and meet another group of diverse travelers from around the world, including many European Jews. Although few words were exchanged on the topic, we shared a new bewildering struggle, surviving as refugees in a foreign land.

Shanghai had an international reputation as a port of refuge and a destination of opportunity for the world's explorers, adventurers, and rogues. Some found their fortunes, living in country-club splendor, while others sank into the city's squalid slums. Shanghai was the sixth largest city in the world, with a population of more than four million—and while most of its inhabitants were Chinese, the rest represented an astounding fifty nationalities, including Japanese, British, Russians, and Americans as well as Jews from Europe and the Middle East.

When the city opened to foreign trade in 1842, Sephardic Jews emigrated from British-ruled areas like Baghdad, Hong Kong, and Bombay, and by the early twentieth century their diaspora was prosperous. When I asked a German fellow I met on board the boat who had studied the topic how Jews had established a foothold, he shrugged his shoulders and told me: "Many followed the British and Americans into the opium trade, but nearly all have abandoned that tainted business and diverted their profits into textiles, land development, and other legitimate endeavors. Some Sephardic Jews in the Turkish Empire fled eastward to Shanghai during World War I, when they became worried of being drafted into the Turkish army. In the early 1900s Russian Ashkenazi Jews joined the Sephardic Jews via Siberia and Harbin, after pogroms. Harbin also saw waves of Jewish refugees during the 1917 Russian Revolution followed by the Russian Civil War. A few made their way to Shanghai."

Shanghai was known as a "treaty port," open to international trade, where nations were allowed to live and trade on Chinese soil. Foreign investment, mainly through British and American creditors, was immense. This relationship between the number of foreigners and their financial importance was the clue to Shanghai's peculiar governing structure. Great Britain, France, the United States, Italy, and Portugal, involved in trade, established their own foreign concessions—territory within China that was governed by a municipal council of the Western powers, although China still held sovereignty over it. Organized crime took hold because a lawbreaker could commit a crime and then walk away to escape to another concession.

I had joined a new wave of Jewish refugees rolling in from Central Europe, but our prospects were as hard to make out as the winding coastline that lay beyond the fog and spray of the China Sea. I'd traveled some ten thousand nautical miles, from Marseille down the length of the Mediterranean, through the Suez Canal, Indian Ocean, and now the East China Sea, to escape Hitler's reach, only to approach Shanghai as his Japanese allies had closed in. The city was beleaguered, but its heart still beat.

As we sailed into port on July 5, eighteen days before my twenty-eighth birthday, I experienced waves of nausea unrelated to sea travel. I felt homesick with an overwhelming longing for my past that took on a fever pitch. I had left Prague sure that I would return, but the little information I'd heard about Europe's deteriorating circumstances made that seem unlikely to occur anytime soon. Worse, I'd received no news of my parents or other loved ones. I was on the expedition of a lifetime, about to be immersed in one of the world's great civilizations, but I wanted nothing more than to eat a bowl of dumplings in my mother's kitchen. I was truly an adventurer against my will.

I gazed at a harbor cluttered with motor ferries and hand-paddled boats, none much bigger than a mackerel. I gawked at the sight of thousands of Chinese people carrying bundles and buckets, leaping from one boat to the next as though hopping between stepping-stones. Every single one seemed to be holding a net full of fish, but the overwhelming stench made me wonder if half of those fish hadn't been dead for days. Dead or alive, they were baking in the intense heat.

When I pried my gaze from the harbor, I saw the Shanghai sky-line above the masts. I sensed that this was a real city, which gave me hope. *Shanghai* means "above the sea," which seems ironic as the city is barely above sea level, but the name signifies that it rose from the Yangtze River (Chang Jiang). Centuries of yellow tides flowing downstream deposited silt at the Yangtze's mouth, and the mudflats formed arable land where people settled. As a natural outlet for the vast Yangtze River Valley, the productive region of Shanghai stretched sixty miles inland. This location might have been the end of the world, as a friend back home had warned me, but at least I hadn't sailed off the edge.

I must have looked out of place in my European knee socks and khaki shorts. I still carried one suitcase, my precious Kodak Retina II, and a small leather notebook. I hoped the proof of my Charles University graduate degree with honors in medicine would serve me better here than it had in Hong Kong and that my original Czechoslovak passport would help me in circumstances where authorities weren't friendly with the Germans. Shanghai had fallen to the Nazi-sympathizing Japanese in 1937 during one of the largest and bloodiest battles of the Second Sino-Japanese War. When I arrived, Japanese marine troops, known as the "Naval Landing Forces," patrolled the harbor. The foreign concessions stayed intact, but there was tension between the Chinese and the occupiers.

11. Chinese laborers, Shanghai, 1939. Photo by Valdik Holzer.

Regardless of whether I appeared to be a tourist, a traveling student, or an eccentric European, I was easy for Leo to pick out of the crowd. My now-trusted guide was once again at the dock, having returned from Hong Kong to his Shanghai home. Leo didn't bother calling a porter this time—he snatched my bag and tossed it into his waiting car. I started taking pictures as we made our way through the maddening clutter of trams, double-decker buses, massive trucks, automobiles, sedan chairs, and bicycles—all weaving around coolies pulling rickshaws and wheelbarrows carrying the poor. Amid it all I watched a wedding procession march down the road, as four people hoisted the bride and groom aloft on a bright-red embroidered chair.

Smells assaulted me—a thousand herbs and spices, burning meats, pungent incense, wood smoke, mildew wafting from cellars dug before the time of Caesar, and the sweat of four million humans and their beasts of burden. The strongest odor was an ever-present fume of methane, a constant reminder that the Chinese did not yet share the European appreciation of public sanitation. As a doctor, I was no stranger to awful stinks, but the intensity, amplified by the suffocating heat, was overwhelming. I tried not to gag, which ensured I would. Leo patted my shoulder. "I could tell you that you'll get used to it, but you won't," he said. I appreciated his honesty, although I'd have treasured one of those Bata gas masks more.

Leo facilitated my move to a boardinghouse in the French Concession after helping me exchange my Lord Mayor's Fund letter of credit for the Chinese currency. He told me I was lucky to have a nice place to occupy as two weeks earlier, on the German steamer the *Usaramo*, nearly five hundred refugees had disembarked, causing great alarm as to how many desperate European Jews could be accommodated. "Shanghai has already been overrun with Chinese refugees who've poured into the city after Japanese hostilities nearby over the past two years," Leo told me. With a morose look he added, "The French consul general told me privately they are beginning to consider through some undetermined method to bar refugees from entering the French Concession."

The foreign area of Shanghai was governed and divided into two sections—the French Concession, with a population of nearly a half-million, and the International Settlement, with a population of over a million. The International Settlement was created through a merger of the older British and American Concessions some seven decades earlier. The French Concession was established later and run under a separate French municipal government. The locals called it "French Town." Over the years it had become an exclusive place to live, full of Western-style mansions, art deco architecture, and gardens that stirred up my memories of Europe. The Russian Jewish community mostly chose to live in the more prosperous French Concession and didn't mix much with the other Jews.

The boardinghouse that Leo directed me to was run by Madame

du Pont, a sturdy woman who claimed to be French (through her marriage) but who spoke Russian to most of her tenants. The house wasn't a mansion, but it was impeccably clean and had a large, elegant parlor. Flora from the local gardens poked from vases and urns that lined the stairs and hallways. I settled into a modest room on the upper floor, big enough for a bed and a small armoire for my clothes. This space more than suited me, as I intended to do no more than sleep there.

On the entry table for visitors, Madame du Pont maintained a pile of newspapers. The June 22 issue of the *Shanghai Jewish Chronicle* greeted me with its headline "Roosevelt Wants Early Action on Neutrality Act." The U.S. president wanted action on the removal of an embargo on the export arms to nations involved in the war. "If war started after Congress had adjourned, it would be difficult to draw up neutrality legislation without it being said the United States was favoring one side or other," the article stated. "This in turn is expected to enable the United States to exert influence more strongly toward the maintenance of peace." I found it odd that the United States considered the world at peace when the most democratic country in Europe had vanished in a hostile takeover.

I set out to explore my new surroundings and found them agreeable. The colonial riverside area was known as the "Bund," or as Madame du Pont called it, the *"quai de France*—the wharf along the Huangpu River." She told me much of the real estate was developed by the richest families in the Far East, the Sassoons, Hardoons, and Kadoories—Sephardic Jews.

The Bund held many foreign banks, opulent hotels like the Cathay, insurance companies, and major trading companies such as Jardine, Matheson & Company. The boulevard was bordered by a park that went to the river's edge, where passengers from ocean liners arrived. At night it transformed from a business district to a party place with cafés and loud music pouring from the many clubs. Shanghai was no longer the anchorage for junks I'd read about in novels.

The French Concession included an array of social clubs and

churches, and many wealthy Chinese had moved in, along with Communist Party members, leftist writers, and intellectuals. Sunday was music day for the community, and I soon gathered with new friends at 5:15 p.m. for two hours of European classical melodies played by local entertainers. A theater, the Cathy, showed first-run Hollywood films. Better still, I was within walking distance of the Czechoslovak Circle, an organization of about two hundred Czechs run by my new friend Frank Urbánek. It was the Czech resistance group in China. I registered with the military organization there, making it clear that I was available for duty with the Czechoslovak army in exile. I completed a formal declaration to the Czechoslovak Committee in Shanghai of my allegiance to the Czechoslovak Provisional Government in London.

Daily walks were routine, both for exercise and mental health. The parade of unfamiliar sights and sounds diverted my uprooted mind from my longing for the familiar. Much of what I saw looked different but felt familiar. In Shanghai, particularly in the foreign quarters, every other building was a nightclub or bordello. In case a fellow in the mood for such entertainment missed the not-very-subtle signs, he could not mistake the look in the eyes of strolling ladies of varied race and shape. Most Chinese lived separately, and what lurked inside their homes and shops was as mysterious to me as their thoughts as I sauntered past.

With my camera always in hand, and with discretion, I created a pastiche of Chinese life—its people, culture, food, and strange scenes. I was instructed soon after arriving that it was considered impolite and unwise for a white person to be too friendly, much less intrude on local affairs. As I approached my intended subjects, I sought their agreement to being photographed. I'd been told that a superstition prevailed in Chinese culture that photographs can steal one's face, but they always agreed through willing eyes or nods.

The landscapes were striking, but it was the colorful humans who allowed a stranger to poke his lens into their midst that I enjoyed most. I was drawn to interesting textures of silk jackets, bold colors in brocade robes, and the delicately lined faces of elders. No matter what people were doing—shaving heads, inhaling smoke from opium pipes, pulling an oxen cart or a rickshaw, riding a donkey, selling live fish and eels from tubs on a dusty street, washing clothes in a mud-filled river—they continued with their activity as if to say, "Just watch!" Taking photographs helped me trust life more and find hope for the possibility of normalcy.

At first this was my primary concern because I neither spoke nor understood the language, so I conducted my affairs in the white district. The International Settlement was international in the sense that it encompassed all sorts of Asians. There were about eighty thousand Europeans in the city. About twenty thousand were Russian, and as many were Jews—and you would most likely meet them all in a month. The biggest surprise was how quickly I became comfortable wandering in Chinese neighborhoods and attempting to communicate with shopkeepers. I even persuaded each new acquaintance, by using gestures, to teach me at least one curse word in Chinese. Until I mastered them, I did my cursing in Czech, which puzzled the Chinese but at least couldn't offend them.

I was appalled by rickshaws. How could one human being allow another to act as his draft horse? But within a week I took my first ride and accepted this way of transportation. The Chinese had a different way of looking at work and at each other. People all around me were hauling carts full of wares or pallets loaded with meats, and none complained or even looked uncomfortable. A Chinese man born to the laboring classes spent his whole life working this way and expected nothing more. Hardly anyone was idle, and I did have a high regard for their work ethic.

I visited a Buddhist temple, where I saw young and old—men, women, and children—kneeling before a shrine and knocking their foreheads on the ground. I watched in amazement as coolies toiled like oxen, lugging loads of rice or vegetables suspended from bamboo poles across their shoulders while dashing as marathon runners to beat the motorcars from traffic light to light.

Sometimes people raced through the streets, fleeing bad spirits, which the Chinese believed attached themselves to the shadow of a person. The way to get rid of bad spirits was to run into traffic and hope the shadow got run over, allowing the spirit to escape. The technique had unfortunate consequences when a car outran a shadow.

Along the narrow streets fortune-tellers sat with little cups full of wooden sticks, which they would shake until one jumped out. The fortune-teller would look up the character written on the stick in the *I Ching* (*The Book of Changes*), which contained all human wisdom of the past and future. I'd heard about the esteemed three thousand–year–old fortune-tellers' manual, the *I Ching*, in my philosophy class at Charles University. The professor launched us students into a lively debate as to whether it should be revered along with the religious Christian Bible, Jewish Talmud, Muslim Qur'an, Buddhist Lotus Sutra, and Hindu Bhagavad Gita. Because of its profound influence on religion, literature, medicine, and philosophy in this vast ancient world and beyond, I weighed in that the *I Ching* should be placed along with the world's greatest religious literature. When I encountered it on a Shanghai street, I wished the book could offer me advice on how to navigate my ever-changing universe. Unfortunately, I had a significant barrier—I needed to speak Chinese to get a reading from the cosmos.

Countless beggars of every age filled the streets, blocking the entrances to shops or sprawling on sidewalks while they pleaded for money. The squalor and circumstance in which they lived made me ashamed of feeling sorry for myself. Small children in tattered clothes hung onto blind, crippled, or elderly men, extending their cups while pleading in words I did not understand. This frenetic stew of humanity mesmerized me.

On July 20, on what started as another windless day, I boarded a bus, but as soon as it began to move forward, the air began to stir in a most aggressive manner. The bus started to shake. With no warning Shanghai was hit with torrents of rain from a typhoon. The bus stopped, and all the passengers struggled out the door.

Sweating like a mad donkey, I ran into the street but got barely a few feet before the wind knocked me to the ground. I rolled in mud, and when I looked around, I saw that numerous gentlemen were moving in the same manner—and they were having a good time, from all appearances. So I had a good time too. Once in a while some gentleman crawled over me with a necessary "sorry." Suddenly there was a loud crash as a roof landed in the street atop some rickshaws and an overturned car. I decided that safety was more important than fun in the mud, so I slithered with the crowd into the nearest passageway.

Over the next six hours I stood or sat in the cramped corridor filled with humidity and humanity, soiled to our very souls. Desperate beggars intermingled with muddied Chinese, English, German, and Russian businessmen along with one Czech refugee—all looking for a dry spot to wait out the storm. The din brought about by the yakking mixture of languages made me flashback to home and the jumble of discordant sounds from Czech, German, Slovak, Polish, and Hungarian conversations at a busy Prague café.

The sounds in our narrow corridor would at times hush when intense turbulence brought violent wind gusts to our waterlogged troupe. One German gentleman with a collarless shirt buttoned up to his neck estimated that the winds were reaching eighty miles per hour, well beyond anything I'd experienced. "Get used to it," he said. "This won't be your last flood. I came here from Berlin a year ago, and this is my eighth typhoon."

In the aftermath it was hard to distinguish the destruction caused by the typhoon from the destruction brought about by the Japanese, who had captured the city two years earlier. The International Settlement and the French Concession were not occupied but were ringed by Japanese forces, which brought on an acid stomach whenever I walked beside these German allies. Some were the personification of Rising Sun arrogance. The war in China had reached a stalemate, but there were occasional clashes within earshot between the occupiers and the Nationalists. Venturing out of my familiar zone always brought the risk of wandering into skirmishes. I often felt light-headedness from the surge of adrenaline. Unfortunately, no haystacks were available to hide in, so I always walked at a hurried pace.

I found plenty to keep me busy in the Czechoslovak Circle, where I encountered many colorful characters. One fellow, known as Malacek, had served in the Czech Legion in Siberia during World War I at the same time as my father. After the war Malacek stayed in the Far East and opened a restaurant in the French Concession. Above the restaurant he ran a nightclub, with White Russian girls all around. Wealthy patrons would arrive in their private rickshaws, pulled by six-foot-tall coolies from North China.

When I met Malacek, grizzled and overweight, his nose with a knob on the end wrinkled in disbelief when I told him I was from Benešov. Thus originated a good conversation. As he was fond of Konopiště castle, Benešov was a village he knew well, but in our banter we established that he hadn't met Dad in the World War I trenches of Siberia. Welcoming me as his countryman, he invited me to lunch: "Do you want duck and dumplings with sauerkraut?"

"Of course!" I replied with delight, I had not eaten the Czech national dish since I left home.

As we entered his restaurant, Malacek turned and started calling out in Czech, "Francis, we have a guest here who wants duck with dumplings and sauerkraut." I was surprised because Francis was obviously Chinese. "Who else speaks Czech around here?" I asked. Malacek grinned his open-mouthed smile, showing his yellowed teeth. He was what they called in Shanghai an "old China hand"—a white man who had lived in China for years, sometimes decades, without bothering to learn even one word of the language. "All my Chinese speak Czech," he replied, sounding cavalier. "I am not going to learn Chinese, so they have to learn Czech when they work for me."

Unlike Malacek, I'd fit in better if I learned the Chinese as the Chinese speak it. Once I picked up a few words, I began trying to converse on the street. I bought a brown leather-bound book entitled *An Introduction to Mandarin* by Rev. J. S. Whitewright.

On the inside cover I stamped my name in Chinese with a hand-carved seal called a "chop." Written in English, the book's introduction proclaimed, "The way to learn to speak Chinese is to commit, commit, commit." The book included a section on etiquette and advice on the "language of manners" so no misunderstandings would occur when in contact with Chinese not yet acquainted with Western customs.

Learning Chinese would have been a challenge at any time, but I couldn't limit my linguistic studies to one new tongue because I had no clue where I might be forced to land next or what my employment prospects might be. I began my English lessons in solitude with a belonging I had carried with me from Prague: a small, blue leather-bound book—*The Dictionary of the English and Czech Languages*. I began to study English and Russian with an old, graying Russian woman in Shanghai. The English was not Oxford English but a cross between Australian and San Francisco English. I thought it might be a good native tongue for my future children—that in addition to my Czech, German, Russian, and French.

Looking for someone my age to share the nightlife with, I sought out Rudolf "Rudla" R. Rebhun. He was a textile engineer in Shanghai whose father was a friend of Dad. I had met Rudla in Prague but did not know him well. When I located the lanky chap with a perpetually unshaven, dimpled chin, he was living in Hongkew (Hongkou), a one-mile-square section northeast of the city, in the International Settlement on the northern bank of Suzhou Creek. Mostly destroyed by the Japanese in 1937, Hongkew was under Japanese control. It was the central area in which many destitute new European Jewish émigrés found refuge among the rubble, along with poor Chinese coolies. Its Austrian bakeries and European-style cafés were so authentic that it was called "Little Vienna."

Rudla's attire didn't match the milieu—he dressed in a stylish double-breasted suit with dark tie, vest, and fedora. When I admired his hat, he shared its purpose: "I brought it from Prague thinking it would impress the ladies. It turns out it was a good choice." With his various get-rich schemes, risqué language, and weakness for wild women, Rudla became a good friend during my sojourn in China. We shared a pipe-over-cigarette preference, and he often bummed tobacco from me. Even if he was out of tobacco, he managed to maintain the aroma on his person in the humid summer months.

Rudla worked with a Viennese man named Walter C. Schiller, who had opened a mechanical laundry. I thought this was a dazzling concept since all the Chinese did laundry by hand. With hair thinning to one side and prominent ears resembling bell pulls, Walter was a friendly chap. Through conversation we determined that he shared common friends with Leo. Rudla, Walter, and I spent time exploring this city, known to some as the "Paris of the East" and to others as the "New York of the West." We enjoyed walking bathed in nighttime neon light on Nanking Road, which the locals called the "Broadway of Shanghai." To the Chinese it was known as "Dao Ma Loo," or "Great Horse Road," because it led to a large green patch of land that included the racetrack and recreation grounds. After sunset, when work stopped and foreigners left their offices, Nanking Road, along its entire length from the racecourse to the biggest Chinese department store, transformed into a promenade. Slender, highly painted Chinese damsels emerged, accompanied by chaperones who served as business managers and protectors. Other young Chinese men and women appeared, some from cultured, wealthy families. They liked to dance and spoke English and sometimes Russian. In the evenings the rickshaws were lit up with lanterns hung near the riders' feet, casting a ghostly glow on their faces.

It was easy for me to learn the legends of China's long history during my excursions, as storytellers could be found on the curbs and at teahouses. Some even told their tales in German and English. It was much harder to receive accurate news of what was happening at home as newspapers were hard to find or were biased. The principal papers were British, American, French, German, Japanese, and Russian. Six were Chinese owned. A couple of German refugee publications were active, too, including the *Shanghai Jewish Chronicle*, which carried day-to-day advice on healthcare, nutrition, employment opportunities, and updates for refugees. The *Chronicle* also reported on depressing international anti-Semitic news and discussions about immigration problems resulting from the influx of refugees. Our vast, not-well-anticipated numbers outstripped available funds to support most refugees who arrived with little or no resources.

The Chinese publications ranged from political propaganda to candid photographs of cocktail parties. My favorite publication was the *China Critic*. I often found old copies on the tables at the Czechoslovak Circle. It was the first and only Chinese-owned and edited English-language weekly newspaper in Republican China, popular with Chinese students in the urban centers and among the English-speaking Chinese intellectual class. They welcomed contributing writers from politically liberal and diverse ideological Shanghai societies and clubs. Articles were in both languages, including one written by American missionary Pearl S. Buck, whose Czech-translated book *Vlastenec* (*The Patriot*) I'd brought with me. It was a fictionalized account of what she'd witnessed in China, much like what I hoped to write someday.

An editorial caught my eye in the *China Critic* from June 8, 1939: "The Anti-British Movement." The story reported on Imperial Japan's attempts to incite anti-British sentiment in China. The writer pointed out that on May 30, before I arrived, the public bodies—the National government administration and the foreign settlements—had decided against commemoration of the 1925 massacre of Chinese workers by British-led troops in Shanghai. The writer purported they were showing "friendly feelings toward Great Britain." I'd taken photos of recent anti-Britain signs and had wondered what triggered it. Leo told me the Japanese were encouraging workers' strikes in various cities across the country, trying to undermine areas where British interests dominated. As Leo did export and import business with both, he felt stuck in the middle.

When I arrived, I began sending letters to my friends back home in some small hope that they would be interested in my travels but in greater hope that they would send news of events from their world that I missed so much. My first letters came from friends who'd left the country as I had. Bála wrote from Regents Street in London, acknowledging a suitcase I sent him from Prague with personal items to store. First, he jokingly complained about the "monstrous piece" and then went on to update me about his life:

> It is a pitiful sight to see all our acquaintances set out for the seven seas, and you particularly I would not imagine on the road Mánes-Shanghai, but then, Hitler has us where he wanted to have us. I am doing, relatively, great. Both Karel Schoenbaum and I are employed by the British Committee; we have a royal income of two pounds a week, with which one can well survive.
>
> We have a lot of work, we are at the office continuously from ten till the evening, and we are registering Czech immigrants and carrying out all kinds of office tasks on behalf of the Czech group. There is no future in it, and even though we are searching for another job, we are still holding onto the committee tooth and nail. The mood among émigrés here is altogether gloomy, prospects none and emigration possibilities entirely negligible. Physicians still have it best, but it is also nothing special. The difference, as opposed to Prague, is only the feeling that here you are safe, even though thanks to the appearance and conduct of our coreligionists the grudge toward emigrants is actively rising.
>
> Otherwise, we live well. We often go to the theater, movies, and concerts. We go to clubs, naturally, we try to make most of the civilization while we still can. Nonetheless, in spite of the care the local organizations give the immigrants, one can observe noticeable cooling of interest toward us.
>
> . . . Regarding the political angle, I think that unless Adolf gets a fit, there will be no war, the English certainly won't even think about going to fight for Gdansk. It is not cheerful here; be happy you are in the Orient. Válda, if you could find some

nice job for me there, I would set out for there right away, keep it in mind, I have doubts that here I will be able to move on . . .

. . . Valdik, I see it is getting dark above the ocean, and the yacht is already swaying. I wish you good winds, the most beautiful girls of China and the archipelago, the best cases of patients, and much, much good luck. I believe that we will once again go down on the canoe from Cholín, and I beg you to accept the display of sincere friendship, which cannot be changed by distance.

I typed, versus handwrote, my correspondence on onionskin using carbon paper to keep track of what I'd told whom. My first post-typhoon report was to Franta Schoenbaum, my childhood best friend stuck in Bohemia. Assured I could trust his discretion on whom he told what, I shared the unvarnished truth about my tumultuous life:

Dear Franta . . .

You have no idea how happy you made me with that letter of yours. You know, when a man does not hear that dialect of ours anymore, at least one can have something for enjoyable reading again. To tell you the truth: that distance is not so big, and it does not seem so huge, but I am damnably homesick for all and for everything, particularly when a man is almost entirely without news and when he does not know when, and if at all, he will return. Such thoughts would develop in your head only after some time. Do not be angry that I am responding to your cheerful letter with such sentimental jabbering, but it is called here "S'ai depression" and supposedly everybody is going through that during their first time. After all, you know that is not my nature.

I hope that in your intended literary pursuits, you will also mention the good physician Osvald, who left his mother country to treat poor little Chinese. In order for you to elaborate on this topic better, I am sending you the following contribution:

So already for three days, I have been partially pummeled with malaria. I caught it some place in Saigon, such an idiotic French Indochina, but it is better than tuberculosis. Hey, one must always be content. I am curing it by myself, chiefly with whiskey, which is dreadfully cheap here. Otherwise, it is possible to catch in this beautiful but strange country everything from measles to leprosy. Hey, so that I won't forget if you happen to talk with my family by any chance, do not tell them anything about these nice things, they would be unnecessarily afraid. It is not so bad.

As you had read *Chuan in China*, 20 percent of it describes things well; otherwise, everything is yet crazier by far. In a week here, you set aside all European social prejudices, you let yourself ride in a rickshaw, you are cursing Chinese, in Czech, of course, you start to booze. In short, you become a white shadow; it is somehow a matter-of-course situation.

Franta, there are 20,000 migrants here, 98 percent of them without money, so the society gave them housing in a quarter completely destroyed by Japanese shooting. From those ruins the Jews built houses, opened businesses, coffeehouses, even Jewish prostitutes are here. But, of course, who will guarantee that the bombing will not start again tomorrow? Those who have a little money live in the French Concession; it is, first of all, safe.

Like in a circus created for adventurers, you can make so much money here in a day that you don't need to do anything else in life ever, and in an hour, you can have all of that go into a toilet. The dollar dropped yesterday and today by 30 percent. That has been talked about here for a week already, so a number of people became wealthy and others lost their shirts in the process. Even the weather is so crazy: I get out nicely in the morning in a white suit, with a towel around my neck as is a fashion here in order to have something for wiping when one is sweating like a pig. I sat on a bus and started moving.

In response Franta wrote about his circumstance—his uncertain future as a person of Jewish heritage under the Nazis. Already they had made it impossible to work. He wasn't alone. I heard this from several friends, many of whom wanted to know if I could find them jobs in China. I knew how desperately they wanted to escape, so it pained me to offer little encouragement. The situation was dire for most of the twenty thousand Jews who'd recently arrived. They lived in a quarter that was abandoned by the Chinese after being destroyed in a Japanese bombing, yet it was remarkable to see the homes and businesses some had already built from those ruins. There were even Jewish prostitutes at work. These sturdy refugees were making a go of it, but most still had very little, and what the rest had built could all be lost if the bombing resumed. Yet each day more refugees were arriving.

In Europe more Jews were urged to come to this place—by people who knew nothing about it. I became aware of this fantasy when a friend in Prague sent me an article from a local newspaper—I believe it was *Jüdisches Nachrichtenblatt-Židovské listy*, a bilingual German-Czech publication—that told of Shanghai's excellent prospects. There was no mention that in Shanghai many professionals like me were on the verge of having to beg for a cup of tea. I wanted to scream at this writer who deceived desperate people.

Pavel Körper, my friend and fellow Charles University Medical School and army alum, was one of those I had to disappoint with this truth. As I started to write him, I recalled his face at our last meeting in Prague after the occupation. His words came tumbling back: "I can't believe we can't get a job. Suddenly we are dirty Jews. I felt a little anti-Semitism before but not a lot." I told him we should get the hell out, but Pavel didn't think that it would get that bad and decided to stay. "I would love to see you in Shanghai," I wrote.

However, I advise giving priority to marrying that American woman you mention. I would do it swiftly. The information you are getting about China in Prague is altogether wrong because the situation here is changing every hour. The possibilities for opening a professional practice in Shanghai are limited . . .

If you do choose to come, I am not recommending either an Italian or French ship. The best ones are Scandinavian departing from Genoa . . . Maybe you will be obliged to take the other because all ships are booked. In addition, I advise you to buy at home at least two pairs of shorts and three white light suits, a dozen T-shirts, a straw hat (not a helmet, that is stupid), and if at all possible some medical equipment, at best the electrical instrumentation (X-ray, uv lamp, etc.) . . . In case you come here, bring Czech medical books. Drop also by my parents to please see if they have some messages for me.

From each letter I received, I excised the canceled postage stamp and put it in a small storage box. Someday, when I saw my father again, I knew his favorite gift from my world travels would be my contribution to our shared hobby of stamp trading, a custom appreciated by all Czech men.

I was starting to doubt I'd find a way to make a living in Shanghai when Malacek asked me if I wanted to visit Tsingtao (Qingdao) for August and act as his paid nurse. He was ill with an enlarged prostate and suffered from frequent urinary tract infections. He wished to escape the heat, as did I—the temperature in Shanghai often exceeded 100 degrees Fahrenheit. With no other employment prospects, I accepted Malacek's offer of a free trip and pay as a medical attendant.

This was not the perfect time for a leisurely voyage. Over the next few weeks the Japanese reasserted control over Shanghai and made it impossible to enter the port without a visa. The authorities saw that relief organizations were overextended beyond what they could provide for so many people arriving all at once. Russia closed travel routes used by refugees to reach China. The Japanese then intensified bombing closer to Hong Kong and cut off direct commerce with the South China area. I'd been lucky to reach Shanghai when I did, but although I would not stop trying, it seemed unlikely my family or friends could join me there.

I couldn't change the circumstances, so I joined Malacek aboard a small Japanese steamer to Tsingtao, about 350 miles north of Shanghai. As advised, I brought a cot and slept on the deck to escape the oven-like cabin. I wasn't alone, as most passengers were Russians with cheap steerage tickets who also slept on the deck. Each day a Russian chess champion played simultaneously with twenty opponents to entertain the passengers. At one point, to show off his skill, he challenged ten opponents and played blindfolded—and won.

The entertaining trip did not take long, and soon Malacek and I were in Tsingtao, where I found a cheap room with a White Russian family from Shanghai. Shortly before our arrival, without any artillery, the Chinese had put up a small resistance to the invading Japanese but were overwhelmed. Japanese ships were as thick on the bay as the soldiers patrolling the streets.

Tsingtao was considered among the most beautiful cities in China. Jagged hills surrounded the bay, a perfect backdrop for the bright-blue water and scenic islands. Buildings reflecting a turn-of-the-century German colonial presence were interspersed with Chinese architecture. Red-roofed houses surrounded by subtropical gardens welcomed newcomers. Making the setting even more appealing was another residual German influence: the Tsingtao Brewery. On the streets were huge vats of red caviar, imported from Russian's Lake Baikal. To the northwest was a newly built Japanese town with bazaars and tearooms. Outside the doors of geishas, Japanese sandals were lined up neatly next to military boots. After curfew the Japanese soldiers and sailors left, and civilians and American sailors from the U.S. fleet would arrive to set out a new arrangement of sandals and boots.

Malacek required little for his prostate complaint other than reassurance and an occasional bladder flush, so I had time during our first weeks to stroll the beaches. That was fine with me as I preferred to be a tourist with a camera than a doctor. One day while exploring, I felt as if I was sinking into the sand, and I barely had the strength to slog back to my room. I didn't need a thermometer to know my fever was back and higher than before. To make matters worse, I felt as though the Japanese army had retrieved all those boots from the doorsteps and was marching across the top of my head.

My Russian hosts took pity and called a Chinese doctor. He confirmed what I suspected: paratyphoid fever, a common malady among those whose systems hadn't yet become accustomed to casual Eastern hygiene. On top of that, my malaria had returned with renewed strength. The doctor was competent and treated me with the available remedies, but my real course was bed rest. This was made tolerable by the attention of my landlord's extended family, which seemed to consist entirely of beautiful Russian girls with apple figures, round faces, and dark brown hair. Their green eyes drew me in, as they seemed melancholy when they brought me hot tea, borscht, and pastila—a pastry reminiscent of Turkish delight.

The doctor visited repeatedly and even tried to cheer me up by making small talk. "How are things in Budapest?"

I explained that I was Czech, not Hungarian, and came from Bohemia, not Budapest.

He nodded as though he understood, but when he returned he again, he asked, "How are things in Budapest?" By the third visit I told him everything in Budapest was pleasant.

The next day he brought me a letter from Budapest, from a Czech radiologist named Dr. Kopfstein. Despite my fever, I was reminded once again how small the world was. Dr. Kopfstein had worked for Dr. Veselý in the same hospital in Berehovo that I'd worked in when I was in the army. As Kopfstein was writing to inquire about work for this Chinese doctor in the hospital in Tsingtao, I could vouch for his expertise.

I was still recovering when news reached Tsingtao that German tanks had crossed into Poland on September 1. Ahead of their slower-moving infantry, highly mobile Panzer units, which included motorcycles with armored sidecars, blasted their way in with what the German's described as a "lightning war," or *blitzkrieg*. The report we heard was they had overwhelmed Poland. Hitler had gone too far. Britain, France, India, Australia, and New Zealand declared war on Germany. For my native land the interwar period of peace after World War I had ended nearly six months earlier. More countries recognized the entrance into this unknown duration of the latest world war—now officially begun for the rest of the world.

It wasn't clear what effect this would have on Japan. Asia seemed to hold its breath as steamers I'd seen docked along the East China coast disappeared. The British withdrew to Hong Kong and Singapore, and the Japanese stayed in port while pulling some boats to Japan. Malacek and I were stuck in Tsingtao for five extra days before the traffic along the coast returned to normal and we could make our way back to Shanghai.

12

A World Apart

September–December 31, 1939

I was excited to find a thick bundle of mail from home when I returned to Shanghai. The first letter I opened was from my parents. Until then my only contact had been a brief we'll-be-in-touch note that reached me in Hong Kong through Leo, plus a few assurances from friends that my folks were doing well. I'd wondered what that meant, as news reports of Nazi behavior spoke of Prague Jews and suspected members of the resistance being interrogated and tortured in the Petschek Palace after it was commandeered for the Gestapo headquarters. Europe was at war, but it wasn't clear how this would change conditions back home. As far as I was concerned, the war involving the Czechs had begun when the Germans invaded, and my parents were already six months into the thick of things.

My parents reassured me in their letters that all was nearly normal, and in doing so, they made me worry that much more. Mom recounted the status of various friends or relatives—one had left for the United States, one for Argentina with her husband, one had died, I hoped, of old age. They described their new routine: "In order to avoid conflicts, we don't go anywhere . . . Don't worry about your father. He is earning sufficiently to cover all expenses even if the prices are higher."

As I read my parents' assurances, I thought of my sweet mother, afraid to walk to the market because thugs patrolled the street. I knew my father would go in her place if necessary. The old soldier who survived the Russian prison camp wouldn't be scared off by the curses of a few street corner bullies, even if they were wearing brown shirts.

The situation in Europe was getting a lot of attention in the foreign press, but it was mostly a matter of politics and chest thumping. Britain and France had declared war on Germany, but not much happened for a while. Both sides wanted to see who would attack first. While they were waiting, Poland collapsed. The Russians invaded it from the East—this when the Germans and Russians were secret allies in dividing Poland. I hadn't gotten over using the term *Russians*, but at that time they were the world's first Communist state, the Soviet Union, run by tyrannical leader, Josef Stalin, who professed the workers of his country were meant to be in control.

Each day I went to the Czechoslovak Circle, where we all shared the scraps of information we'd turned up and debated the meaning of rumors and half-truths. We passed around yellowed newspapers that sailors had brought from Europe and the United States. Within old issues of a British tabloid, the *Daily Mirror*, I discovered insightful columns by Winston Churchill, before he became first lord of the Admiralty.

August 11, 1939: "A great fortress-like Singapore, armed with the heaviest cannon and defended by aircraft and submarines, is in no danger of a purely naval attack. High military opinion in France and England inclines to the view that China in another two years will have defeated Japan."

August 24, 1939: "There can be no question of buying peace. No further concessions can be made to threats of violence . . . If the Nazi regime forces a war up in the world, the existence of free government among men would be at stake. Such a struggle could not end until the reign of law and the sovereign power of democratic and parliamentary government had once again been established upon these massive foundations from which in our carelessness we have allowed them to slip."

In the background of our conversations at the Circle was always the hiss and whistle of far-off radio stations in whatever language they were broadcast. Our most abundant source of information was unreliable. The Japanese news service, Domei, broadcast constant reports on world events—all propaganda unrelated to Bohemia. When it seemed the situation in Prague had ceased to be news, as though the Czech people were erased along with the country's name, I read a disturbing article.

The *London Times*, under the headline "Martyred Czechs," reported that one Sudeten German authority admitted the Nazi policy aim in Bohemia was to "smash the brains out of the Czechs." According to the article, the growing Czech "intellectual strata" had "disturbed the desirable relationship which used to exist between German employer and Czech employee." This explained the closing of Czech universities. The Germans wanted to prevent our young people from receiving a higher education, ensuring we could only practice trades, conducted not in Czech but in German, so they could put us and keep us in what they perceived to be our place.

I was not about to display wounds inflicted from afar by the Germans. After all, I wasn't the first Czech to endure unpleasantness. Ours was a history full of uprisings, occupations, liberations, and betrayals. Yet with our characteristic wit we always prevailed to make light of such situations, to ridicule our despised rulers not with a sword but with a joke. At the Circle we tried our best to find humor in our desperate situation.

During the late summer Leo left Shanghai and returned to Hong Kong, but he never abandoned me. Through Leo's contact I applied for an assistant's position at the mental hospital in Hong Kong. I received an instant rejection. I tried to see the humor, that my Charles University medical diploma from the second oldest university in Central Europe wasn't good enough to qualify me for this not-so-cerebral job. Soon after that rejection, Leo wrote of a promising possibility:

There is one job at this time that most probably could be given to you. It is in Kwangsi Province [Guangxi] at a newly planned emergency hospital in Kwan Yuen with American missionaries and French Canadian padres. Near this place is a railway junction that is seldom the object of Japanese air attacks and bombing by these aircrafts. How far the town itself is in danger cannot be told responsibly; it can only be said that it has no strategic importance. A further question about which I have to inform you is the question that the Japanese would attack Kwangsi from this side. In such a case, it is possible that they would try to advance against Wuchow and Nanning, isolating Kwai Yuen. There are no indications at present that such an offensive would take place, and I mention it only for order's sake. Besides, it is not to be overlooked that the cutting off of a place in a war here can't be compared with such events in a European war, and I believe that here is always a way to get out.

My way out this time was to not go there in the first place. Leo discovered there was fierce fighting nearby and suggested I withdraw my application. It was a reminder of the fluid nature of my situation.

As days became weeks, I'd had limited success getting information directly from Prague, but friends elsewhere in Europe were more forthcoming. My cousin Hana, working as a domestic in Staffordshire, England—being a maid or nanny the single way the Gestapo allowed her to emigrate—relayed word that her previously well-to-do parents, Uncle Rudi and Aunt Olga, had lost the apartment they owned when a German colonel took it.

As news trickled in through letters, it became clear that the reluctance of my parents and friends to speak out wasn't a result of putting up a brave front, nor was it a Švejk-like facade of ignorance. The Nazis gradually shut down all contact between the Czechs and the outside world, as though drawing a curtain to eliminate the possibility of witnesses. Major steps were undertaken a few days after I received that first letter from my parents, when the Gestapo ordered all Jews in the protectorate to surrender their radios. They timed the proclamation no doubt to coincide with

Yom Kippur. A series of increasingly harsh measures were enacted in the weeks and many months that followed, including confiscation of driver's licenses and required forfeiture of apartments in the best areas of Prague as Jews were moved to flats or houses already occupied by other Jews. Their residences were then taken over by Nazi officials. This was the awful reality of my city under siege, the city where my parents remained.

While I furiously scribbled pleas to my contacts abroad, I intensified my search for employment with the help of my friend and surrogate father, Leo. With his assistance I'd attempted to identify and contact as many medical employers as possible before I left for Tsingtao. The possibilities ranged from physician's assistant to hospital surgeon to ship's surgeon. I felt sure that at least one positive reply would be waiting for me on my return, but I was wrong. Not only were Chinese avenues closed; the war in Europe defied my expectation that all physicians would be in demand. I renewed my offer to join the Czechoslovak army in exile, again signing all the declarations and applications. I looked forward to the second Czechoslovak resistance also being successful, as the first had been against Austria-Hungary. I held faith in a beautiful future. My physical distance from the conflict didn't diminish my interest, although I would have preferred to leave for Europe immediately. Our Shanghai army unit had placed itself at the disposal of the Allies, but I was told there was no need for me in Europe yet. I tried to join the British army. Enlistment papers didn't distinguish between a doctor and a regular recruit. I guess a Czech from afar of any sort didn't fit Britain's requirements, as I got no reply.

I was furious and frustrated by the world's complete lack of interest in me either as a trained physician or as cannon fodder. I couldn't remain in China without a job, yet I had nowhere else to go. Living in Shanghai with no income made me feel like a peasant visiting Prague. At last, near the end of September, I got wind of an opening with the Red Cross, which hired me as chief surgeon of the outpatient department at a small ambulatory hospital it operated. It was a part-time position, but it paid a salary equivalent to five hundred Czech crowns, a good sum prior to the Nazis devaluing our money. It was more than enough to live on. This sudden good fortune reinvigorated me. The Red Cross approval allowed me to obtain a medical license in both the French Concession and the International Settlement, where I established a small private practice, sharing an office with an Austrian doctor.

I worked hard to make my practice a success, but my patients were mostly poor immigrants who couldn't afford to pay, and there was no shortage of doctors willing to accept as little as thirty cents per visit from those who had it. No matter how I tried, I couldn't make enough to pay my rent share. I wasn't alone in having trouble supporting a medical practice in Shanghai: in early November the Red Cross closed the hospital where I'd been working. I was again unemployed.

My situation seemed like nothing compared to the news I got from Leo. He informed me that traditional Independence Day celebrations had broken out spontaneously in Prague on October 28, 1939, despite official Nazi condemnation, with students from my alma mater leading demonstrations against the occupiers. The Nazis stormed into the crowd and killed a Charles University medical student named Jan Opletal. His death sparked a new wave of protests. In response the Nazis arrested nine students, stood them against a wall, and shot them dead. Then they arrested twelve hundred more students and shut down the Czech university and all other Czech higher education institutions. I felt an overwhelming sorrow mixed with a sense of loyalty and great pride in my fellow Czechs. I cabled Leo that I was ready to fight alongside my comrades, but I received his reply before I could pack my bag. Leo wrote that he had reluctantly withdrawn both suggestions as he'd received word there was still no need for my services as a soldier.

The news of turmoil in Prague elevated my anxiety, and I tried once again to pry information loose. Most letters I received were from friends who were as frustrated as I was about the lack of updates from their families. Closest to home was Aunt Válda

12. Medical license for Valdik Holzer, Shanghai, 1939.

Mařík, my father's youngest sister, who lived in Neveklov, outside Prague. Like my parents, she did her best to conceal any concerns. Meanwhile, my friend Karel Schoenbaum, who was studying for his Ph.D. degree at Oxford, complained that he was also in the dark about his family but had heard two friends had been dragged off to concentration camps. The camps I'd heard about were brutal places for vocal dissidents of Nazi philosophy. Several outspoken Czech nationalists from Benešov were in the first group taken. I worried about my father's state of mind.

I wrote to my cousin Hana in Britain of my hope that our family would overcome the storm without ruin and that we would all safely meet again in our dear homeland. I begged her not to hesitate to ask me for monetary help and told her to contact my friends Bála and Karel in London, both of whom had connections to leading Czechoslovaks in exile. Exhibiting her admirable feisty independent nature, she did neither.

I shared with my cousin Rudla Fischer, hiding out with his wife, Erna, and son, Tom, in Néris-les-Bains, France, that my father was still working and that he and my mother had reported they had "enough food." All the correspondence arrived opened by censors, and as my mom didn't always edit herself, I wrote to Rudla, I feared they might lock her up. I also told him what I'd heard from Shanghai immigrants after the last uprising: that the Nazis were evacuating those they deemed not "dependable" to Poland.

As this life-changing year of 1939 drew to a close, I continued to report to the Czechoslovak Circle each day, just as I continued to report to my Czechoslovak army post after the surrender. I expected to receive an order, or at least a suggestion, to point me toward some way to help my country and loved ones. Just as I'd realized it was time to strip off my uniform and move on from Brno, I now realized it was time to leave Shanghai. As I intensified my inquiries, I learned of an opportunity as chief physician of an American Mission Hospital in Pingting Hsien (Pingding County), smack in the middle of North China.

Well over a thousand miles inland from the great Pacific Ocean lay the vast province of Shansi (Shanxi), where Pingting was located, nearly 210 miles southwest of Peking. The region name meant "West of the Mountains" as it was located west of the Taihang Mountains. The area was in high flux, as was the rest of China. The ancient pattern of control by local warlords had been disrupted by Japan's invasion of the Chinese mainland in 1937. Shansi had been controlled for thirty years by Yen His-shan, a warlord loyal to the national government, until the Japanese invaded, and the area became loaded with Communist guerrillas. To resist this invasion, the Chinese Nationalists, loyal to Chiang Kai-shek, and the Chinese Communists, loyal to Mao Tse-tung, had joined forces, temporarily as it turned out.

The Japanese invaders were better armed, but their strategic problem was the sheer size of China in relation to their own limited numbers. China's vastness offset their military superiority, and the result was a near stalemate. The Japanese held coastal areas, railroads, roads, and towns, while the Chinese controlled the vast inland and tended to dominate the countryside, from which they could launch their attacks. The United States supported the Chinese, who hoped to keep the Japanese off balance until the United States entered the war and forced the Japanese to direct their energies away from China. There appeared to be nothing backing up the Chinese hopes.

By the time I was scheduled to arrive, Shansi Province was in its third year as contested territory. The Pingting County seat was occupied by the Japanese, while the surrounding countryside was in the hands of Chinese Communists. The conflict between Communist forces and the Japanese invaders was not a matter of distant gunfire, heard in safety from within the hospital walls, but a practical concern because Chinese guerrillas showed up regularly seeking treatment.

In "normal times" Pingting had around twenty thousand inhabitants. A Brethren church had been established there in 1912. The hospital was founded two years later, along with primary schools and a women's Bible school. The head physician at the hospital, Dr. Daryl Parker, was leaving with his missionary family for a two-year respite in the United States, so I was offered a two-year contract.

I was amused by Christian missionaries offering such a job to a Jewish refugee, but I'd met many missionaries since arriving in

13. Caricatures by Valdik Holzer
(China, 1939–40). Often signed
oh for "Osvald Holzer."

China and found most to be pleasant. None had expressed the slightest concern about my religion or lack thereof. The security of an extended contract during all the disruptions in China and the world made the offer impossible to resist.

I was suffering from a growing case of immigrant psychopathy and would sometimes kick a rickshaw for no apparent reason and then regret my outburst. I saw this happening throughout the Shanghai Czech community. I'd grown sick of the backbiting among the Czech émigrés. I was rebuked for all kinds of things—for having too many foreign friends, for the fact that my favorite book was *The Good Soldier Švejk*, for lukewarm patriotism, and who knows what else.

I began to feel adventurous, ready to try somewhere different. The primary reason was economic necessity; there were so many physicians in Shanghai that one doctor could almost care for another. I was such a greenhorn that the remote Shansi assignment seemed better than walking around the city with my hands in my pockets. So I left behind the final vestige of the familiar—the Czech refugee circle in Shanghai. I would travel to the dangerous backcountry of northern China, where an airfield had recently been built by the Japanese invaders outside the town where I was seeking refuge. Knowing no one else in my situation, I sometimes doubted my sanity but told no one.

On December 31, 1939, I celebrated my last New Year's Eve in Shanghai with my friends, who put on a party for me in the French Concession. The toasts centered on my plight. In his thick Czech accent, Rudla envisioned what my future would be: "Stranded in faraway Pingting Hsien with the Brethren teetotalers, Valdik is caring for the poor Chinese. While searching for something to read, among the Christian Bibles he finds a lamp, rubs it, and a genie offers him three wishes.

"'I want a cold bottle of Pilsner for my Bohemian way of life,' says Valdik.

"A bottle of Pilsner appears, and Valdik drinks it in one swallow. Magically, the bottle refills.

"'It's a magic bottle for you, Valdik,' says the genie. 'It will never run dry. What do you want for your other wishes?'"

Offering a smirk before giving the punch line, Rudla reported my self-styled response: "Two more beers."

The smug Rudla had a way of causing me to see the ridiculous side of life. Because my friends didn't think I was tough enough to handle living alone in the interior of China, they gave me two Lhasa apso puppies, which looked like golden, silky, self-propelled toupees. Lhasa apsos were originally bred as sentinels in Buddhist monasteries in Tibet. The Dalai Lama gave them in pairs to the emperors of China as gifts, thus my gift of two puppies. Curious and clown-like, the lion-colored dogs seemed suited for what I assumed would be my upcoming monastic-style life with the Brethren. I was ready to willingly suffer the hardships of my expedition into the northern wilds of China.

13

Snowdrifts, Machine Guns, and Prayers

January 1940

I set off for the Chinese interior on January 6, traveling first by steamer boat and then by third-class train coach, colloquially referred to as "cattle class." Wartime China was not up to modern standards for shipping industrial waste. Passengers sat on worn but hard wooden benches, separated by an aisle so narrow our knees sometimes touched. My face was mere inches from that of my fellow travelers, who were covered in dark soot from head to barefoot toes. A broken window that spilled cold air into our midst made us shiver, making it impossible to doze off. If anyone around me spoke a familiar language, I would gladly have started a discussion on any topic, but I was the solitary foreigner. So, in the darkened compartment, I listened to the sound of my heartbeat and the agonized cry of a nearby infant and fantasized that I was traveling back to Prague.

After a most unpleasant journey ended with our group having to pry the train door open, I arrived at Tientsin, which was drying out from floods and under Japanese blockade. My first impressions were of mud marshes and mud houses along with staring people transfixed by our arrival. There I met up with Mr. Gray, a missionary who was responsible for taking me to the Brethren hospital. He was a delightful grandpa who, in turns, burped, farted, and hiccuped. Mr. Gray had during his thirty years of life in China adopted Chinese customs and told me he only spoke Chinese at home. At times he spoke to me in Chinese, to which

I responded with Czech to gently call attention to his mistake. Luckily, he spoke enough German to give us a common tongue for basic communication, although he'd promptly forget and revert to Chinese the next time he spoke. This is how we made our way to Peking, where we waited for four days for the next connection. As it was my first visit to what I considered the actual capital of China, I hoped to see this splendid ancient city—moat enclosing moat, wall around wall. But Mr. Gray was fatigued and requested that we remain mostly at our hotel.

On a Sunday evening we started out to the railway station, which was a fifteen-minute walk. The first five minutes we enjoyed a frozen road and sharp wind. Little by little the road became slippery and strangely black. This was due to oil pollution from some factory, so we rolled up our pants, and in this way we shuffled to the platform's gate. There we stood in an impoverished crowd of delightfully soiled and foul-smelling people for about two hours until we could enter the platform.

My farting companion had remembered too late that morning that it was necessary to buy the tickets in advance. So there was nothing left except third class again, or what white people then called "coolie class." This was by Gray's design so he could avoid the extra cost of second class. He gave me the impression that it was unbecoming for a missionary to have his baggage carried, which allowed him to save the expense of a porter. I went along with this on the first few legs of our journey, shouldering the load until the last transfer, when I insisted on getting help. As a result, the old fellow was forced to part with ten meager cents for a coolie.

As we waited on the platform to open, we bought Chinese treats for the journey. Sandwiched uncomfortably in the crowd, Gray took it all in stride. "God must indeed love the Chinese," he said. "He has made so many of them!" The gates swung forward, and the sweaty human herd rushed ahead, trampling a woman who moved too slowly. Policemen with rifles rushed to her rescue, but they were shoved aside. We seated ourselves on the train and dutifully shared our snacks with fellow passengers, as their

Snowdrifts, Machine Guns, and Prayers

thin frames were alarming. In turn they shared the stench emanating from a peeling crust of dust and sweat that covered their bodies. Later we bought some rice and vegetables and Chinese tea from the circulating merchants. Then, on the hardwood seat, I fell asleep peacefully in the disgusting odor.

When I awoke, the missionary was still snacking—this time on a bag of cinnamon-sweetened peanuts known as "monkey nuts"— and offering commentary on the passing scenery, which he assured me surpassed the grandeur of Yellowstone Park. I'd never been there, so I could provide no confirmation. Mostly what I saw passing by was illuminated by the few faint streaks of moonlight that managed to penetrate the soot-smudged windows.

I suspected Mr. Gray had already been made aware of my Jewish heritage by the Brethren's Shansi Mission, but as a missioner, he felt compelled to share some religion. From a jowly face came a voice that sounded as thick as hearty potato soup as he told how there had always been philosophies opposed to Christianity and its teaching: "China has more or less always been in turmoil, but nothing has been worse than the current disaster." He claimed that 80 percent of China's millions live in the countryside, mostly as poor peasants, and that we were headed for the country also. We would settle in the county seat of a rural area, where "Dr. Parker, who you will work beside, is a kind, gentle, and generous man." Pausing as if to rewind the audiotape of his life, Gray stared out the window at the rugged countryside. After taking a deep breath, the old man's eyes twinkled again. "Dr. Parker works to create a better life for those who are often forgotten," he told me. "He'll teach you how we minister through medicine."

I interrupted Mr. Gray long enough to extract some more pertinent information, and he peeled back the curtain: to get to the hospital after our six-hour train ride, we'd first have to ride eight miles on a donkey. Also, there was an outbreak of typhus, known as "spotted fever," at our destination. Most significant, heavy fighting was still taking place along the route we were traveling into the Shansi Province, as Mao's Communist army repeatedly clashed with the Japanese. It was why we were going at night, as the train became a less visible target in the darkness. This explained why Japanese soldiers carrying heavy machine guns guarded each car on the train.

When I entered our compartment, I placed most of my considerable luggage on my side of the aisle. On the other side, in the overhead bin, I positioned a covered basket with my two sleeping Lhasa apso puppies. After we had settled in, a Japanese colonel took the seat below them. The thick-browed colonel made brief eye contact. I didn't attempt to speak with him in Russian or German, wanting peacefully to read my copy of *A Restless Border*, a novel about the Orient by Czech author Dr. Miloslav Fábera. After we had traveled some miles with the clickety-click rhythm of the rails in the background, something started dripping from the basket onto the colonel's bald head. The colonel looked puzzled and glanced at me; I smiled back. Wiping a few drops from his brow, the colonel continued reading his Japanese book. All was peaceful until we arrived at my destination. I picked up the basket, and the dogs started barking. The colonel gave me a menacing narrow-eyed glance and, taking his rifle in hand, began to stand. With a pounding chest I exited the train at Yangchuan station with Mr. Gray in hot pursuit, farting in rapid fire as he rushed.

Elder Frank Crumpacker, a missionary from the hospital, was waiting for us. "Sorry, if you had any difficulties getting here," he said. "The railway system is on the decline again because of war conditions." Frank was an evangelist and director of the Men's Bible School, and his wife, Anna, was the dean of the Women's Bible School. He had hired rickshaws to transport us to the hospital. "The donkey ride will be saved for later," he chortled. Thank goodness it wasn't snowing, although the winds pelted us with snow from the drifts piled beside the road. I missed the stench of the train, which at least had been heated.

As we bumped along, Frank made certain in a one-way conversation that I knew we were both there to further the Lord's service. Leaning forward, as if I was the first person to hear this,

Snowdrifts, Machine Guns, and Prayers

Frank gave me a reverent glance and said: "The church's responsibility to carry forth the good news of life and peace does not lessen because of war, or any other sin. In fact, our efforts need to be increased. History is being made here. We missionaries have a ringside seat for this most impressive performance." Leaning forward as well, I nodded with fake enthusiasm.

As I wasn't sure if he knew of my heritage, I remained silent, but it didn't seem to quell his enthusiasm. "The area where you will live," he told me, "has a past marked by droughts, floods, famines, and poverty. Of course, discouragements come. But the sky is not falling. God is still on the throne. There is a good deal of goodness and mercy all over the world. We are still in the garden even though a few beans may fall on our heads occasionally." I muffled a laugh at the image of my dark curly hair covered with beans.

The greeting at the hospital was suitably low-key but cordial. I learned that everyone was aware of my unique background as the hospital newsletter had noted, "Dr. Holzer had fled Central Europe's anti-Semitic atmosphere with others of his race."

I was assigned to a small, well-heated room in a villa occupied by a local evangelist, along with two Chinese housemen. The furnishings in my room consisted of a firm bed and a small oak secretariat desk. The desk held a typewriter bay and three drawers for the clothes I'd brought. On the desk was a table lamp with a parchment shade and a radio. On the bed were two towels. The door had a lock, which I found odd amid missionaries.

In contrast to my China travel experiences so far, everything and everyone connected with this place at first appeared spotless. I stumbled through the day's obligatory introductions and explanations in a daze, exhausted from my journey. Despite this, I took part as the first assistant during an operation before running out of things to do. I napped in my well-heated room and enjoyed it so much that I skipped dinner and slept comfortably in my new surroundings until the morning. After being awakened by the sound of a howling rooster, I poked my head out the window and inspected my new principality in greater detail until my stomach began to growl.

I reported to the communal breakfast table eager to learn my new routine, only to discover the routine started with the unfamiliar practice of prayer before each meal. I'd prayed a few times but not regularly, as we weren't a religious family, and I certainly wasn't familiar with the Christian missionary version. I had no objection, however. Buddhist meditation or any spiritual practice would have been equally fine. It seemed to me that the blessings of anyone's deity should be welcomed under the world's sad circumstances. I bowed my head as the others recited the words that I was yet to learn and then began to reach for my cup of tea before discovering that our holy contemplation wasn't over until a Bible verse had been read. The same ritual was repeated at each meal, causing me to learn patience before having a bite to eat. In the evenings we all sang gospel songs. It suited me as I had no better social prospects in the remote confines of Pingting.

There were altogether eight American missionary families with plenty of children. One family collected old Chinese knives and razors, and I gave them a couple of unusual antique carved bronze knives I'd procured in Shanghai. Afternoon tea was drunk, hosted by a different family each day. They all lived like one big community, into which I was kindly accepted. In the evening we'd listen to the radio and play cards or chess. They weren't stiff. Naturally, they did stop to pray from time to time, but that's fate. Otherwise, they enjoyed a jazz band or a spicy story. One had a collection of gramophone records with all possible symphonies, so life was not merely bearable as I settled in but pleasant. Dad's advice echoed: "Keep in mind, things change in big chunks in life like music. But if you love music, you will love life."

Surrounded by mighty bulwarks and impressive mountains, the walled city was a scaled-down Peking, where inhabitants lived and toiled. The war had taken its toll, and the place seemed grimy and lacked in enterprise. The hospital, together with three missionary villas, was outside the city walls and surrounded by a barricade. The gates of each wall closed at 6:00 p.m. so no one could get in or out. Inside our sealed compound, the only single white women I encountered were sixtyish missionaries with thin lips. This was disappointing because while I was living with what sometimes seemed like monks, I hadn't become one. Back in Shanghai and even on my trip to the north with my older male patient, I'd enjoyed the company of several charming and attractive women of all backgrounds. At this point I wasn't choosy, but there was nothing to choose from, and this added to my sense of social isolation.

I'd brought a bottle of brandy with me, but since the missionaries didn't drink, there was no one to share it with. They were hospitable, but I spoke little English, and they spoke neither Czech nor any other language I recognized. Typical dinners were of baked beans, sandwiches, olives, synthetic orange juice, ice cream, and cake. After our evening gospel sessions, we might play cards or chess, but then I'd retire to my room, light my pipe, acquired during my short stay in Paris, pour a drink, and write in my journal.

I began to boost my morale by entertaining the idea that I was gathering experiences for a book about my exploits. Thinking about my sea journey led me to the thought of writing about people I'd met, like some real pirates, a sea dog from Shantung (Shandong), and an undercover photographer for *Life* magazine. This tale would involve a farting missionary who spoke Chinese, to which I responded in Czech. The story played out against a backdrop of cruel warfare and travel in blacked-out trains. I worked on this material for months, writing notes and planning to add illustrations, impressed by the colorful aspects that my life had taken on.

The pleasant surprise in Pingting was that, considering the sad state of affairs all around me, I'd landed at what appeared at first to be a proper medical facility. The hospital had about 150 beds, central heating, electric lights, and an operating room better than any I'd seen since leaving Europe. It even had a working X-ray machine—the Brethren took their obligation to help the local poor seriously. My starting salary of four pounds was about what a surgery room assistant in Prague would have been paid, but it was good enough for me to get by for the time being, and I expected to move up in compensation and status once I completed my initiation. This was delayed by a tragic circumstance that preceded my arrival. Mrs. Myrtle Pollock, the hospital's American nurse, was stricken by typhus while visiting the Brethren's satellite hospital in Liao Hsien. Dr. Parker, whom I was to replace, set out to attend her. The road had been bombed by the Chinese and Japanese and blocked in many places by snowdrifts. Thus, it was unsuitable for a car, so Dr. Parker had to make a three-day trip by donkey. He was at her bedside when Mrs. Pollock, fifty-three, passed away on January 12, 1940.

The thought of spending three days on a donkey winding around bomb craters filled with snow depressed me, and I became troubled with the notion that I'd be sent to that miserable place. Adding to my early disappointments was the mystery of my luggage. I'd registered my large trunk with the railroad in Peking, but it hadn't arrived, and I feared that my best clothes, my photos, and all the odd and curious reminders of my journey were lost. My blue mood was lightened by the mental image of a coolie pulling a rickshaw while dressed in my khaki shorts and knee socks.

In another week my outlook brightened with the return of Dr. Parker, fit and lean, impeccably dressed for this ultimate nowhere-place. I was grateful to find in this wilderness such a talented doctor to learn from, whatever his faith. It was interesting to discover his skill as a cataract surgeon, with a reputation for restoring sight to nearly blind patients. Despite the rigors of travel, he appeared energetic and excited by my arrival at such a time of urgent need. We managed to communicate in English, with common medical terms helping to bridge the language gap. He told me that Nurse Pollock had come to the China field in 1917, to nurse and evangelize. She'd spent most of her twenty-two years in the Liao Hospital (Liaozhou) and was caring for over thirty refugee children there when she passed on to her "eternal reward." With his glasses perched on his nose, he added that she'd left a signed message in her room: "Grieve not for me; rejoice with me instead! God always knows what is best no matter how hard it is to understand." The good nurse, Dr. Parker pointed out, "was called from her earthly labors to a higher service in the Father's Kingdom, and it was up to us to go on with life."

When I inquired about mail service and my desire to let Leo Lilling know that I'd arrived safely, Dr. Parker advised me to send a cable noting the hospital address and warn Leo that mail sent to Pingting would be censored. If it was in "a less comprehensible language" (he meant Czech), "it may be censored by the waste-basket." He suggested we write either in English or German. To improve my English, my cable to Leo suggested English and included a request that he send me summaries of my parents' letters until we were sure mail would reach me.

Dr. Parker was concerned about the fever outbreak, distressed about the death of Nurse Pollock, yet charming at the same time—so lovely, in fact, that I forgot all my apprehensions when he proposed I join him in returning to Liao Hsien.

I did have one concern: Who would take care of my Lhasa apso puppies while I was gone? As they are bred to be indoor watchdogs, my dogs were suspicious of strangers until we'd arrived in Pingting. Having gone on several excursions among the missionaries and patients, with most of the people they met wishing to brush and comb them, I could see where these resilient little dogs from Tibet were starting to become acclimated, as I was. Together, our attitudes were adjusting. When I put out the word that I needed help for dog-watch duty, a long line of volunteers showed up. I would even say there was a greater welcome for the dogs than me.

My mind was further eased when Dr. Parker mentioned the snows were clear and enough bomb damage had been repaired to spare me the donkey ride. I knew I'd be more useful in his company than in Pingting. Nurse Pollock was supposed to have been my trainer and interpreter. There was no one else to fill that role, and her replacement wasn't expected for another month. I was eager to make the better acquaintance of Dr. Parker, who promised to alert me to any suitable positions in the United States when he got there. Best of all, my trunk of meager belongings arrived. I took this as a sign of better days ahead.

We set our departure for January 25 to give my typhus immunization time to take effect. This vaccine was made outside Peking by the Trappist monks. All the missionaries were immunized against typhoid, cholera, and smallpox. They carried certificates whenever they traveled in the occupied territory because the Japanese required vaccination for these diseases, so proof of immunization was significant.

The outbreak we were concerned about in Shansi Province was another consequence of the country's abysmal hygiene, as body lice transmitted the disease. The resulting fever was named for the eruption of rose-colored spots on the skin and often resulted in high temperatures, with a high mortality rate among some populations. Such outbreaks were most prevalent among the poor during the coldest months, when people huddled in close quarters and were least prone to bathe.

Our mission was to make headway in treating this outbreak at the source before it spread throughout the province. I was eager to join in, although my enthusiasm was tempered when I got a close look at our intended chariot—a black 1928 Model A Ford that drooped and sagged as if it wanted to lie down and take a nap. The rusty old sedan with running boards had been used as taxi, tractor, and truck by the mission staff for twelve years. My inquiries about its trustworthiness on a long trek were answered with distinctly negative head shakes by everyone except Dr. Parker, who assured me it was more than up to the task. I was not sure if his confidence was based on sound mechanics or on the expectation of Divine assistance.

The doctor and the Ford had made this winding, ninety-mile trip many times, and I'm certain it was never much fun. The road was built not long before by the Red Cross for famine relief and was not intended for the faint of heart. After the Japanese-Chinese hostilities had begun, the thoroughfare was repeatedly blown up and riddled with machine gun holes and artillery fire from both sides. At Dr. Parker's request I painted an American flag on the car's roof, chained two badly worn spare tires to the front, and placed a huge can of gasoline in the back. Coolies stuck five small American flags in the car windows, and our group carried a Red Cross flag and a large American flag for additional protection against attack by Japanese or Chinese Communist forces.

No more than two years earlier, a Baptist physician from England had been shot and killed in Shansi. No one was sure whether he had been fired upon by Japanese who mistook his group for soldiers from the Communist Eighth Route Army or by Eighth Route Army soldiers who mistook them for Japanese. (The Eighth Route Army, formerly the Communist Red Army, at that time was named as such in a Nationalist joint initiative of the Chinese to defeat the Japanese.) After the incident the American consul in Peking had sent an advisory warning to the missionaries to "stay off the roads of North China in cars." We hoped that wearing Chinese gowns and using the flags would ensure safe passage along this treacherous route by indicating that we were neutrals traveling the dangerous path. We felt through each nerve the grim unspoken truth—we were taking our lives into our own hands.

I was told the road would climb six thousand feet into barren mountain lands and then disappear under dry riverbeds. It ran crazily between hanging cliffs and stretched grandly in many branches into the flat country. We launched our journey at the small, quiet railroad station in Yangchuan.

I held my breath as we chugged up mile-high mountains, scattered across barren peaks, and then freewheeled down the other side. I'd done my share of mountain driving back home but always in a good Czech car designed for such things; there's a reason the Tatra automobile is named after the Tatra Mountains. I slid out of my seat as the Ford's skinny tires slithered around curves that sloped toward a sheer drop. The scenery must have been more pleasant before the bombings, which left scars everywhere on little fortresses, Buddhist temples, and ruined cities, where ancient gates gaped from the rubble. Along the road thousands upon thousands of Chinese coolies with a layer of sloughing dough of sweat and dust worked as slaves repairing war damage. We shared the road with slow-moving caravans of two-humped thick-coated camels and donkeys as well as army transports camouflaged by the dust and dirt that clung to their sides. Open mines, where coal lay thick on the ground, were unusable because of the lack of transportation. When we did pass through a village that was still inhabited, the Chinese, who had seldom seen a vehicle of any sort, stood in our path, encircled us, and stared.

Once we stopped when bullets whistled across the roof, seemingly shot from nowhere. We waved the white rag we had ready for that purpose. Several times our path was blocked by Japanese guards who demanded to see our papers, which Dr. Parker promptly provided. We passed miles of telephone poles, erected in daylight by the Japanese only to be cut down at night by Chinese guerrilla bands. We slipped by a multitude of bridges constructed in the day by Japanese engineers and blown up at night by Chinese peasants. After six hours of tedious travel in our rattling Ford, each mile documented in photographs taken with my trusty Kodak, our tiny band of mercy arrived at the place of the raging epidemic.

Dr. Parker and I began the round-the-clock work of examining and treating the sick and immunizing those who weren't yet infected. Our area included a refugee camp with several hundred children, many of whom had contracted typhus. Children were more vulnerable than adults. I also saw several cases of smallpox. After we'd worked together a few hours, above the pandemonium, Dr. Parker turned to me with a look of gratitude and said: "I think you have something beyond your fine training. You're a keen diagnostician of the old school. It is a unique gift that will serve you well in this life."

I was less helpful than either of us had hoped. An endless line of desperately ill patients spoke Chinese, and I could not understand what they were telling me, no matter how loudly they shouted or how wildly they gestured. Crying babies, sobbing grandmothers—they all looked at me, and I could merely look back. None of the hospital staff had the time to help translate. Few would have been able to help even if they weren't so busy.

Snowdrifts, Machine Guns, and Prayers

On the return trip Dr. Parker admitted that seven years earlier, when he and Mrs. Parker had arrived in Pingting, he'd faced the same language problem, knowing no Mandarin. He wanted me to learn Chinese and become more familiar with Chinese culture and offered to ask the Brethren to give me time off to immerse myself in the study of Chinese. I agreed, and we completed the arrangements with surprising speed. The Brethren decided that I should be sent to Peking for three months to the College of Chinese Studies, where I would not solely learn the language but would also become acquainted with the Chinese culture. The school was known as the "California College in China" and taught foreign missionaries, diplomats, doctors, and nurses, along with others. At the same time I would get a letter of recommendation to the Peiping (Peking) Union Medical College (PUMC) so that I could practice there in my spare time. The mission would cover the school fees and other expenses, and in return I promised to serve a full year at the hospital upon completing my courses. This was the closest I'd come to having a plan of action since I left Prague, a proposal that set me on a reliable professional course with a new language that would allow me to take advantage of other opportunities in this vast country. The dogs had been deliriously happy when I returned from the trip up north, but once again I needed them cared for during my planned time in Peking. The volunteer line again formed rapidly for what the missionaries called the "masters of the house."

Leo's first letter arrived with no problem. Written in English, it summarized the contents of two postcards and two letters that had come to Shanghai from my parents. Most reports were of family and friends, with no cause for alarm. One description caught my attention:

> Your father mentions the news concerning the evacuation of Jews seems to be exaggerated and that they are to be accepted with a certain reserve. He says that according to information, only Jews from Mahrisch Ostrau have been forced to evacuate.

The tendency in Bohemia is that as many as possible and especially young people leave the country. The parents of Mr. Rebhun were prepared to leave during the Christmas week, but your father says that their position was different. Mr. Rebhun has lived for thirty years in Prague while he remained a Polish subject. Further, your father says for any case of the future, he prepares slowly all in such a way that an order in this respect should not surprise him. For such a situation, he would like to get your information about whether and what would be possible to undertake in Shanghai. He wonders with your mother whether it would be possible to make knitted goods here for export. He would like to know what capital would be necessary for it. Uncle Rudi is interested to know whether he could start here in his line of construction. In case of emergency, if need be, he would learn in Prague a suitable handicraft for China.

Your father also thinks about another possibility: if you decide to stay in China, he would prefer to live near you and not to depend on your sabbaticals to see you once in some years. He mentions that they have enough of all the goods you described in your letter and that it is not necessary to send something. Besides, it would mean spending money for other people.

After reading Leo's summary, knowing that my father missed my presence, I felt a lump in my throat the size of a lemon. Leo continued in his letter to offer his advice on what Dad had inquired about—a means of support if all fell apart at home.

To this I mention for my part, that to know what capital is needed for the production of knitted goods, it would be necessary to know how big the production is to be established. Besides, it is to be considered that already different people started such a production, which means increased competition. But it is not to say that a success is impossible. Such things have to be thought over, and it is hard to advise somebody by letter. Concerning Uncle Rudi, for the moment the situation in his line is not bad, but still it is not as it was before the war. I cannot tell you whether there will be a chance for him to get a job with a construction firm. You know yourself that all depends just on accident and on luck.

Besides, it is hard to understand the meaning of the letter, as all previous letters say the conditions are not so bad for our people at home. Therefore, I think this message may be influenced more by Christmas mood and feelings than by reality. It does not please me to write to you the contents of this letter from your parents, but, on the other hand, I don't feel sure whether it would be fair not to inform you. My impression, which I got from this letter of your parents, is that there is no reason to be worried at present about their fate.

With no other choice, I took Leo's words to heart, hoping for renewed peace of mind as I settled into the remaining days before the next leg of my journey. Dr. Parker's kind concern for my well-being extended so far as to insist that I move out of my modest room and into a villa suited to my station as the hospital's new chief. In addition to my hiring a Chinese woman with bound feet who took care of my room and laundry, the villa offered a softer bed and bigger desk, on which I could spread my notes and display my photographs. In back was a field of vegetables and another little house for servants. I received a selection of hens to lay eggs, goats to give milk, and rabbits to be broiled, stewed, or baked into a pie if I wished. One evening, as I was eating a Chinese dinner with my chopsticks, the missionaries honored me with Czech music. A slim missionary daughter with a voice resembling a pipit songbird sang "The Christmas Lament," to the tune of Dvořák's Humoresque No. 7. I started to think this might be a nice place to be master of the realm once I learned Chinese. I wondered what it would be like to have a wife to keep me company and share my happiness and my servants. These last days in Pingting might have passed most pleasantly indeed if I hadn't received an uncharacteristically chilly letter from my friend and mentor Leo.

In it he related the news from Prague—the Gestapo was brutally enforcing an 8:00 p.m. curfew for Jews—and passed along a summary of letters my parents had sent while I was in transit. The first few letters were general: my parents were healthy, in a good place financially, and carrying on with their lives. It was meant to be reassuring, yet that impression was impossible to reconcile with the image of the Gestapo raiding homes where they suspected visitors were engaged in such criminal acts as sharing a cup of coffee after 8:00 p.m. The latest letter mentioned that Jews in parts of the protectorate were being pressured to leave the country and abandon their homes and valuables. My parents insisted that no such order applied to them but again asked about Shanghai living.

It made my head spin to realize my family was being lured by the same false hopes about Shanghai that I'd warned others against. I would do what I could to help them if necessary, but I took heart in Leo's earlier remark that the situation was not dire. I'd never had reason to doubt Leo's judgment before, and I wanted to believe he was right about this. I needed more time to complete my Chinese studies and establish myself in my new job. Then I could send for my parents without any of us having to worry about the market for sweaters knitted in Shanghai.

The tone of Leo's letter bothered me more than the substance. I saved it because it was an important reminder that we were neither completely insulated from the turmoil in Europe nor beyond the Nazi's reach: "I beg to ask you once more to instruct your parents to address their letters only to Dr. O.H., P.O. Box 1591, Shanghai, without mentioning my name, and to give also to your other friends only this address without my name. Further, I beg to ask you not to mention my name in your letters home and to ask your parents not to mention my name in their letters. When you write about it to your parents, you can let them understand this without mentioning directly my name."

It was clear that kind, generous Leo had grown concerned that Nazi censors in the Protectorate of Bohemia and Moravia might alert German Nazis or Japanese Nazi sympathizers in Shanghai and Hong Kong about his activities. This could have endangered his business, his family, and even his life. If Leo didn't feel safe here in the vastness of China, how could I be sure my parents were safe in Prague? My soul was torn and filled with discontent.

I had no choice but to hope Leo was right as I left Pingting and embarked on an eight-mile donkey ride in the snow to board a train for Peking.

14

Learning to Love Peking and Its Forbidden City

February–April 1940

After the long train ride, I entered Peking on a rickshaw through a gate in an ancient stone wall that suggested a fortress of Asia Minor with warriors fending off clashes of the ancient world. Thick enough to house a garrison and sufficient to withstand the force of invading armies, it was the first of many clues to why its Imperial Palace compound is called the "Forbidden City." Shivering in the air near the freezing point, I wondered if the Japanese believed they could hold Peking for long.

During my last, brief stop in Peking, I'd been distracted by thoughts of what lay ahead. I was getting my first sense of what would be my home for three months, and I realized it was not a city but a hundred cities or a thousand. Peking's character changed from one street to the next, as did the streets themselves—broad boulevards crisscrossed with alleys so slender it was impossible to presume a breeze could pass through, much less a person. As in Shanghai, I again watched an endless parade of human forms and conditions, from emaciated beggars to self-styled princes. The contrast in appearances was as striking as the disparity between the paupers' shacks as fragile as rice paper and the dazzling, pleasure dome palaces that seemed to have been lifted from a storybook.

As much as I wanted to take in the rest of this exotic panorama, I was so eager to start on the next phase of my education that I nearly leaped off the rickshaw when we arrived at the Peiping Union Medical College. The sight as I stepped through

14. Peking (Beijing), 1940. Photo by Valdik Holzer.

the front door was just as startling. Everything I saw was modern and thoroughly Western, as would befit an institution supported by the Rockefeller Foundation. I was told by Reverend Parker that John D. Rockefeller Sr. and his son, a Junior, for many years had with their fellow Baptists held a high interest in missionary work in China. The college was founded in 1906 as part of an effort to revive American and British missionary work disrupted by the Boxer Rebellion at the turn of the century.

Established with the goal of training Chinese doctors and nurses, the college's program was based on the Johns Hopkins model of providing first-rate medical practice combined with the latest research. It became respected worldwide as the finest and most modern teaching hospital in the Far East. The 1920s-era buildings, built in the tradition of Chinese architecture on the seventy-acre site of Prince Yu's palace outside the Imperial City, were still the city's most modern when I arrived two decades later. It was obvious from my tour on the first day that the place deserved its reputation. I marveled at the impressive new instruments and machines. Here, for example, you could take an EKG yourself of a patient directly on the operating table—something beyond our dreams back in Prague.

I would not only be working in a top-flight facility; I'd be living there. The Brethren paid the reasonable equivalent of fifty-five American dollars a month to provide me with a room at the college's Wenham Residence Hall, although they would not give me this money until I returned to work at Pingting, an insurance policy to guarantee my return.

My most intense involvement in Peking was at the College of Chinese Studies, an extension of the University of Southern California on a street called T'ou T'iao (Tou Tiao). At that time Peking had about 1.8 million residents, but just a few thousand were foreigners, and a minority of those were European or American. Yet I found myself installed in the city's two most Western-style institutions. The language school off Hatamen (Chongwenmen) Street was accessible by a modern electric car line that shared the street with camel caravans from the West, people riding donkeys, rickshaws, and Chinese in 1933 Ford v8s. The school seemed even more modern than the hospital. There were rolling lawns and tennis courts to serve the American missionaries, who made up a good deal of the student body. A few of these dedicated people became my close friends, notably Ken Kohler and his wife, Phyllis, who were preparing to go to a mission field in Hunan Province.

I am confident I was the first son of my nation to be educated at the College of Chinese Studies. Of course, my nation no longer existed, so I'd best say, "I bought a pheasant, and it had fish eggs," a common Czech saying, meaning "Things came about differently than expected."

I never figured out whether my first language teacher, dressed in a flowing silk robe, spoke English or any language other than the Peking dialect of Mandarin Chinese because that was the language spoken in class. Our dignified teacher and the wisdom bestowed made him "teacher for the rest of our lives." During the first days and weeks of our course, he communicated entirely in sign language or by picking up objects and naming them in Chinese, yet he made it clear that we were to bow when he entered the room and again when he left. You could always hear the swish of his robe before he entered or after he'd gone. One day, after I'd left class, I had a chance encounter with my professor. Watching as he crossed the street, I saw him lift his dark-blue robe when muddy water ran beneath his feet. In a compromise with the modern world, I noticed he wore Western leather shoes. As his hands spread his skirt, we caught eyes. I didn't want him to feel awkward when I saw his carefully guarded secret, but as a faint smile formed at the corner of his mouth, I felt a barrier between us fall. Whenever we met again, our never-omitted greeting bows became less formal.

The intensive daily classes started at 8:00 a.m., with a small interruption at 10:00 a.m., when we students played volleyball for about fifteen minutes. At noon we entered the school's dining room and sat at a table with one of the Chinese teachers and were not allowed to speak anything but Chinese. After lunch we returned to class until we had finished for the day, at about five o'clock. It was the best-run language institution I ever saw.

After about a week I could go out on the street and bargain in stores using my new language. In about three weeks I could speak Chinese to patients at the medical college, and they understood me through my thick Czech accent. I became adept at cursing in Chinese, incorporating various body parts into my new language just as I would in Czech. Rickshaw boys became my first targets for long conversations as I practiced the four melodic tones of voice that all-resounding Pekingese, the prestige dialect of Mandarin in Peking, combines.

Despite the many hours of study involved in adding this new language to my growing repertoire, I managed to fulfill my obligations as a part-time "observer" physician while joining in many of the hospital's social functions. I was invited to dinners and to great parties, where I made the acquaintance of more outstanding doctors. I not only enjoyed their company; I hoped to tap into their international connections, which most offered to share. I even managed to meet some fascinating characters outside the hospital, mostly because of my relentless search for other Czechs in exile. One interesting fellow was named Max Engel. Max, a chemist, had graduated from the Technical University in Prague in 1908. He'd immigrated to China sometime after World War I and lived in Kaifeng, where he manufactured milk, cheese, and meat substitute out of soybeans. Max was well-known among Czechs for having sent a cable to former President Beneš during a temper tantrum resulting from some now-forgotten crisis. The cable read, "Kiss my ass!"

Max had been a Czechoslovak consul but was relieved of his position when he issued a passport to the Hungarian spy Esterházy. Then he founded a new republic in Peking and issued passports and visas to people traveling around the world. The Japanese would let people go to Japan with these phony passports, and he had a lucrative business. He lived a comfortable Chinese existence, married to a Japanese woman who at that time was about twenty-three years old, even though he was over sixty. He had several other Chinese girlfriends and two mixed sons who spoke Chinese.

I joined the Peking Club, an active social club for foreigners in the Legation Quarter near the southern Tatar walls. It had a clubhouse and tennis courts. I used to go there for lunch on the weekends to enjoy their foreign newspapers and magazines. I invited Max to join me there on my first few visits. After lunch I'd return to the hospital, and Max would travel by rickshaw to Chien-men (Qianmen) to an opium den. There he would smoke and spend an afternoon of delusional bliss as if there was no suffering and all was well in the world. Max tried to talk me into going with him, and I gave in. I observed people in great peace sitting on a couch smoking away leisurely. Why not shroud my circumstance with delusions?

In the dimly lit, smoky opium den with lovely dragon art on the walls, I was as intrigued by the comatose men of all ages lying on their sides as I was by the ritual of preparing the tar-like drug for consumption. The process needed two people, as one used a candle flame to heat the opium ball while the other made sure it wasn't sucked into the pipe. Once ready to inhale the mostly vaporized morphine released by the heat, the drug fizzed and hissed down the pipe as if an angry bee was being squeezed down its narrow curved neck. I realized why the patrons were lying down. I could neither stand nor sit and slumped in a relaxed haze onto the soft mattress of my divan. I'd expected happy thoughts akin to what Max described as he enticed me to his smokehouse, but I got so deadly sick that I never tried it again. I did keep the pipe as memorabilia.

After five or six visits to the Peking Club with Max, I was called into the office and directed not to bring him back anymore. He was persona non grata because of his unethical and immoral activities. By then my social circle had expanded to include a respectable and famous American paleontologist, Dr. Amadeus William Grabau. A stocky, white-haired, bespectacled man in his early seventies, Grabau was energetic despite using a cane due to debilitating arthritis. A former professor of geology at Columbia University, Grabau was teaching at the Peking National University while conducting a geologic survey of China. He was so respected by Chinese geologists who studied under him that he was called the "father of Chinese geology." Dr. Grabau was best known for giving a name to a group of fossil specimens unearthed in the late 1920s at Zhoukoudian, thirty miles from Peking. He called the discovery *Homo erectus pekinensis*, famously known as "Peking Man."

Dr. Grabau and I conversed in his family's native German, although he had been raised by Lutheran ministers in midwestern America. At his vast Peking brick home west of the Imperial City, the professor held an open house tea party every Sunday afternoon attended by many international intellectuals, including several who had taken part in the Peking Man excavations. Among them was Pierre Teilhard de Chardin, a French philosopher and paleontologist. He was a grandnephew of Voltaire, the French Enlightenment writer and philosopher. Teilhard had been a Jesuit priest and lived in Tientsin before moving to Peking.

His courageous thoughts regarding religion and science became his legacy. Professor Grabau told me that at the age of five, Teilhard set up a bar of iron and worshipped it as God. When the iron rusted, he lost his faith. For fifty years Teilhard had made it his life's work to bring earth and spirit together in his thinking—to make them one, as he believed they should be.

Other visitors at Dr. Grabau's house included Mrs. Johnson, the wife of the American ambassador, and Dr. Vincenz Hundhausen. Before World War I Hundhausen was a high government official in Imperial Germany. He came to Peking in the 1920s on business and decided to stay. He bought a small island in a lake outside the city walls, built a house, and brought a gang of Chinese workmen to farm the land, growing enough food for himself and his workers. He translated German classics by Goethe and Schiller into Chinese and Chinese poetry and drama into German. He gave me copies of several of his books, which I thoroughly enjoyed. On his island Hundhausen manufactured his own paper and set up a printing plant so he could produce his books. The plant was big enough to print all the material for the Catholic University.

Meeting these brilliant people opened my eyes to the possibilities in Peking. Reminiscent of Prague, the city attracted foreign writers, scholars, and artists, and I found my creative side reenergized. I began to regret my obligation to return to desolate Pingting, but I put it out of my mind while I practiced my newly attained language skills, reaching beyond my comfortable cluster of European friends to see more of this enchanting city. As a boy in my country, I'd read about the Venetian explorer Marco Polo, the first Westerner to write about this great Mongolian capital city of Khanbaliq, as it was called in Kublai Khan's era. By the time Marco Polo arrived, in the late 1200s, the "City of the Khan" was one of the world's greatest cities. I had a chance to see where he traveled and to experience the challenge and wonder of trying to understand this alien culture. Over many centuries Tatars, Mongols, Ming, and Manchus all ruled and influenced this ancient city. These waves of occupation reminded me of the Huns, Avars, Bulgars, and Magyars who had pushed my Slavic people westward. I felt a kinship with the population struggling under Japanese occupation as mine was struggling under the Germans.

The mighty leader Kublai Khan, the grandson of Genghis, built Peking's finest palaces, but they no longer existed when I arrived. When the Yuan Dynasty fell, in 1368, the capital moved to Nanking (Nanjing, meaning "Southern Capital," in contrast to Peking, meaning "Northern Capital"). By 1403 a son of the new Chinese Ming emperor established Peking as the imperial capital. The Imperial Palace was the grand design's focal point. Around the palace was the Imperial City, with its various governmental buildings and palace structures. What I saw in 1940 was how the old and new worlds coexisted.

Outside the Imperial City walls was a moat with access to the enclosed area through sixteen massive gate towers. Two streets ran east and west and two other roads north and south, all filled with rickshaws, camel trains, and automobiles stirring up dust. The city was modern in parts. The streets and stores were supplied with electric lights, yet most of the metropolis still got its water supply in five-gallon oilcans or great squeaky wheelbarrows. An electric streetcar brought students to the language school, but nearby you could still see mangy camel caravans and people on donkeys amid modern Ford v8s. The most prevalent transportation was still human powered: men pulling rickshaws, pushing huge wheelbarrows, and shouldering cargo-laden poles. There was always a soldier or two reminding me of ongoing national and European unrest.

Between the main streets were many narrow alleys called "hutongs," a Mongolian word meaning the "space between two tents," barely "nine horse steps wide." Most people lived along the shady *hutongs*, where high walls enclosed a courtyard garden. A screen at the entrance stopped the spirits, who were said to travel in straight lines. Occasionally, from inside, you could hear an *erhu*, a bamboo fiddle that imitated the sound of a bird or horse or produced a soulful violin-like sound, making me wistful for the violins of Prague's symphony. I bought one to give to my father.

Without warning, sandy winds from the Gobi Desert surged through the Peking streets, resembling a mountain runoff, and the sky turned yellow. The sun shone red, my eyes burned, the sand rasped between my teeth. On one occasion I saw a dead body covered with a straw mat, weighted down with a stone—a coolie who had fallen while working. The encircling dust reminded me of the powdery snow in the High Tatra Mountains of Slovakia.

A walled area housing the foreign embassies and some foreign residences stood to the south though still within the city limits. Known as the Legation Quarter, it became an international territory under its own administration after the Boxer Rebellion in 1901. When I arrived, the area was peaceful, with broad tree-lined streets and beautiful gardens. The quarter was a city within a city, exclusively for foreigners. It housed the French, Russian, Italian, American, Belgian, and English embassies, each with architecture reflecting their country.

The French embassy had an entrance like a modern hotel, with a floor of French parquet and French-style telephones. The American embassy housed a radio tower, marine barracks, and an indoor basketball court. The building was well heated and popular for the entertainment of missionaries to art dealers, especially in the winter. On occasion small and quick Mongol ponies paraded around, to be used later in polo matches. A marble obelisk near the Legation gate was the single remnant of the two-month siege during the Boxer Rebellion.

The Boxers were named for the use by the group's members of kung fu–style boxing exercise. They originated from the Chinese countryside and were opposing the presence of foreigners. The Boxers had grown violent out of fear and resentment of acts of arrogance by foreigners, especially diplomats and missionaries. Missionaries and Chinese converts were murdered. In 1900 the Boxers converged on Peking and the diplomat's fortified residences. Several hundred foreign soldiers were protecting them. Eight countries sent armies to rescue them. Afterward the foreign troops plundered the city, creating even more animosity, which lived on with many Chinese. The Legation area also remembered the bloody assaults that happened. The British embassy still displayed a sign, LEST WE FORGET.

I often explored well beyond the city wall. About two miles south was a large complex constructed in the early 1400s called the "Temple of Heaven." The blue-tiled temple was where the "Son of Heaven," responsible to celestial power for the success or failure of his government, would inform Heaven of the status of his rule. During mist or snow, day and night, I returned for photographs as the sight of bright curving roofs against the sky was astonishing.

Northwest of the city was the majestic Summer Palace, a misnomer because it was much more than one building. Built in 1153, it was decorated with extensive lush gardens, graceful multicolor pavilions, with a system of lakes and a famous marble boat with a wood structure painted to look like marble. Legend said the Empress Dowager Tz'u Hsih (Cixi) paid for it with money intended to improve the Chinese navy, which allowed Japan to defeat China in the First Sino-Japanese War of 1894. Calling it the "garden where peace is cultivated," she used the royal residence for rest and relaxation much as the Czechoslovak officers used their Tatra Mountain retreat.

Most weekends I hiked through the Summer Palace or to the Western Hills. On the same latitude as southern Italy, Peking had a broad range of seasonal temperatures, but I was able to enjoy much of the outdoors during my time there. With my father I had spent my Bohemian youth hiking the two-mile path from Benešov to Konopiště Castle, and my excursions in and around Peking made me feel at peace for the first time since my arrival in China. I shouldn't have been feeling peace because I was told after my first visit to the hills that bandits were in control of parts of the area. There were violent kidnappings, and many nearby villages were deserted as residents fled with whatever possessions they could take.

My contact with ordinary Chinese during these random wanderings was most rewarding. I would always dress casually and go armed with a bag of film. It was impossible to tell whether their friendliness was genuine or a defense against showing their true feelings to an intruder, but I enjoyed them and found the way they conducted their business quite intelligent—and I found their artistry beautiful and refined. This was a revelation, as most of us in Europe were raised to view Asians as simple people who shuffled along with their heads bowed, muttering meaningless riddles. I saw what a provincial, conceited simpleton I'd been. How strange to think the lunatic Hitler with his stupid opinions about racial superiority had opened my eyes to this by casting me out into the world! Adolf provided me with at least this profit, albeit I dearly paid for it.

I always returned from hiking to Room 121 Wenham Hall invigorated, only to become depressed when I opened my mail. As much as I treasured any word from home, particularly from or about my parents, what I learned often raised new concerns. My friend Bála kept up a steady stream of reports from London about events back home, including a drumbeat of arrests of intellectuals, politicians, and even some of our friends. Most startling to me was the arrest of Karel Agular, an old schoolmate from Benešov who'd spent two years in an insane asylum. Yet the bastards dragged him off to a concentration camp and killed him.

I was receiving mail directly from my parents in Prague. They didn't write anything noteworthy except that, according to a new Nazi decree, persons of military age—men about forty-five or younger—could not leave the protectorate. I had several friends or cousins who were still trying to get out, and I wondered what this meant, particularly for Hana's cousin, Pavel Kraus.

Bála reported from the Czech Committee in London that the mobilization still existed on paper. "We are slowly getting ready to charge at Adolph through the field," he wrote, adding that within the army in exile, "there is one officer per one fellow and for those two, there is one physician." With that ratio they were not accepting physicians. The Czech Legion's chief physician, Dr. František Langer, who was stationed in Paris, was Bála's relative through marriage. Bála's Jewish father-in-law, Dr. Leopold Langer, was still free at home but not able to practice law. Bála disclosed that many acquaintances had been dragged away to concentration camps, among them my friend Dr. Sobička, whose father was a clerical party member of the Parliament at the Reich assembly in Vienna, and Benešov's Dr. Taussig, a friend of my dad.

Bála and Leo kept me updated on the continued transformation of our homeland into a police state modeled after the Reich. By March businesses and stores had been "Aryanized," meaning Jewish owners were forced to sell their companies and shops for nearly nothing or abandon them with no other way to make a living. Jews were forbidden to go to movie theaters, museums, and libraries, and banking hours were severely limited. More Jews were driven out altogether and forced to become refugees, but it was becoming harder to escape Nazi fervor no matter how far the displaced persons traveled. This fact was driven home when I struck up a conversation with a local police official during one of my excursions. He told me the German consul had instructed authorities not to honor Czechoslovak passports. Anyone who held one should be told to apply to the German embassy in Shanghai for new documentation after proving loyalty to the current government. I assumed anyone foolish enough to follow such instructions would be subject to deportation back to Prague.

Leo continued to monitor mail arriving for me in Shanghai. He forwarded a friend's gift of two small boxes of tobacco and photo paper and asked if I knew of a job for a forty-year-old German gynecologist. The doctor was arriving by ship after six months in a concentration camp, the brother of a shared Shanghai friend, Dr. Grossmann. I added his name to my long list of people I felt guilty about not being able to help.

In a depressed state, my reply to Leo began accordingly:

Damn it that so many people from Bohemia are coming to Shanghai, God knows how this all will end. Plus, those already from Shanghai would be most happy to run away from there. Dr. Kurz asked me to help him get a position of a missionary physician. There is nothing here in Peking at the moment but more advantageous to start from here for a doctor. The only reliable way is to enroll at the College of Chinese Studies and study Chinese for several months, and then get a job. There are plenty of physicians from the closed-down British hospitals who, of course, have priority.

Leo wrote, thanking me for my "positive response."

Concerned about my unacceptable passport, I kept a low profile for the rest of my time in Peking, which I savored. The arrival of spring gave the city a poetic quality that deepened my appreciation of its beauty. Japanese cherry trees, known as "sakura," blossomed in the Summer Palace, clothing its stark whiteness with a rosy-colored veil. Under the flowering trees, with their sweet smell, girls in brightly colored kimonos pranced about.

The warmer weather brought outdoor socializing to the Legation Quarter. I often went to the Commerce Club, where they set up a large Mongolian grill in the garden to broil lamb and beef. The people attending these parties were mostly diplomats stationed in Peking at different embassies, including the British, American, and French.

I spent time at the French embassy, where an acquaintance kept me informed of what he knew. He gave me a copy of the "Yellow Book," a study of the French Republic government of the origins of the European war (1938–39). It detailed the Führer's assurance to the world three days before his attendance at the Munich Agreement that the incorporation into the Reich of the Sudeten areas was the "last territorial demand" he would make upon Europe. Hitler added: "As soon as the Czechs have reached an understanding with their minorities, and I mean by peaceful methods, not suppression, I shall have no further interest in the Czech state."

Especially for Britain's Chamberlain, Hitler included this final mockery: "And that I guarantee him: we do not want any Czechs."

Because of those words, I was a Czech in Peking.

I enjoyed the excellent company around Peking as I did the conversation of scholars at Dr. Grabau's home. I was invited to cocktail parties and even played tennis at the U.S. embassy. For future job applications I managed to get a meeting with Dr. Henry Houghton, director of PUMC. A handsome man, slightly older than my father, with thinning hair and round studious glasses. Born in Ohio, he'd graduated from the prestigious Johns Hopkins University Medical School in Baltimore. He'd overseen the development of the teaching hospital, stayed for a while, and then returned as its director shortly before I arrived and was disturbed about the effects of the war with the Japanese on China. He'd treated Imperial family members and was a great collector of Asian art and porcelain, of which I shared his interest. My interview lasted more than an hour, which was a great success considering that he usually kicked everyone out in a few minutes. He asked me my opinions on what I'd seen at PUMC, what I thought about bilingual instruction, and how I viewed Chinese and Western faculty members. He provided me with an excellent reference letter. I knew that when my language studies were completed and my command of Chinese was good enough to work with Brethren staff and patients, I had a job to do in the interior, even though I was leaving as a "Chinese half-learned."

On April 25, 1940, I traveled like a melancholy stork on the darkened train back to Pingting's nowhereness, gazing at my brooding reflection in the window, never uttering a word.

15

Outback of Nowhere—Pingting

May–July 1940

With Dr. Parker on furlough to America, I was the head physician of the Brethren Pingting hospital and the satellite hospital in Liao Hsien. After my experience at such a model institution in Peking, this one no longer impressed me, but I was determined to do my best. I was soon to see all the disadvantages and difficulties of this institution—challenges unthinkable in the hospitals I'd worked in before.

Our missions were located on the east border of Shansi Province, between the provincial capital city, Taiyuan, and the provincial capital of neighboring Hopei (Hebei) Province, Shijiazhuang. Shansi had a population like Chicago—some three million people. Our hospitals had two American doctors, about a dozen qualified Chinese doctors, and sixteen nurses but no dentists to serve this section of Shansi. The average Chinese knew nothing about dental hygiene. In addition to the regular population, there were Chinese refugees, many of whom were ill or suffering from the ravages of war. Not long before my arrival, the Japanese smashed the dikes to the river and flooded the countryside to our south. The result was not just a fresh wave of refugees but the destruction of crops the province desperately needed.

The good news was the language school had worked miracles. I could, in the Pekingese dialect, question my patients, give out orders in the hospital and household, and even joke with the missionaries. I could tell the meaning of about six hundred signs and

write about four hundred. It didn't mean much since to understand a newspaper I needed to know about twelve hundred to
fifteen hundred signs. But I could contribute to the cause—my
accepted mission—and they needed me.

We were overwhelmed with patients. We did our best to delouse
and then treat, immunize, and educate them about hygiene and
nutrition, but many had to be content with one meal a day of ran-
cid scraps that should have been thrown away. Malaria and dysentery caused much suffering during the summer months, and
a whole range of infectious diseases raged throughout the year.
Tuberculosis and syphilis were widespread to a terrible extent, and
the few people who escaped them were still vulnerable to cholera, leprosy, and many other diseases.

Each day unfolded with a new story or two that I considered
worthy of consideration for my future book. Several miles from
us was a new road being built under Japanese supervision. Since
there was fighting going on in this region, the engineers had a
team of Russian bodyguards for their protection.

One day I was sitting in my hospital office about two in the
afternoon reading some papers. Someone knocked on the door,
which was unusual because the Chinese usually burst in. A white
man in a khaki Japanese uniform appeared, and he wasn't exactly
clean or groomed. A youngster about twenty years old, blond fluff
on his chin, he clutched his cap in his hands as he smiled at me.

He let me ask questions in Chinese for a while and then said:
"Hey, please, I not sick, but I was told there was a Czech doc here,
so I came around to see ya." I froze—the chap spoke Czech! A
strange Czech with a touch of Russian. "My name is Vejvoda,"
he says. "My daddy left fifteen years ago for Prague, he wrote me
once and then nothing. I wanted to ask you where I should write
to reach him and how to talk to him."

He was from Charbin (Harbin) and worked as one of these
bodyguards, but I was happy to have a chat in this mixture at least
that I understood. He spat that he did have a "pain," the one that's
always talked about last: syphilis. I treated him and recorded the

story in my journal. I heard later that he was "permanently rest-ing," courtesy of a Red hand grenade.

With the old Ford at my disposal, I made the long, lonely, and often terrifying trip between our two outposts by myself to keep up with the patient load. I'd been told the medical center at Liao once had ninety-nine beds full but had to abandon it at a moments' notice. In a year and a half, the city had a change of controlling powers seven times. When the Chinese authorities left, they would force the local people to leave with them. Thus, the medical work stopped for a while as the Chinese staff went with them. The need was appalling in the mountain villages, where refugees were in terribly crowded, unsanitary conditions. Many were getting by with one meal of bad food a day, with dysentery and malaria-causing misery during the summer.

On many occasions I encountered sick people with easily treat-able conditions, but I was at a loss because they had no money for medicine, and I had none to give away. The local peasants were so destitute that even several cents was a large sum for them. The Brethren's resources were so thin that I sometimes had to operate without gloves because we couldn't afford them. I took what com-fort I could from the truth: even if there was little we could do for these people, it was better than nothing. Although I read Ameri-can medical literature, I tried to spend my leisure hours painting, writing, and reading books my parents sent me. It helped, but as the weeks passed, my restlessness turned into anger, compounded by the threats to my well-being from diseases and the Japanese as well as from the Communists and Nationalist Chinese, who were still fighting each other and then banding together to battle the Japanese.

The Japanese would visit the hospital after the 6:00 p.m. cur-few to make sure no guerrillas were getting treatment. They would count the number of patients, and each morning a patrol would come in for another head count, reasoning that if the evening and morning numbers were the same, no guerrilla had been admit-ted overnight. We used to keep a bunch of Chinese farmers who were ready for discharge and let them go during the night, and then we would admit some peasants, who obviously were in the Chinese Communist army, if they needed any medical care. Our census at night matched the count in the morning and vice versa.

Upon returning to Pingting, I cheered myself up by hosting a celebration on the anniversary of my emigration. I used my semi-mastery of Chinese to instruct my cook to prepare schnitzels, fried potatoes, American corn, and apricot dumplings made from our garden's bounty. The missionaries introduced the corn, but I recognized it as the so-called popcorn that used to be sold at the fair in Benešov. After dinner I feasted on peaches better than at home and then retired to my room and drank a half-liter of gin in total solitude. When I realized to my great disappointment the bottle was empty but I was still sober, I started sniffing cologne, which was the only alcohol I had left. When that did not help, I put my feet in a potash kettle and talked to myself loudly.

The greatest source of my frustration with my ability to do my job was the cultural differences that interfered between the Chinese and me. People I otherwise admired and respected for all they had accomplished and suffered through seemed determined to reject not just modern science but even common sense whenever it clashed with superstition. The struggle against Chinese superstition and incomprehension sometimes brought me to a state of mad abhorrence, at other times to a state of apathetic resignation. I could not force the staff to use their superior elocution in Chinese to explain to the patients the treatment objective, why the checkup, the hygienic conditions necessary to keep their—with great difficulty attained—health.

Time after time I tried to coax a patient who had a severe case of tuberculosis to open a window in a hospital room filled with thick, unbreathable air. But the moment I left, he'd close the window again. The reason was that an open window would allow his "home ghost" to escape. I couldn't change his mind, so I recommended he sit out on the balcony to get some fresh air. He refused because the other patients on the balcony were below his social class. I didn't have a separate place for the privileged to lie down.

Another time I was told not to remove worms growing out of an old varicose ulcer because "healing will slow down."

Twice a week I ran an X-ray clinic. This was attended by the sick and their relatives and acquaintances. At first I could not understand why there were five times as many onlookers as patients in the room. Then I discovered the whole extended Chinese family wanted to see their grandfather's lungs. Sometimes I was pushed to the periphery as discussions about Grandpa's health expanded into the corridors and even the street.

It was not rare for a sick person to send someone, a stand-in patient, to see the doctor in his place. Most often, it was a husband, but sometimes a son or servant would come to explain the sick person's pains and request a cure. Women often came with their husbands and nodded silently as the men related their wives' tribulations.

Even the educated Chinese I worked with often refused to abandon their most dangerous habits. I'd scrub up for an operation, only to find the room filthy and the patient lying in dirty linens. To explain or preach was futile since I was greeted by a smile so innocent that it would make me cry. Soon after arriving, I was about to perform a lifesaving procedure when I realized the nurse had laid out the same instruments I'd used on the previous patient. I reminded her about the importance of using sterile instruments, but she merely blinked at me, so I walked around her to get a clean set. She had also not changed the water in the sink in which we washed our hands. She handed me a towel that was in such a state that I would be afraid to polish my shoe with it.

The next day I encountered a Brethren's administrator in the hallway and received an impromptu lecture about the need to respect Chinese culture. I felt I was being punished for my virtues. I blew my top. "That isn't culture; it is ignorance," I shouted. "Unless germs learn to respect it, I won't either." I should have controlled my temper, but my studies at Charles University had taught me to be vigilant for the patient by ensuring sterilization and aseptic operating conditions.

After that incident I was involved in a surgery and requested silence while listening to a tubercular patient's chest. Everyone was talking as if I weren't there at all. I needed to do my knocking and listening, so I asked for silence. I repeated my request two more times, and then something I could not understand happened. Two of the Chinese staff responded by speaking more loudly. I felt it was a deliberate provocation. I erupted in strident English, which they understood, and the others could tell from my shrill address that I was not in the mood for cozying up.

I was rebuked for "unchristian" behavior. Worse—because my intent was excellence in the service of medicine—my attempt to reorganize the duties of assisting staff met with opposition due to tradition, incomprehension, and the convenience of the missionaries. They displayed more understanding for the Chinese, among whom they had lived for years and whose habits they took for their own. Yet I knew their intentions were honorable from their vantage point.

I felt excluded from both the missionaries who had gone native and the Chinese staff who had embraced Christianity because I'd done neither. The situation battered my confidence. My mood kept swinging as I dealt with all this. Sometimes I was content; other times I swore or was overcome with homesickness. When I was in such a nostalgic mood, I sat down at a piano and played the drinking songs I remembered from U Suterů, a hotel pub in the center of Prague. I drank wine given to me by the French priests of Hopei. Once, while I was in such a miserable disposition and cavorted alone, an old teacher came to visit me. She sat down in the next room and listened to my entire repertoire. When I finished, she begged me to write my songs down and even brought me music staff paper. I listed "Would We Drink?" "What a Girlfriend I Have," "Unhappy Caretaker's Courtyard," "Bricklayer's Building"—well, I wrote down about fifty melodies. Later I came to the local chapel and beheld the children's choir singing Chinese words to the tunes of my drinking songs. At the end of one song I couldn't control myself. I sang back to them in my most perfect Czech song voice until they ended the program with wild clapping. Dad would have been proud.

My disenchantment with Pingting reached the breaking point when I learned that an American physician in a similar hospital was drawing a salary three times higher than mine, $160 per month compared to my $52, even though he had less experience. From what I'd heard from friends in Shanghai and elsewhere, there was no rhyme or reason to what anyone earned in this puzzling and infuriating country, except that a refugee was at the mercy of everyone and thus was paid a pauper's fee. As contented as I thought I'd be before I departed for Peking, I could not accept the plan of spending one day longer in Pingting than my contract required.

Leo tried to make my temporary existence more bearable by sending my requested exigencies for living. From Shanghai he mailed some cheap cloth for a white summer suit to be made by a local tailor for my hospital costume. I'd ruined the white clothes I'd brought with me. He also mailed buttons, since they were unavailable, along with a mosquito net and a toothbrush. Sometimes he hid in a towel a bottle of alcohol. To add humor to Leo's days, I sent him the feuilleton I wrote in response to a *Jüdisches Nachrichtenblatt–Židovské listy* newspaper article from Prague about Shanghai in which I smeared its take on the refugee situation. It was a review written more for fun than in the likelihood they would publish a "from the ground" report.

I did share with Leo news in my effort to locate jobs for people on my "desperate physicians list": "I managed to find something for Dr. Grossmann. It's nothing definitive, but should he get the job, it would be good. In Taig, that's about fifty miles from Pingting, they are looking for a physician with a practice in surgery. The young American doctor who had been there contracted spotted fever and died two weeks ago. The hospital is slightly bigger than ours, also with two subaltern Chinese physicians. I am writing it to you as it really is, so he wouldn't by some chance be surprised should someone tell him that his predecessor got infected at the hospital. As far as I know the physician was not inoculated."

From my friend Rudla Rebhun I asked for accoutrements that couldn't be bought in Pingting—two ounces of Prince Albert pipe tobacco and Kodak paper for enlargements. I would reimburse him through Leo's assistant in Shanghai, Mrs. Terekhin, who was keeping an accounting of my debts. Rudla updated me on changes in Shanghai since I'd left, one of which was the Germans now sponsored a Shanghai radio station, WGRS (GRS for "German radio station"), in the German Concession. Rabidly anti-British and pro-Japanese, they continuously broadcast Nazi speeches talking about the "ultimate victory."

Where to go next was a puzzle, but I had no time to waste in trying to solve it while also making sure my parents could join me. They'd written soon after the year-end holiday season that the situation at home was getting worse and they were preparing, as a last resort, to leave Bohemia by evacuating to Poland. Soon afterward they wrote that things had gotten better. They continued to insist there was no urgency, instructing me in their letters not to spend money trying to obtain visas for them. They worried about what they would do to support themselves in China. They repeatedly told me they did not want to be a burden.

Despite their reassurances, I knew better because my father began mailing me bundles of books instead of keeping pace with my reading. He was trying to send his entire library before the Nazis could burn it. Expecting that my folks would agree to come once I had the arrangements in place, I applied through all available channels for entry permits, but neither the Chinese nor the Japanese wanted to encourage any influx of foreigners. I managed to obtain a residency permit for the Japanese-controlled territory in northern China.

I'd contacted the Far Eastern Jewish Central Information Bureau for Emigrants the previous year, and I heard back from them after returning to Pingting. The bureau assured me of its help in arranging for my parents to join me if I could prove that I could support them—and if I obtained something called a "landing permit," which meant paying for their fare in advance. That would require a deposit of eight hundred dollars in U.S. currency, about the price of a new Ford Fordor automobile in the States. I had nowhere near that much money and no prospects for saving it with my salary of fifty-two dollars per month.

I'd already learned about the landing permits from my friend Rudla back in Shanghai and was expecting his help in obtaining one. I wrote to him again, but he could offer no encouragement in reply: "You are holding me for such a bad friend when you write that I have not done anything about the permit for your dear parents. It is more not true. But neither you nor I can do anything because there is one and only one way to get that permit, and that is to be able to put forward U.S. $400 per person. As neither you nor I have that kind of money, I have not wanted to make your heart grow heavy unnecessarily."

The truth was that my heart could not have become much heavier. I felt trapped deep in the war-torn, disease-infested interior of China while my parents were caught eleven thousand miles away in Nazi-infested Prague. I'd failed to join the fight against Hitler, and now I was failing to help my parents outmaneuver him. From my correspondence with friends, I knew that others were having qualms about what was happening—or what they feared might happen next. Bála in London had gotten word that he'd be able to join the Czechoslovak army in exile, while Franta Schoenbaum back home thought he'd arranged passage to Bolivia but then learned that no one under age forty-five could get permission to leave the protectorate.

I wondered how long it would be before this European theoretical conflict burst into flame with outright fighting. It had been more than six months since the Allies declared war on Germany, but Hitler was yet to feel so much as a bee sting in the occupied territories. Britain had begun rationing food, but it seemed like a precaution, or were they stockpiling for a major offensive? I searched the few international papers that came my way and listened to the church radio, which received broadcasts from Nanking in English. I yearned for any hint that the Allies were ready to drive Hitler out of Europe. I tried once again to volunteer my services, this time contacting the French consulate in Peking. I got no reply—and as far as our Czechoslovak émigré army was concerned, I continued to be of value as its only reserve officer in Pingting Hsien.

After my parents the one I'd most hoped to help was my Uncle Leo Holzer, my father's younger brother. Leo didn't indicate he'd decided about emigrating, simply that he was "deliberating" while gathering information. He had many questions that dealt with details such as how much luggage he could bring on the Manchuria Railway and how payment for passage could be arranged through Moscow, given the currency differences. I knew little about this route, except that it involved a dangerous crossing from Russian territory to Japanese-held territory. I did my best to provide answers and suggest other sources of information, knowing Uncle Leo was resourceful enough to overcome obstacles. If Uncle Leo could find a way to bring his wife Elsa, and young son, Hanuš, to China, this might encourage my parents to consider joining us. (Unfortunately, Uncle Leo never tried to leave. He and his family were transported to Terezín concentration camp. On September 28, 1944, he was sent to Auschwitz and then to Dachau to perform labor. He was the only one of the three who didn't survive.)

Another name that sticks in my mind is Dr. Ctibor Erdélyi. He was my Aunt Erna's brother-in-law, a few years older than I was and a former military surgeon like me. He was so eager to leave Central Bohemia and start a new life in China that he offered to bring his considerable store of medical and dental equipment with him, including his X-ray machine. My reply was realistic, detailing the reasons he'd find it difficult to obtain a work permit and why it would be impossible to earn a living even if he could get one. I heard no more from him. (Years later, after the war, I realized his letter was like submitting to me a résumé for sustaining life. I learned that he had remained in the protectorate. He must have been one tough guy because he somehow survived both Auschwitz and Buchenwald, but his wife did not. I've often wondered if their outcome would have been different if perhaps I'd painted a less honest picture. Deceitfulness on occasion could have been a better choice.)

It would have been difficult for me to convey a rosier view of China, as I was determined to find somewhere else to land. The United States of America seemed the most attractive choice but also the least likely option because so many others felt the same way. I had applied for a U.S. visa before I left Prague and registered with the American consulate when I arrived in China. My quota number came up in the spring as I returned from Peking, but the consulate made no great effort to find me in Pingting. By the time I inquired again, a bureaucrat coldly informed me that my number had expired and I had to start over again. While I tangled with this red tape, I applied for positions at several California hospitals. All responded that they could not use my services.

For all my Czech pride I no longer considered returning to Prague after the war. I'd grown disillusioned with my homeland. From my new perspective I saw how the ideal of full assimilation had collapsed and how Jews were being mistreated in what was Central Europe's most promising democracy. I doubted assimilation could be a reality in Europe. For a while in China, during my initial throes of homesickness, I'd continued to look back on the idyllic scenes of my Bohemian childhood with great fondness and remembered nothing but happy times. Darker memories rushed back. I didn't want to dwell on old wrongs, but there had not been a time when I, as someone of Jewish heritage, was not an unwanted stranger. I never had full rights in my homeland; wherever I went, I was tolerated. Whether at primary school, high school, university, or in the army, on occasion I was met with a sneer, although I tried hard to belong. I was a second-degree citizen.

Maybe I was making a mistake, but it was my truth—a tragedy of the assimilated ones, of the second and third generation who'd tried so hard. I had such unfailing trust in and love for a country that had never absorbed me entirely, and even though I loved her and felt home within her, all others considered me this stranger. As I lay staring at a ceiling beyond the range of anyone who could advise me, I pondered what the core of my identity was—a Czech, a Jew, or something else?

Endless interrogation of my dejected self-produced no sound answers. What set me apart? I spoke the common language; I ate the same food as everyone else; I played the same sports and laughed at the same jokes. Yet the people who sensed that I was different enough wanted to get rid of everyone like me, to oust us from society. Escalated to dangerous levels of hatred toward international Jewry spurred on by the crazy Hitler, the circumstance at home seemed to purport that our main crime was breathing. His racist ideology was built on his premise of Aryan (German) race superiority. An aggressive nationalist ideology that put the nation over the individual and demanded Germany first extend to what Hitler and his followers perceived as its natural territorial borders was unfolding. This all seemed clear from a distance, but it was hard to digest. Maybe I was fooling myself again, but I felt more accepted in China, where I was a white man among many races but still judged by my personal qualities and not by my curly hair. We all had one enemy: the degenerate Nazism and racism and totalitarian ideology, fascism. In this outpost human dignity was alive.

This consumed my thoughts as I struggled with the realities of my position at the hospital. My soul was torn and discontent; I missed something all the time. Only God knew what I wanted—I didn't know it myself. In my letters I asked my far-flung friends: "Where will this all lead to?" "What will come out of this?" "Will those set against each other be able to unite in some future toward the positive work of embracing our differences and one another?" Caught in dismal circumstances, none had any answers. Was there still a covenant between God and humanity? I sat alone, accompanied by my devoted dogs, nightly in my room and scribbled notes for my novella, naturally with illustrations, and toasted to a dreamed-up utopia until my muse abandoned me.

It was with Franta Schoenbaum, in missives transcribed on frail onionskin paper, that I could be myself. Across a colossal distance I sent thoughts and updates of how I'd managed to teach our Chinese doorman to greet me in Czech with "Kiss my ass" and named our missionary Ford "Fart-Fart." By teaching the smallest boys at the mission how to unknowingly say *ass* in Czech, for a time I created a haven, escaping for a moment war-torn China and worries from home. My friend Franta also sent packages of books and newspapers and reports of acquaintances to arrive in Shanghai on ships comparable to the ss *Conte Biancamano* of the Italian Lloyd Triestino Line. (The Italian ship was seized by the United States Navy at the beginning of World War II and converted for troop transport. It carried nearly six thousand troops, who landed at Casablanca in North Africa in 1942.)

Twice a month, for supplies, I took the train through Peking to Tientsin on the coast, a three-hour additional route that carried me with a knot of emotions through Japanese-occupied territory to the British Concession. At my expense I purchased first-class tickets. In these parts white men were expected to travel in first class.

When I arrived in Tientsin on the first supply trip, I was snookered again. Instead of taking a taxi, the trusted porter suggested I hire a rickshaw for my luggage and myself. It was half the price of a taxi but had its disadvantages. On the way we had to pass through a blocked-off concession. In a taxi this was possible without any inconvenience, but rickshaws could not enter the concession. So the suitcases had to be carried for about a hundred meters to another rickshaw, and in that expanse one had to undergo an inspection. While not strict, it was not pleasant.

For eighty years, until 1938, when the Japanese arrived, and for a short period of the Boxer Rebellion, part of Tientsin had been under Western control. This situation followed a series of military defeats of the Chinese by Britain and France in the Second Opium War. There were several foreign concessions that operated or had operated in the city, including those of Britain, France, Japan, Russia, Italy, Germany, Japan, and Belgium, and each had its own distinctive architectures in a clean and modern appearance. Along the Hai River banks the French had châteaus and the Germans red-tiled Bavarian villas. The area streets with tree-lined borders followed suit with names like Woodrow Wilson Road, Victoria Street, and Kaiser Wilhelm Strasse. Important industries of fur and rugs in China were centered in Tientsin.

The Japanese accepted my German protectorate passport, the one with the sticker put on by the friendly Czech policeman who had issued it to me in Prague. The British recognized only my Czechoslovak passport. That meant I had to keep removing and then reapplying the sticker. This worked until I lost the label during one trip on my way back to Peking. I then went to a Chinese print shop and had about ten stickers printed so I would have spares. I had several Czech friends in Peking who had been living there before the occupation of Bohemia. I became popular because I had stickers for their old Czechoslovak passports and dispensed them freely.

On another supply trip I took the usual train again through Peking some ninety miles southeast over to the coast, a seven-hour arduous route that carried me through Japanese-occupied territory to the British Concession. My frayed nerves weren't entirely due to the periodic brutish behavior of the Japanese. Warnings always existed about the risk of holdups by bandits and kidnappings, so I was never certain I would reach my destination. To add to, or should I say subtract from, the traveler's general welfare, at most rail stations were swarms of houseflies. With their grimy legs and microscopic hairs that cover their body, each one was a possible carrier of the dreaded cholera, tuberculosis, or typhoid. If a station attendee suspected a passenger suffered from one of these diseases, they'd quarantine the entire crowd for days under not-so-desirable conditions.

When the train stopped at the border of the British and Japanese Concessions in Tientsin, I noticed a Japanese truck distributing rice to Chinese peasants. Thinking it would make a good photograph, I stepped across the line and out of the British zone, and Japanese soldiers armed with bayonet rifles arrested me. They dragged me to a small, windowless building nearby, where some Japanese noncommissioned officers began yelling at me. They tried to grab my prized Kodak camera, but I held on tight, as sweat beaded my forehead and adrenaline-fueled pain filled my stomach. I didn't understand Japanese, but soon an officer arrived with a round face that looked identical to a vicious Japanese Tosa dog bent over a meaty bone. He tried to interrogate me in English, but his English was worse than mine, so the conversation didn't get far.

After a while the officer returned with a young Russian, one of many who'd emigrated from Imperial Russia in the wake of the revolution and civil war. The officer spoke to him in fluent Russian, expecting the trembling fellow to translate it into English. My Russian was better than my English at that time, but I didn't let on that I understood because I was afraid they would think I was a Russian spy. The quivering guy translated from Russian into English while the large-eyed Japanese officer kept telling him: "Ask him if he is a spy! Ask him if he's a spy!"

Whenever the Russian exclaimed, "He is not a spy," the dog-faced officer with gritted teeth and twitchy muscles yelled back: "I am not asking you. You don't answer this. You ask him!" The sound reverberated in the small room, and then we'd stare at each other to see who would yell next.

Like an absurdist drama, it was almost comic, except I knew my life hung by a thread. After about four hours of detention, the same Japanese officers who had arrested me came in and demanded the film from my camera. I understood their gestures and knew that opening the camera's back would expose the roll unless it was rewound back into the cartridge, but I did as they asked. Even if the Japanese tried to develop the film, there'd be nothing to see, but they seemed satisfied with confiscating it. I could have vanished into a Japanese jail, but they returned me to the British line and chased me back over. If they'd have kept me or put a gun to my head and left my brains on the wall, my demise would have been a mystery. Instead, it became a part of my *shuoshu* (*ping-shu*)—my storytelling.

May 1940 brought more bad news. Hitler's occupation of Luxembourg and the Netherlands was followed by the surrender of Belgium. Amid these calamities my two Lhasa apso dogs, faithful companions who stayed by my side calmly as I made my hospital rounds, became febrile and refused to eat. After about three days they died. I was totally unprepared for losing them, as they were from a hardy breed and I had expected to have their company for some fifteen years. My loyal dogs were victims of yet another of this country's scourges, kala-azar (visceral leishmaniasis, or black fever), a disease that shows up first in animals and spreads to humans the following year. My great loss and the thought of what lay ahead because of this latest infection further depressed me.

June grew even darker as I got word that the building where my parents lived had been "Aryanized"—given over to the Germans. My parents were forced to move to an apartment in a Vinohrady neighborhood building on Slezská Street designated for Jews. Before I could determine details of their new circumstances, news reached Pingting that Paris had surrendered and the British were rounding up every fishing trawler and skiff they could find to ferry their retreating soldiers back across the English Channel.

Days later Hitler posed for a portrait in the shadow of the Eiffel Tower, exactly where I had stood a year earlier. I was shocked by the loss of such a great city and angered that the Allies had allowed this gangster with the comic book mustache to get so far. It gave me no pleasure when I learned the price the French had paid for their part in betraying my homeland: every third tank the Germans used in the invasion of France had been built at the Škoda ironworks in Czechoslovakia.

I wrote to a French friend in Peking, Miss Fernande Saizeau, a sophisticated French artist and antiques dealer I'd met several times at Dr. Grabau's tea parties. Nearly forty years of age, she ran an exquisite curio and Chinese art shop on Wu Lao Hutong, where I had acquired a greenish bronze deer dating from the fourth century BC. Our conversations had once been about what might be considered unimportant things but now turned to France's gloomy political situation. At those moments I was haunted by the sadness in her eyes. With the deteriorated situation in her homeland, I felt compelled to write her: "I don't want to lose my confidence in the final victory of right and democracy and complete independence of yours and my people. I am asking you to accept my sympathy and hope with me for a better future." At this point words were the entire defense I could offer her.

Miss Saizeau's response was heartwarming. She appreciated "from the bottom" of her heart my great feeling for her country and wrote: "Our civilization is experiencing more than we could expect, undoubtedly because we have been too blind. Now that we begin to awake, we must unite and each of us, in our own little sphere, fight in the best way we can to kill the barbarism that is invading the world. Victory depends not only on the group of militarists and technicians but on all of us, and for that we must master some great truths and act accordingly . . . America is too slow and too weak, I should say. Keep your courage as I keep mine and never stop fighting for our shared cause: the wheel is bound to turn."

France's colorful statesman Gen. Charles de Gaulle had joined Edvard Beneš to set up a government-in-exile in London, a city crowded with self-exiled leaders. With the fall of France, Britain stood alone against the Axis powers. As I attempted to occupy my mind elsewhere, I reached out in a letter to Dr. Miloslav Fábera in Prague, Czech author of *Neklidná hranice* (The Restless Border), to offer advice from the field. Fábera's book was inspired by his father's diaries as a soldier and legionnaire. With a passion for Asia, it manifested in his work, and I shared his wanderer's desire to travel. My parents had mailed the book from Prague via Siberia as they suspected I'd appreciate the novel's backdrop of China. My letter read:

Dear Dr. Fábera,

It is not my habit to write to the writers of books I have read. In this case, I nonetheless do so, only out of interest. I live in the region and in the circumstances you write about. My hospital is in the interior of China, in a region alternatively controlled by the Japanese and the Chinese guerrillas. I almost cannot believe you have not been to the area you describe, it clicks so well. However, in details you tripped a few times nonetheless. You changed the fighting units into the uniforms of the former Czechoslovak army, Siberian hills you transferred to Krkonoše a bit. But generally your account fits, even for us here in the East. Particularly the mentality of the inhabitants of the Far East, the international atmosphere in the mercenary company is good.

And now how I got to your book: it was sent to me, "via Siberia," directly from Prague. Of course, I will not keep it, and it will travel farther, to a Czech brewer in Peking, a doctor in Tientsin, a Skodovak in Dairen, and so it will slowly make its way down south, it will wander like your fictional character, Hall. Finally, I want to offer you some cooperation. Should you write something more about the Far East, I will be happy to answer all questions so you could avoid some "mistakes of regie [direction]," which would not benefit an eventual translation.

Please, I ask you to use this letter only for your private purposes, as I absolutely do not wish my name be publicized in any way.

I didn't think I would hear back from the author, but a month later he answered. Agreeing to be a source, I typed a five-page response, attempting to share pertinent on-the-ground information for his next book:

You can't know how happy I was to receive your letter; correspondence in Czech is my only conversation in my mother tongue. The milieu I live in is entirely Chinese. Chinese is also my language of communication, and I can use English only rarely, when in contact with American missionaries, and lately also Russian, which I speak with a few fellows who are wandering around in the surroundings and about whom I shall write to you. I beg your pardon if my letter is longer than such dispatches tend to be and if I allow for the dam of my self-retained glibness to burst.

I will answer your letter, when possible, point by point: Czechs are present in the Far East in respectable numbers. However, they are mostly settled in large towns on the coast. There is a large Czech colony in Charbin and in various places in Manchuria. These are either immigrants from Russia, who came here during the time of the revolution, or legionnaires who did not return to the motherland. Next to Skodovaci and Batovci—Škoda and Bata employees working abroad— you will find various characters here, from a city policeman in Shanghai to the director of a noodle factory, a makeup artist in the theater in Charbin, the owner of a dry cleaner's in Tsing Tao, I could list a number of these characters and minor characters from Manzuli to Colombo. But where doesn't one meet a compatriot?—I have already seen a nice-haired beauty bow down in the Blue mosque in Constantinople and heard her talk in a Prague accent; I ate ice cream at an ice cream maker, formerly a clerk in the Abyssinia bank in Addis Ababa. I think that you, in your novel, borrowed the address of the only Czech in Peking, Mr. Kara, and put old Hall there, the only difference being that Mr. Kara lives on Kuang An Men Wai and not Way. This *wai* means "outside" in Chinese, the address thus means that it is outside of the gate of Kuang An (huge, spectacular) and, therefore, has nothing to do with the English *way*.

I went on at great length to describe my place of work in the atlas of the world and how it looked:

Scenery is varied and changes its character with every mile; dried-out rivers several miles wide run through deep valleys and form important communication links, on which caravans of donkeys, mares, camels, and human carriers travel.

. . . red mountain roses cover the rocks in places, such strange mixtures of minerals of all geological stratum, with a generally lateral black stripe signifying where the coal reached the surface of the earth. And what kind of coal—the best anthracite lies here at one's easy reach, iron ores and who knows what else—

but there are no roads to take them away, and the deposits that lie near the railroad are so plentiful that it just doesn't pay to transport minerals from so far. This winter I paid 70 cents for coal in Liao, i.e., about 1.10 Czech crowns. The social conditions are according to that.

I described my Brethren workplace:

For the completely penurious we have a missionary committee that covers the fees in necessary cases. Naturally, the hospital and the whole medicinal apparatus receive substantial grants from the United States. These are brief notes on the social and medical conditions in my surroundings; I will surely find an opportunity to describe these conditions to you in more detail and commit some interesting stories to paper.

. . . The populace lives on a desperately low standard of living; the average income is equal to several cents a day, in that I refer you to Buck's novels, which cogently describe the life in the interior. Recently the monetary politics also added up to all this, of both of the warring camps, whose victims are only those small peasants who toil the weak fields their whole lives. For years the country has been ravaged by wars, by seditious generals, predatory hordes of bandits, and finally, by the third year between Kuomintang Chinese and Japan. The so-called culture entered the Chinese interior in the form of kerosene lamps, tin cans, and as of late, dive-bombers. Even though the population in places feignedly accepted the Christian faith, they did not leave their superstitions and resist our doctrine regarding hygiene and all sanitation efforts.

Social diseases like tuberculosis and syphilis are widespread to a terrible extent; only a few individuals can be found here who are spared from having one of those. Infectious diseases: typhus, typhoid fever, dysentery, cholera, leprosy, etc. It rages mercilessly. Sanitation is prevented not only by the atrocious hygienic conditions in dwellings but also the mentality of the populace.

I added multiple stories of people I'd met and even became philosophical, attempting to prophesy the future of China:

> I, for myself, know that China will be a land of opportunity
> at the time the Chinese-Japanese conflict will be ended. Then,
> here will be great progress. The land is waiting for organized
> work. Every hand that will help build the new China will be
> welcomed, I hope. Then they will find many helpers through
> the immigrants' technical hands. Soon there will be important
> industry because the richness of the land is inexhaustible.
> It needs only to be organized. I hope then that the cultured
> states will wonder what China is producing and China will
> export it to all the world markets and trade fairs, and the
> Far East will not be lost to their export market. You only
> have to acknowledge where you live, get in touch with your
> surroundings, and not omit being a part of the culture. You have
> to admit the Yellow Race is no second-class citizen. This is an
> excellent thesis about immigration to the Far East, a position
> that none of the writers has written about so far.

Miloslav Fábera's response from Prague XII, Saarská st. 15, was
immediate and nearly as lengthy as my letter to him. He told me
how he'd developed his first book and was planning his second:

> Dear doctor Holzer,
>
> Accept our sincere greetings, from me and my wife, Helena. We
> thank you for your letter dated June 6 of this year at Ping-Ting-
> Hsien. We received it, with the seven photographs, on July 7.
> The photographs were masterful, we were looking at them for
> a long time, but your letter was even better. You know how to
> write, allow a man of this craft to tell you that. You should take
> notes and write down everything that you see around yourself.
> Once, a whole book could come out of this—but your book.
> Your life and your work. It would certainly be interesting, and
> you would surely be able to sell it well. Proofs of your medical
> artistry will lay their bones somewhere among yellow rocks and

if you don't have the exceptional luck as the personal physician of Tutenchamon [Tutankhamun], the Egyptian pharaoh, after your death no one will appreciate your medical craftsmanship. A good book lives much longer.

. . . Regarding the interest in the Far East, we are like two trains on the same track, traveling in the same direction— with the difference that while you are already whistling at the final station, I am still crawling far behind you somewhere on the tracks. You wrote a long and beautiful letter to me, and I am your debtor. For that account to be settled, I shall write something about myself to you today. Becoming acquainted through letters is like poker. One does not know what one gets to receive. Take it like that. I already told you in my first letter that my fates are not too interesting, in comparison to yours. Therefore, you will likely have a feeling that you are drawing mediocre cards, and I am aware of that. I already know in you that I drew a "street" at least.

This account can be settled only by my second book, all the while my letter was traveling to you by Trans-Siberian railway and yours was going in the opposite direction, I decided to extend my own deadline till the fall of 1941. The book poses many interesting questions and pleases me. I would not want it to leave my hands unfinished. The year 1941—that's still far away, isn't it? I am in no rush. Everything that is to be finished will be finished, what should be severed will be severed, I view haste like a born Oriental . . .

Neklidná hranice (The Restless Border) was the reliving of my father's life but also my wanderer's desire. When it came into being, one can't say. Maybe in the years 1936–38, but that is just the fact; intellectually, this subject matter has permeated my mind since high school gymnasium. *Nobody's Mountain*, my second novel, was coming into being together with the first theme. I studied school in Rokycany, law studies in Prague, military service I got through in Beroun, and now I am at the Czech-Moravian bank in Prague II. Na Poříčí 22—you might know it under different names. That's all. A concise curriculum vitae—nothing more.

He wrote of countrymen we knew in common and about our circumstances, thrown to a bitter wind by the Nazis. He closed with philosophy and good wishes:

> You did a good thing that you did not stay in Shanghai as a "fashionable physician." This ascetic life in Pingting will bear interest to you many times, about that we are both, I and my Helena, strongly convinced. We have no other option but to keep looking forward so that once we will get to see each other, that we will really stand in front of each other and not over the distance of several thousand kilometers, and that we will talk about it. Then we will be able to more or less philosophically analyze it. Paper would not suffice for that. Be certain that we often talk about you and hope from the bottom of our hearts that no harm comes to you there and that you survive it there in full health.
>
> These "forts" or outposts of civilization are a nice thing, the men who are carrying out their duty there are worthy of admiration, but there is a time when the garrison needs to be changed. You will realize that yourself. Later, with time. But the old cannot be thrown away. As you see, I know many people from the Far East, but I realized one thing about them—they all came from this tiny country in the heart of Europe, and after years they all came back here again. I know, it is better "to sing elsewhere from the choir than eat sweets at home," but even that has to have its end. Then my house will be open to you, as is so nicely said by the Mohammedans [Muslims].

Our wholehearted greetings and best wishes,

Dr. Miloslav Fábera

In any case, the exchange with this famous author had escalated my simmering interest to someday write a book—a travelogue-style memoir exploring my adventurous journey, supported by images. But first I needed to find my place in the world. With America seeming less likely to be my next destination, I considered an alternative I did not want to face but saw as possibly unavoidable. I wrote to my contacts in Shanghai. I hoped they'd inform me that conditions there had improved or at least that I might have some prospect of a decent living. As if the letters crossed in mid-air, Leo Lilling wrote about the worsening situation in Shanghai. The British War Office had decided to shift forces from Shanghai to protect the Dutch East Indies, Singapore, and Hong Kong. As the British had for years protected the safe flow of commerce, Leo's concerns for his livelihood grew. There were a small number of United States Marines to fill in for what the British had provided since Shanghai had opened to foreigners at the end of the Opium Wars, nearly a hundred years earlier. I was worried about Leo's safety, as well as all the European immigrants and marines, as it wasn't clear how the Japanese would react.

My misery turned physical when I came down in early August with pneumonia once again. I felt as weak as a fly and too nauseated to eat. You might think that as hospital chief I'd get first-rate care, but I only got what I could provide for myself. I yearned for the kind presence and skill of Dr. Parker. The missionaries took turns offering their concern, but none stayed more than a few minutes. I felt that even this limited attention was provided out of obligation, not real sympathy—and that was the best I could hope for, as our medical staff was rapidly decreasing. New clashes between the Chinese armies and the Japanese were occurring nearby, and civilians were in flight through dust and smoke. The battles roared with bursting shells from big guns on both sides. When I felt strong enough to get out of bed, I discovered that we had five patients and two nurses left in the entire hospital. I read in the papers that the Red regiments from the south had been moved to the railroad and our occupants started to move out.

I had no idea how to get replacement staff, but the fighting ensured that more patients would be arriving soon, regardless of whether we had enough people to treat them. I had no choice but to gather my strength and leave on my scheduled train ride a week early to replenish our supplies, particularly drugs. I was in Peking for what was to be a three-day trip when the Brethren sent a cable referring cryptically to a "red catastrophe" that had resulted in upheaval throughout the region and caused the railroad to be shut down. It took a while for the scope of what had taken place to become apparent. The Chinese Communist guerrillas of the Eight Route Army had mounted a major campaign, destroying hundreds of miles of rail line and a valuable coal mine that was vital to the Japanese. The Communists briefly celebrated the territory emancipation, but the Japanese fought back and carried out a campaign of ruthless retaliation against the civilian population.

I had no choice but to postpone my return to Pingting and wait in Peking for the fighting to subside. There was no end in sight—a second cable arrived suggesting I not return at all. The Brethren granted me a month's pay and their best wishes for finding a new position. Although I'd offered my best healing talents to their endeavor, I felt my services were better suited for Peking.

16

Love Breathes Life into the Heart
August–October 1940

The missionaries back in Pingting instructed my servants to pack my belongings so they could be shipped to me in Peking. The servants, in turn, were kind enough to keep nothing for themselves even though I'd abandoned them without showing my appreciation with a coin or two, as I would have if given the chance. It was a miracle that all the photos, artwork, and whatnots I'd lugged around China made their way past the war zone and caught up with me a month or so later.

Through a friend's contacts I got an offer for a position in Tientsin with room and board and $250, but only for a month or two, until their physician was to return from Shanghai. My friend, named May, was a well-connected and wealthy woman, half-Chinese and half-Jamaican, who promised me that she would bring me Chinese clientele if I took the offer. She was older than me but pleasant looking. She drove me around to do shopping, fed me ice cream, and in general wanted me to open the practice there, but I was nervous. Although I appreciated her company, I wasn't in love.

As I wrote to my friend Karel Schoenbaum, "Nothing lasts forever, not even the love for one miss."

I was happy to be out of Shansi, where I had grown to think they were treating me as a "refugee doctor." In Peking the salaries of European physicians were starting to adjust to the U.S. dollar base, but I was sure that would not happen at the Brethren Pingting hospital.

Peking remained different from Shanghai, as it wasn't overrun with European immigrants. As far as I could tell, I was one of four refugee doctors, and the other three seemed to be doing well. I'd paid a visit to the Peiping Union Medical College to catch up with my friends and former colleagues. I asked each for any hint they could offer of a job. To my delight I discovered the school's distinguished and charitable president, Dr. Houghton, was impressed with my part-time research work there the previous spring in vitamin and skin diseases. He offered me a job in the department of dermatology and syphilology, and I accepted. He even sweetened the pot by offering me free room and board at Wenham Hall until I found my own place.

Deep in the gloom of my final days in Pingting, my streak of bad luck began to change. Leaving on that last supply run had saved my neck, and losing my job had freed me from the obligation to stay—and sink—in that infectious quicksand. I appreciated that the missionaries were dedicated to making a difference in Chinese lives, but the tides were surging against them. I felt remorse that I hadn't been able to help build a better future for the many Chinese they sought to help. I was proud that I didn't compromise my standards. I'd gained significant experience for wherever my medical profession would take me.

Now I had a new job that lacked only the prestigious title of "chief," which I traded to rejoin the professional company of top-flight personnel from around the world—just as I traded evenings alone sipping gin in my bedroom for the company of intelligent and gracious people like Ken and Phyllis Kohler. Soon Ken had to leave us for his mission assignment in Lakeside (Huping), near Yochow in Hunan Province (Yueyang City), and to prepare for Phyllis and his two children to join him.

Until then Phyllis made sure I didn't get lost in my work. One day in mid-September, a few weeks after my return to Peking, she invited me to join her on a train ride to Tientsin Harbor to welcome three American women arriving on the Japanese passenger liner *Nitta Maru* to study the Chinese language in Peking before taking to the field in Lakeside as missionaries. They were part of the German Reformed Church China Mission from Philadelphia. I would happily have gone along, but my work schedule didn't allow it. I made up for my absence the next day, when Phyllis hosted an afternoon tea in honor of these three young women.

My recent reversal of fortune had lifted my mood, so I must have appeared confident when I sauntered into the parlor. Attempting to look much the big-city surgeon in my pleated linen trousers and starched white shirt, I entered the room not on a cloud but within one, as white smoke billowed from the Digby pipe I'd bought in Paris that I clamped between my teeth.

I spotted Phyllis and lifted the pipe from my mouth so I could say hello. She was a few steps away from me, but I never reached her because Phyllis and everyone else in the room faded into a black-and-white background the instant Ruth Lequear came into view. She stood near the expansive front window, framed by the afternoon light that illuminated her shimmering red hair. With no makeup except for a hint of red lipstick, she was the most natural beauty I'd ever seen, athletic and trim yet feminine and poised. With pale blue eyes as clear as a mountain stream and curly hair cropped short, she reminded me of Amelia Earhart, not simply in her appearance but because she radiated a serene self-confidence. As a bouquet of her perfume reached my nose, I looked straight into her eyes, and to my delight a smile spread across her full lips as she looked back at me. We held our gaze until I reached her side.

"Your pipe smells like cake," she exclaimed as her smile lit her freckled face.

"I guess it's from herbs the Chinese mix into the tobacco," I replied in my best broken English. "Or maybe it's something I'm better off not being able to identify."

Ruth laughed, and luckily for me she continued to laugh at about all I said. I wondered if she found me witty, or maybe my Czech accent and a garbled mixture of English and Chinese were the source of amusement. One of the first things she uttered was "Ni hao," a sound similar to *knee haow*, which means "hello" in

Mandarin. I was amazed that she already spoke Chinese at all. Although she insisted her Chinese speech was rusty, I thought she spoke like a native—and it turned out she was. This was the first of many pleasant surprises as Ruth filled me in on her background.

"I was born in 1916 in Hunan Province, where my American parents were Christian missionaries. I'm a missionary-in-training," she said with her shoulders back and a gleam in her eyes. Her father had arrived in China in 1909. "My mother, who was a nurse from America, turned up at his mission in 1911. They married in 1913 and learned the Chinese language through the Bible—from characters translated into English." Ruth knew all about her homeland, from the towering Himalayas to the eastern flat plains to the northern Gobi Desert and the rainforest of the south. "When I was born," she told me, "the population of China was around four hundred and fifty million. They tell me that one million people have been added since I left. That gives me a lot more students to teach writing!"

With a high chin assuming a teacher's pose, she described where she was going to the mission field. "Hunan is located in the south-central part, south of Lake Dongting, which is why they named it Hunan, which means 'south of the lake.' Do you know, the most famous Hunanese native at the moment is the Communist revolutionary leader, Mao Tse-tung." She lived her youth in Hunan under looming threats from bandits and ongoing famine until her family took flight in 1926, during one of the country's periodic spasms of violence against foreigners. At age ten she began a typical American childhood in Virginia that in many ways sounded like my typical Bohemian youth, with a few variations: I loved to ski down my favorite mountains, while she rode a sled down hers—"a big, boy-style sled," she added, to be sure I knew she could handle it. We both played tennis, but I also played football, "soccer" she called it, while she learned to throw a baseball similar to that Babe Ruth fellow. It turned out we were both great sports enthusiasts, which led us to wonder if we might have met at the 1940 Olympic games, which were supposed to be held in Japan before war changed the world's plans. At the language school she'd already signed up for the tennis and volleyball teams.

I learned I was not so far off in associating her with Amelia Earhart. Ruth not only admired the great aviator; she had been taking flying lessons at the time Amelia disappeared over the Pacific in 1937. Far from shrinking, after that Ruth became more confident of her own course. She graduated from Virginia's Bridgewater College and taught school for two years and bravely returned to China at age twenty-four, despite the civil war and Japanese occupation. She chose to continue the work her parents had begun before she was born. Because she was a missionary's daughter, she didn't need an official sponsor church, but the Reformed Church of the United States, known as the "German Reformed Church," her mother's church, acted as a caretaker for her with the China mission. She was a person of deep and lasting faith, which I admired even though I didn't necessarily share it.

Whenever she uttered a word in Chinese, it surprised me. "I was bilingual as a child and wondered when I got here if I would remember my Chinese," she told me. "But the first thing I heard from the ship's railing when we got to port were coolies on the shore shouting to each other. I understood all they said because their dialect was the same as I'd spoken as a child. Mine, called 'Southern Mandarin,' has a different accent—sounds of *shhhh*'s versus *sssss*'s."

We would have talked all night if the party hadn't ended with the whole group taking in a movie. Ruth and I had to be silent during the show. I found excuses to visit the language school the next day and for days after that, offering to escort the girls on city tours while stopping for tea and candied walnuts or a duck liver delicacy. I was an awkward companion, as the girls rode bikes so effortlessly, but since I had never learned to ride one, I followed alongside them in a rickshaw.

Ruth's companions, Kitty Funk, a nurse from Pennsylvania, and Betty Jane Howell, a teacher from Ohio, all single and in their twenties, seemed to find me as amusing as Ruth did. The reason, they later confessed, was my given name, Oswald. They kept asking me to repeat it, and they giggled each time I did because it reminded them of a cartoon character called Oswald the Lucky Rabbit, who was popular in America. After they had got one final chuckle out of this humiliation, the girls agreed I needed a more suitable nickname. Everyone in Peking called me "Doc," but that wasn't distinctive enough. Riding through the Peking streets, we saw many Russian grandmothers, known as "babushkas" for the shawls they wore over their heads. With the crisp fall air taking hold, Ruth took to covering her head with a scarf, so I called her "Babushka," referring to the old women. From that, Kitty and Betty Jane dubbed me "Bubbie," which stuck. They had no idea the Yiddish word for "grandmother" often turns into the nickname Bubbe. By then I was comfortable enough to call Ruth by her preferred nickname, Chick, a cute moniker she had chosen twenty years earlier around a campfire when the children selected their favorite animal names. (So I don't confuse you, for the rest of my tale I'll call her Ruth.)

I worked up the nerve to ask Ruth on a real date on September 20, as we were touring Peking. I scribbled a note on a cigarette wrapper and reached from the rickshaw as she reached from her bicycle. A stranger on his own bike passed between us, and my hand knocked his hat sideways so that she had to snatch the note. It read, "YMCA dining room at 7 p.m." Ruth smiled and slipped it into her pocket. I hoped that meant yes, but I began to doubt it when I found myself sitting alone at the dinner table a half-hour after our appointed time. When I saw the waiter approach, I was expecting him to refill my water glass, but instead he told me I had a telephone call. It was Ruth. It hadn't occurred to me that there were two YMCAS: the Chinese Y, where she'd gone, and the American Y, where I'd gone. I swiftly arranged for a rickshaw.

My luck held as Ruth found the mix-up amusing. We chatted until the dining room emptied, and then we strolled back to the language school and talked some more, until it was time for the doors to close. She did more speaking than I did that night,

Love Breathes Life into the Heart

partly because her rusty Chinese was still much better than my half-Chinese mixed with Pidgin English, but mostly because I wanted to know everything about her. She described camel rides in the Gobi as a child with the same adventurous vein as the stories about her flights over Virginia. When she described her father in China shooting muskrats, her eyes widened, identical to those of an expensive china doll. She told me many stories about her childhood in China, two of which I recall with great clarity.

"The fields around my family's outpost in Yochow were carefully kept by the farmers and their families," she described.

One principal crop was rice—a strong, bright-green plant that needed constant watering and care. I remember walking through a rice field on a beautiful sunset evening, under the attentive eyes of my "amah," as the Chinese call nursemaids, when we stopped to watch an unfolding drama. A young woman interrupted her field work and squatted. Then she reached down and picked up a newborn baby. The mother held it briefly, then placed it in the water and gently pushed it away from her. The baby's cry dissolved as its little form disappeared in the water. Amah shook her head and said to me in a quiet voice, "Ai ya!" She cannot take care of another girl. I learned much from my amah about the Chinese way, some of it that made me sad, but I try to understand.

Of her devoted father, Horace, Ruth spoke warmly:

One evening, when the sunset on the Dongting Lake was exceptionally beautiful, my dad took me and my sister, Rachel, for a ride in his outboard motorboat. We headed to a rocky promontory, passing a tiny island called "Bienshan." The island was covered with small temples and pagodas and was considered sacred, so no foreigners could set foot on it. As we neared the promontory, we saw dozens of white dolphins cavorting among the rocks. Several dolphins nudged the little boat, which capsized! It wasn't scary, as we knew how to swim and the dolphins were friendly. The water was shallow, so it was easy to walk along the shore, but we had to be careful not to trespass on the sacred island while hurrying home before dark. Father led us silently along for more than an hour as the fiery sun disappeared over the horizon against a purple sky. We knew we were home and safe when he began to whistle his favorite tune.

Unlike me, an only child, Ruth was the oldest of four children. She had grown up with a strong sense of duty to protect her siblings and set a good example. To my inquiry about what her best trait was, she didn't hesitate. "My feeling of self-worth," she answered. "As a child, I was taught to respect and revere all the qualities that make a person a strong personality with character. If we could instigate a tiny bit of that in our schools and homes around the world, we would go a long way to settling the problems that seem unsolvable now."

She introduced me to a different world—the family life of a minister. Some things I knew well, though. She described her passion for hiking in Virginia's Blue Ridge Mountains while we climbed up pagodas on one bright Peking night: "I love the countryside and drink up those mountaintops. It was great fun meeting the dozens of people who hike and find such joy and delight in feasting on the scenery and the air at each turn." I imagined myself putting on hiking boots, walking with a swagger as I led her up the much taller Krkonoše or across the four thousand–mile–long Great Wall of China.

We discovered we had something else in common as she described why her suitcase was filled with favorite books. "How much happier the readers of this world always are," she told me. "Never a day without an adventure of choice, a thought for digesting, or a beautiful escape from the mundane." I thought of my father madly mailing me his books, trying to save what was so precious to civilized people.

In our conversations we discovered a shared China link. The Brethren's elder, Frank Crumpacker, who'd picked me up at the train station, had ties to Virginia's Bridgewater College, where

Love Breathes Life into the Heart

Ruth had received her teaching certificate. Years before she graduated, Crumpacker was a student there. She described him as "a pioneer missionary to China, much like my father."

I loved listening to Ruth and that she was willing to listen to me. I told her as best I could in our shared languages about my journey and my worries for my parents and country. I told her I was Jewish by birth, although not by practice. I tried to describe my Czech pride and what assimilation was all about in my country, although I wasn't sure at that moment what it had meant for me. "Perhaps many of my friends, family, and I never fully assimilated," I said, "which was why we have been so easily cast aside."

She listened without interruption, holding my hand the whole time. I felt her reassurance and unconditional acceptance. From that night on we spent every moment we could together. We climbed the city's ancient walls and hiked far beyond them to picnic on the hillsides. There was no better romantic place for lovers than that old metropolis. The Peking autumn of beautiful willows, white pines, and rusty red and pale yellow chrysanthemums the size of dinner plates offered our budding romance an exhilarating backdrop. According to Chinese superstition, Ruth described why chrysanthemums were her favorite: "Their clean scent prolongs life. It is the flower of immortality and knows how to die with dignity and grace."

On one gray, cold rainy afternoon, as we strolled along, despite the evil being perpetrated around the world on the innocent, I felt as though I was walking into a room where all the lights blazed from a desert sun and a fireplace welcomed me with a cozy rocker. Her presence healed and transformed my crippled life, and the need to linger by her side overtook me. As the well-read Ruth guessed at my mood, she often shared a favorite quote that matched the moment.

"What lies behind us and what lies before us are tiny matters compared to what lies within us," she said now. "That's from Ralph Waldo Emerson, you know?" I imagined my mother's face and encouraging voice: "Love knows no obstacles."

Five months earlier, I told Ruth, during my first sojourn in Peking, I'd achieved some level of social success in the expatriate community that centered on the Peking Club, with its clubhouse and tennis courts exclusively for foreigners: "The Peking expatriate community is congenial partly because they've shut out the degenerate Nazism and racism, totalitarianism, and the suppression of the free mind. Through my hard work to learn Chinese and accompanying hard play, I've become an official world citizen in this fascinating circle—a mixture of scientific, medical, religious, and International Legation friends. Do you want to meet them?" A vigorous nod of her head indicated yes.

I introduced Ruth to my friends the Kandels and the Komors. Dr. Kandel was an Austrian dentist who'd practiced in Peking for about five years when I arrived. The cosmopolitan Hungarian Mathias Komor, with a doctorate from the University of Grenoble in France, had become a leading authority on Chinese antiquities. He was a purchasing agent for several museums in the United States. His wife, Lila, had befriended me first. Ruth became curious about the people I'd met involved with the Peking Man, including Franz Weidenreich, a German anatomist, paleoanthropologist, and renowned scholar. In 1935 he became honorary director of the Cenozoic Research Laboratory of the Geological Survey of China. From his work on the fossils of Peking Man and his observation of anatomical characteristics in common with modern Asians, he originated the "Weidenreich theory of human evolution." This led to his polycentric evolution model of racial origins. Franz directed the well-to-do American sculptress Lucile Swan's bust reconstruction of the female fossil "Nelly." Lucile was a close friend of the handsome, aristocratic priest Pierre Teilhard de Chardin.

For tea on Sunday I took her to Dr. Grabau's house to witness the continuing intellectual debate. Fascinated by the deliberations, she paid attention intently to Pierre Teilhard de Chardin as he expressed his religious views, his evolution of faith, and his thoughts about evolution in general. Ruth stood spellbound as the lean and charming French priest-in-exile spoke of what he

Love Breathes Life into the Heart

believed and didn't believe, which he described as "springing from my involvement with unbelievers."

Startled, I heard Ruth speak out to the patrician priest. "It is through seeking the truth that one finds the beauty of life," she told him. I swallowed hard as I tried to decode his facial expression. In what felt like forever but was only a moment in time, Teilhard's close-set eyes studied her face—a face unknown to him until that afternoon. Looking uncomfortable, he adjusted his collar. I thought it felt tighter when he heard someone speak the truth. Then from his sober facade sprung an approving smile: "But yours and my truth is not everyone's truth. And yes, the search is a gift of life."

"Yes, I suspect you are correct in that we perhaps have a tendency to seek out evidence that supports our existing beliefs," she coyly replied. As I observed her in action, I recognized that self-identity plus healthy self-esteem had a powerful impact on Ruth's behavior.

It was clear to me at these salon gatherings that Ruth preferred this philosophical conversation to the others about fossils and sculpture, but with each person she met, she radiated outward with sincere interest. There was a genuineness about her—an acceptance of another person's fundamental worth. Her desire to help people reach their full potential through their strengths and virtues, nurtured by the guidance of her "higher being," became a recurring theme in our private conversations.

With the corners of her mouth lowered, after I'd described what I'd endured, she disclosed her view of the positive aspects of my situation: "It has been shown that people's character can be strengthened through adverse experiences." With my upper lip raised, I didn't share what I'd learned from the writings of German philosopher Friedrich Nietzsche, who believed that Christianity's emphasis on the afterlife made humans less capable of handling life in the present. I did, however, disclose his relevant quote pertaining to my circumstance, "What doesn't kill us makes us stronger." It was received with cold silence.

What I admired most was that with her ready tongue she stood her ground on her convictions and did this with a charming blend of tough and tender-mindedness. If she didn't concur with what I'd said, she'd listen carefully. "At Pingting, in their hierarchy of priorities, I don't believe the missionaries cared about cleanliness," I told her. Then she'd make her case—"Missionaries' hearts are full but our purses always empty"—and we'd finish the disagreement peaceably, usually with her having the last word. "Washing our hands can make us harsher moral judges of others."

She made me realize that I may have been looking at the world through inflexible rules by which individual parts interact. Better at empathy, Ruth understood the emotions of human motivation. We debated what best described *mind* versus *brain* and *heart* versus *soul* and agreed on one important motivation for the behavior: self-preservation. It ran deep in her family, as it did mine. "My father taught me," she said, "against all odds, after repeated failures, you must dust yourself off and try again. After seventeen years in China, he was still politely referred to by the Chinese as 'guest man.' His longtime Chinese servant told him as he packed our family to leave that he was destined to return to his own country."

One of Ruth's greatest qualities was her infectious brand of enthusiasm. Wherever we went, we searched for a piano or an organ, as Ruth played both beautifully and eagerly. I loved listening so much that I didn't even mind that she never played Dvořák. She played her favorite hymns and sang along, and I clapped my hands even though I didn't understand more than a phrase or two of the lyrics. I kept on clapping as she played "God Bless America" and a new tune, "Over the Rainbow," from a famous American movie that hadn't reached me in Pingting.

I recall during our first intense days together, when Ruth and I held hands, the autumnal afternoon sun shining over ancient clay rooftops. I went to work at the hospital at seven in the morning and spent the late afternoons and early evenings with her. The perfect photographic light accompanied us everywhere she and I walked and talked. It was a month before the height of fall leaves, but whenever she saw a leaf with hints of gold and scarlet

萬壽山

15. Valdik Holzer and Ruth Alice Lequear,
falling in love in Peking (Beijing), October 1940.

she most admired, she stuffed it in her pocket. During the evenings a chill crept into the air, which gave me a chance to put my arm around her shoulder with the pretense of offering warmth. As she didn't pull away and leaned into my body, I knew things were going well.

Since my return to Peking at the end of summer, I'd felt little chance of escaping the shadow that followed me. Now, three weeks later, the jewel-toned season brought this gilded young woman who made me believe joy may be retrievable. On a bridge bookended with dragon statues, the sun shining on a smooth lake, Ruth blurted out her enthusiasm: "Close your eyes tight and think of your favorite autumn. Tell me how it smells and looks."

I didn't want to sound trite, but *this* was my favorite autumn. I told her so. In my best Australian-British English, I babbled on about my feelings: "I feel as though the year's mistakes have been washed away. I have a fresh start, and anything wonderful and unexpected for the world is possible." Her eyes sparkled as I described an autumn from my past. "In our Bohemian village I smell the earth scents that one encounters when the countryside is filled with changing colors. At home, in good times, the big square is alive with a feast—a festival with a street band performance where my father sings beside an outdoor stage upon which fairy tales are enacted with colorful puppets. All around us are delicacies such as duck liver in fat and blue cheese on toast and the smell of yellow and bubbly beer. In the second half of September, if we are lucky, summerlike days with crystal-clear blue skies create picture-perfect moments that we call 'Babí léto.'"

She giggled. "I think you mean what Americans call 'Indian summer,' when the warm days melt into cool days?"

I knew the cold weather in the next weeks would bring clouds, snow, and then an icy dust-wind to Peking that would lay us all underground again. But for that second before the smoke trees turned dark-red and purple after the first frost, for the first time in months, I felt hope. I sensed my heart, which had hardened within me, grow soft again.

When we ate, she kidded me with Chinese traditions—for example, I had to start eating before her because I was the oldest (by four and a half years). She made sure I knew the symbolism of food—in China oranges mean a lucky life, and noodles represent a long life. As we ate our stir-fry, I impressed her with my dexterity using chopsticks, my first encounter having been a year and a half earlier in Saigon.

Ruth continued to tell me many stories from her childhood in the Hunan mission fields: "When I was six years old, I watched my mother trying to help the dreadful famine-induced poverty by giving out special gifts at Christmas. Our cook, Da shi fu, reluctantly went out on the street with my mother one day, with baskets of hundreds of tiny pennies and small coins, individually wrapped in red paper to bring good luck. As they entered the street, they were mobbed by peasants frantic to get a few coins. They tumbled my mother and Da shi fu into the seething streets

Love Breathes Life into the Heart

along with their baskets. Watching out the window from the compound wall, I will never forget the tear-stained look on my mother's face when she realized the helplessness of their plight. I was young, but I understood how desperate the poor Chinese people were, and I wanted to help them. It was a valuable lesson for my mother, one that neither she nor I will forget."

I didn't have to ask why Ruth had come back to this turbulent country—I saw it in her love for China and its people. "We are all responsible for one another," she'd say. As we sat together on an ancient bridge that appeared to be lifted out of a seventh-century Chinese painting, her eyes filled with tears. She spoke of devoting her thoughts to heaven and her actions to works of kindness. I found it inspiring that her religious faith could lead her to such complete dedication despite the wartime challenges we understood so well. "It's more than religious faith," she confided. "You must have confidence in yourself, in your character and abilities. People who have faith in themselves go a long way toward cushioning the bumps that inevitably jolt them. If you have firm faith in yourself, other people feel it too, and they believe in you. I have watched it work over and over."

Since childhood I'd been naturally confident when I took on a challenge. Some professors described it as arrogance, although I always thought of it as self-assuredness, but the "jolts" I'd recently experienced were the greatest of my life, and there was no doubt my confidence was lagging. I wasn't sure what lay ahead, but Ruth's faith intrigued me.

I thought of my frustrations in Pingting, where I struggled with limited resources and stubborn superstitions. I understood the importance of carrying on that struggle. For me the goal was healing; for Ruth it was teaching. We continued our conversation the next day as we walked along a dusty Peking street, sharing our feelings about tending the sick and feeding the hungry, and I began to think: "Why not in China . . . with her?" I told Ruth that I dreamed of running a small charity clinic, and she responded with tears, "My heart swells with all there is to do."

I could think of only one thing and blurted it out: "I would like to be married with you."

It was an awkward proposal, but it was the best I could do with my limited language skills. I was about to try again when a beggar walked up and pushed his way between us. Neither of us had any money to give him, so I attempted to shoo him away while repeating myself.

"I would like to be married with you."

"Are you proposing to me?"

"Yes. Yes."

To my great surprise, with the beggar still between us, Ruth at the top of her voice answered, "Yes, I would like to be married to you." We had known each other for eight days.

A busy street spectacle followed. Pulling her into a dramatic embrace, I dipped her backward, kissed the top of her head, and planted another kiss on her lips. Tears of joy ran down her red cheeks, while the wide-eyed beggar scurried away as if we'd lit a firecracker in our midst. His reaction sent us into uproarious laughter, while others around joined in with applause followed by more laughter. With the world in turmoil, we all needed a good hearty laugh.

Czech words were a new thing to Ruth, but as we strolled away, she enjoyed what I told her in my mixture of broken English, Chinese, and Czech. Although most Bohemian Jews refused Yiddish as a jargon, I shared one expression that had crept in: "There's a Yiddish expression my grandmother used when something was destined or fated—*Bashert*. She'd say if she were here, you are my match made in heaven. It doesn't mean our marriage will be trouble free. Like everything else in life, we'll need to work at it, but I'm confident we can have a long life together."

"Ming," she replied in Chinese. The dynasty that presided over China's age of enlightenment called itself *Ming*. "Our destiny, or allotted time, is sealed with *Ai*. Love breathes life into the heart until the door closes on life." I'd learned that the Chinese character *Ai* speaks to the love that one person feels for another. More enlightened, Ruth informed me it also can be considered as a form of giving, extended to more distant members of society.

Neither of us saw any point in waiting longer than necessary to wed. After all, we were living in a world at war. No one knew what tomorrow would bring. So we decided to be married in one month and started making arrangements. I'd blurted out my proposal without even having an engagement ring in hand, so that was the first order of business. We went to a street market to see what might be available with my limited funds. A restaurant there had an oyster tank that became a tourist attraction because the oysters were seeded with cheap beads to produce pearls. For a small fee a visitor could buy an oyster and keep the pearl. Ruth picked a lucky oyster that held not one but two pearls. We took the larger pearl to a jewelry shop and had it set in gold as an engagement ring. I had the smaller bead made into a tiepin.

The following day Ruth wrote to her parents. I have no doubt they were more than shocked when they began to read her words displayed with a typewriter ribbon that allowed for periodic emphasis in red. The teacher-and-daughter-turning-missionary they'd just bid goodbye to weeks earlier in America let them know our life-changing news in what I came to know as her consistently confident, upbeat manner:

Dearest family . . . .

By the time that you receive this letter it will be old news . . . for things are happening so fast around here that I have hardly had time to breathe . . . This time next month I will be Mrs. Holzer . . . the wife of a former Czechoslovakian army surgeon . . . and then of course to think that when I see you again, I may present you with a family . . . Now don't faint or be afraid that I am doing things too fast . . . you know what I told you, Mom, what when I finally got married, it would be fast. Well, it is true.

She had a beautiful way with words and made me sound like

a prize, going into detail about my Czech background, my medical skills—and my good looks!

> And now I will tell you of your new son . . . He is dark . . . black
> hair and gray eyes . . . has a winning personality . . . five feet
> eleven tall . . . weighs about 186 pounds . . . or maybe less . . .
> He isn't sure . . . anyway it is distributed well . . . ha . . . ha . . .
> he is 29 years old . . . and more fun than a barrel of monkeys . . .
> which, of course, you knew would have to be true . . . and the
> rest of it is that I cannot believe that it is true . . . I feel as
> though I must be walking in a dream all the time . . . I simply
> cannot understand how it all happened unless some higher
> power was saving us for each other . . . we fit like old shoes . . .
> and when he is with me I don't give a hang what the rest of the
> world might be doing.

She went on to tell them that I read and wrote German, Czech, Russian, French, and Chinese, but that my English was yet weak. Her description of my parents—"They are both Bohemian, living in what is now part of Germany against their will" and that "Mr. Holzer owns a chocolate factory, which right now is not in operation and what will happen no one knows"—was part right. I knew she loved chocolate, and I think my description of my father's businesses must have drifted from accuracy in my poor English.

Two things she got entirely right included my hope to reunite with my parents so I could introduce them to Ruth and what our lives would be like: "Someday we will return there and make a stay but we cannot know when that will be or for how long or anything. One thing I do know is that for the rest of my life I will not know much ahead of time where I will be or what I will be doing."

When news of our impending wedding was announced at the language school, a few of Ruth's missionary friends were floored by the information that she was about to marry a Czech Jewish refugee, and they were shocked that she would act so impulsively. To spare my feelings, she refused to tell me much of what was repeated to her. She assured me she'd never be part of group polarization. With a big grin she mocked their questions: "Did you ever dream you'd commit to someone outside your faith?" "Does this mean you'll abandon your teaching in the mission fields?" Neither was surprising to me, and she reported her answers were a calm "no" and "I'm not sure."

There was a serious objection from a missionary who'd met me in Pingting. He told Ruth that I was a strange fellow who made hospital rounds accompanied by two dogs. More important, he warned her the marriage would never last because I was an alcoholic.

The mere mention of my dogs made me forlorn, and I recognized the rumor's root the instant she told me the story: I'd returned to Pingting from one of my supply trips with a half-dozen bottles of champagne. The champagne was produced by a group of Trappist monks in the mountains outside Peking. The monks were French, Spanish, Polish, Hungarian, and Italian. They had an exemplary farm. The Japanese didn't bother them. They grew French grapes and made delicious wines, which they sold along with a drink called "7 Grain Liqueur" that was like Benedictine. The monks had a laboratory where they were making typhus vaccine, a tedious process in which lice infected with typhus were killed and dissected. Observing this process was the primary reason for my visit. I found their work in the lab intriguing, and the monks gave me champagne to take back to the interior.

I had not yet realized the Brethren were fanatics about alcohol abstinence. So I chilled a bottle, brought it to the mission's dining room, and poured it into small glasses for the other diners. Everyone looked at me as if I were crazy but stayed silent. They weren't going to join me, so I emptied each glass. I took the remaining half-bottle to my quarters and finished it that night. The busybody missionary who later turned up in Peking was in the dining room that evening. He decided that only an alcoholic would do such a thing. He undoubtedly felt he was doing an excellent service to my future bride by warning her. Ruth was not dissuaded.

While we were planning our wedding, the U.S. presidential campaign was under way, with debates about isolation or intervention between President Roosevelt and Wendell Willkie. Within our Peking international community it was a big part of the conversation, along with other unfolding events. In early August, prior to my return to Peking and Ruth's arrival, the British government had withdrawn its China military troops not just in Shanghai but also in Peking and Tientsin. They were needed back home and for their Mediterranean fleets. Japan had won permission from the French Vichy government to access airfields in northern Indochina and joined the Rome-Berlin-Tokyo Axis with a ten-year military pact. Concerned, the United States enacted an export embargo on scrap steel and iron to Japan.

Our wedding invitations were printed double-sided, in English and Czech, by the Poplar Island Press of Vincenz Hundhausen, the island-inhabiting friend of Dr. Grabau. We sent a large batch of invitations to each set of parents to distribute, and letters soon flooded in from surprised but happy relatives and friends. To reach the greatest number of our eclectic Peking friends, foreigners and Chinese alike, we gave Dr. Grabau's secretary, Trude Schack, a supply of invitations, which she offered to disseminate widely. "The invitation is at a premium," she liked to say. Trude, who taught English at the Catholic University, was a German refugee from Stuttgart. The Chinese students who took her course spoke English with a German accent. Trude took the liberty of announcing the details of our upcoming marriage in the *Peking Chronicle* within the Social and Personal column. Ruth wanted to get married on the steps of the Temple of Heaven, long regarded as the most sacred place in China, but the unpredictable Peking weather made that impractical. So, on October 19, 1940, we were married first at the American embassy, where we were presented with a legitimate American marriage certificate signed by Vice-Consul Alvin E. Bandy.

This procedure satisfied all legal requirements, but it didn't satisfy Ruth, who wanted to be married in a church. She chose the interdenominational Peking Union Church at Nan Ho Yen and requested the altar be surrounded by enormous yellow chrysan-

Love Breathes Life into the Heart

themums like the ones she'd enjoyed on our walks. I made sure her dream was fulfilled. In Chinese tradition a gift of a single chrysanthemum means you view the person as honest. The large golden yellow blooms, held perfectly upright on strong stems, seemed a perfect representation of my Ruth.

As the distant strains of traffic could be heard on the streets outside, the 11:00 a.m. Saturday service was performed by a friend, the Rev. Edwin "Eddie" T. Plitt, an ordained minister of the Reformed Church of the United States, who was part of the young group going to the mission fields. One of my surgeon colleagues, Dr. Chen, was the organist. The wedding of Miss Ruth Alice Lequear of Bridgewater, Virginia, and Oswald A. Holzer, MD, of Prague, Bohemia, was the topic of conversation and gossip throughout the international community, so an egalitarian crowd of Americans and Europeans filled the church, along with Chinese friends. The Western men and women wore formal garments, and the Chinese women were in stunning short sleeved, high-necked robes. Ruth was the most beautiful woman in the room, with her cream-colored dress, shining red hair, and sparkling blue eyes. I will never be sure why she answered yes, but it was that day that I knew she meant it and that our love and admiration for each other would last a lifetime.

At the ceremony's conclusion, after Reverend Plitt slipped two silver crosses into Ruth's hand, she and I signed our official church certificate of marriage, while her missionary girlfriends, Betty Jane and Kitty, served as witnesses: "Elizabeth Jane Howell and Catherine L. Funk." The words on the certificate spoke to the future.

> Hand in hand, by grace of God
> You will start this happy day.
> Down the path where Love hath trod
> Making sweet the way.
> Hand in hand, through golden years,
> Each with Love-light all agleam
> Reflecting ever in your hearts
> Life's glory and its dream.

As we left the church through a shower of rice, Ruth noticed a large black Cadillac whose driver seemed to be signaling to her as he opened the door. Thinking it must be a wedding surprise that I'd planned, she hopped into the car and slid into the back seat. I had made plans for us to leave in a cheap Chinese taxi. Just then the American ambassador's wife, Mrs. Nelson Johnson, arrived. Although I'd seen her at Dr. Grabau's house, I had met her formally only in a brief encounter at the Peking Club, when I brought Max Engel as my guest. As she leaned down to enter the limo, her head tilted and her eyebrows raised. Mrs. Johnson was puzzled to see Ruth. I reached between them with a crooked smile, nodded politely at Mrs. Johnson, and escorted my bride to our more modest vehicle.

Our honeymoon destination was in Patachu, outside the city in the Western Hills, in a resort long popular with the legations and other foreigners. I'd reserved the finest room in a hotel managed by a White Russian actor who was active in Chinese theater. I'd stayed there before, when I wanted to take peaceful hikes on the winding tree-laden trails. Eight Buddhist temples, built one above another, stood along the winding gorge. The highest, the Pearl Grotto, rose twelve hundred feet above the sea. The picturesque scenery featured peaks and ravines with ancient shrines and monasteries on every side of the range of blue hills. I could tell by the jaw-dropping expression on my new wife's face that she was impressed with my choice of where we'd spend our first days together as man and wife. "They look like the foothills of the Blue Ridge Mountains of the Shenandoah Valley, except with temples," Ruth observed, bouncing on her toes to admire our view.

We arrived to find the hotel empty except for a few staff. When I asked the manager where the other guests were, he sidestepped my question with a dramatic show of appreciation for our visit. The area had periodically been involved in fierce skirmishes between Chinese guerrilla forces and Japanese troops. But as contested locales regularly changed hands between warring parties and he made no further comment, I opined, "How nice it is to have the

Love Breathes Life into the Heart

place to ourselves." With a shrug he insisted on giving us a tour of his impressive living quarters. The highlight was a flamboyant bedroom with black-painted walls. In the center was a bed carved as a black swan, with a black silk bedspread that matched the drapes. His bathroom included a large recessed tile tub, all in black tile with Chinese red trim.

We persuaded the manager to show us to our room, which had doors opening onto a terrace overlooking the hillsides—a fairy-tale world filled with sweet-smelling green pines and dancing red and yellow leaves. As we marveled at the sight, the manager told us the sightseeing of the red leaves was a custom dating back six centuries, to the Yuan Dynasty. A terrace table complete with white tablecloth and silver was already set with a sumptuous lunch of steaming bowls filled with local specialties served with a mound of fragrant rice. We ate well but in haste, then went back inside and got undressed. We'd no sooner gotten into bed than the earth moved, but this had nothing to do with marital bliss. Our meeting of heaven and earth was interrupted as the whole building trembled and swayed—an earthquake had intruded on our honeymoon.

As we held onto the bedpost waiting for the shaking to subside, I shielded her now naked body with my arms and tried to tuck her beneath me. Simultaneously, I reached for a pillow to cover our heads. She found my protective maneuver humorous— her shoulders heaved with laughter while I heaved a sigh of relief. I'd seen people curl into the fetal position when an earthquake rolled through, but this was the first time I'd seen someone laugh during the turmoil. I knew I'd made the right choice. Ruth was refreshing. When her laughter subsided, she calmly lay back on the bed and opened her arms and then her thighs in what I can only describe as uninhibited joy as the earth moved again.

When we were satisfied that the tremors and aftershocks had passed, we went for a walk in the hills. The sun was a bit lower in the sky, and with evening approaching, I anticipated a breathtaking sunset. My camera stayed busy as Ruth willingly posed from one rocky promontory with a temple to the next as she sniffed the pine-perfumed air. When we reached the top, a strange buzzing sound startled us: machine gun bullets whizzed over our heads from the other side. With racing pulse I pulled Ruth to the ground, and we crawled along the craggy summit while artillery from both sides fired over us. This time she didn't laugh. Her body trembled, and she admitted she was frightened for our lives.

I learned the Communists had staged an offensive and were stopped by the Japanese at the Western Hills. We had landed smack in the middle of the fight. News of the first new skirmishes was reported in Peking before our wedding, which explained why the hotel was empty when we arrived. Others had paid attention to the news, while we were aware of nothing but each other.

We managed to get to the hotel safely, packed our things, and hurried back to Peking.

17

Leaving China

October 1940–February 1941

I have heard people say they were so much in love that the world stopped. As Ruth and I were reminded of our close encounter with artillery on our honeymoon, none of the dire events threatening our world slowed down while we snuggled and smooched through the early weeks of marriage.

When we returned to Peking, we settled into Ruth Yang's boardinghouse, where I'd been staying since moving out of Wenham Hall. In typical Peking style our room overlooked a lush courtyard behind a big red gate filled with evergreens and a goldfish pond. As drinking water was a health concern, with the consent of our friends we brought gallon bottles of water from the embassy compound. Ruth returned to the language school, and I continued my work at the hospital.

Our plan was to move in a few months to the mission school in Huping, in southwestern China, where my wife was born and where our friend Ken Kohler was stationed. It was located eight hundred miles up the Yangtze River from the Pacific Ocean. After our wedding Ken wrote us a note from the mission field that became Ruth's favorite: "Dear Speed Demons . . . your romance has already become an epic in the story of missions in China. With all my heart, I wish you a rich and satisfying married life. And regardless of conservative shakings of heads and wagging of mouths, I believe all who know either of you are of the same mind."

As our marriage had caught many by surprise, we continued

to receive wedding gifts, one from a dentist acquaintance, W. B. Prentice. He gave us three books by Teilhard de Chardin. With jewel-toned earth covers designated "for private circulation," Teilhard had written them while in Peking: *How I Believe* (1936), *The Spirit of the Earth* (1936), and *A Personalistic Universe* (1937). In addition to espousing his beliefs, the writer-mystic expressed his eccentric philosophy of mankind's evolutionary progress using his scientific and spiritual passions. Ruth considered the small booklets one of her most treasured presents from our union.

Although with threats growing, the international social circle was shrinking in Peking, we picked up with our rhythm of having tea at five o'clock with a walk afterward. We joined friends at outdoor cookouts in the Legation. In the cold air women sported thick fur coats and the men wore thick wool hats as we talked over philosophical ideas and China's latest hostilities with the Japanese. There was much discussion among the diplomatic core when the Western Hills was proclaimed off-limits.

As we settled in, I stayed tuned to world events through all available channels—radio, newspapers, and letters and even eavesdropped on conversations at various legations.

The plans we were making were liable to change in an instant. The bulletins from Europe depressed me, as Hitler's Luftwaffe had begun the terror bombing of London that became known as the "Blitz." With a few friends of mine in London, I couldn't turn away from the news, no matter how difficult it was to hear. My parents continued to insist they were well and safe—in fact, they had persuaded me to quit all efforts to secure landing permits—but as I read and reread their letters, I was troubled by the details that were either being withheld or censored. I couldn't even tell if my father was still working, as he made no mention of it. From correspondence I learned that two of his friends had been tortured to death in concentration camps.

In the meantime Germany's arrogant dictator concluded yet another agreement with his partners in Italy and Japan, the so-called Tripartite Pact, in which they decided on how to carve up the world after their glorious victory. Exactly what role Japan would play beyond China was unclear, but already there were rumblings in the international press about secret plans for Japan to join Hitler in attacking the British or perhaps to strike at the Americans before they had a chance to arm themselves adequately. Ruth became distressed at the uncertain nature of what lay ahead. Her insecurity, to make matters worse, was reinforced whenever she spoke with other Americans. As the tensions between the United States and Japan mounted, the word leaked that embassy and consulate wives in Peking were preparing to leave.

Then, sometime in November, something altered all the speculation. The Chinese Nationalists reportedly shot down a Japanese plane in South China. Supposedly, it carried three Japanese generals who had plans for the invasion of the Philippines, Hong Kong, and Singapore. The unconfirmed rumor was that Chiang Kai-shek's Nationalist government had passed these military documents to the Americans and to the British. A November 14, 1940, Shanghai newspaper that reached the Peking Club bore a headline "Japan Removes Troops in China." This caught my attention: "Japanese military authorities announced today their troops had been withdrawn from southwestern Kwangtun Province, as they already had done in neighboring Kwangsi Province, strengthening the belief in foreign circles here of another impending move against French Indo-China."

It was hard to discern what might be propaganda. One article from the Australian newspaper the *Vargus* with a November 5 London report described Japan's effort as "a small snake trying desperately to swallow an elephant." The troop numbers provided in the article by W. Y. Tsao, vice-consul for China, amazed me. "Japan has had casualties totaling 1,750,000 and 83 percent of Japan's able-bodied men have been conscripted. China has 5,000,000 troops in the field, and of 50,000,000 men in the limited military age group, 30,000,000 have already received preliminary military training." I'd seen some in the Chinese military age groups who appeared to be children around the age of ten.

This information about a secret Japanese attack plan might have been dismissed as rumor or even paranoia had not the U.S. State Department warned all Americans not working for the government to leave the Far East—not just Japan and Indochina but China as well. The news touched off a near panic in Shanghai and other ports, as Americans rushed to get passage back to the States, while shipping lines ferried more boats across the Pacific to handle the demand.

Kitty and Betty Jane were considered brave to continue their mission work in Chinese territory still controlled by the Nationalists. The Kohlers had already gone to a missionary outpost in the interior. Ruth was torn about what path to follow. She had come so far and showed great passion for her work. But she also remembered her family's harrowing escape in 1926 amid an anti-Christian and anti-foreigner movement growing out of the emerging nationalist and socialist ideologies along with anger being directed at Western nations. As they huddled on a burning dock waiting to depart along with hundreds of fleeing Europeans and Americans, ten-year-old Ruth and her family were encircled by angry mobs setting fiery explosions.

I was prepared to follow her anywhere. Reluctantly, she decided to return to the United States while that was still possible, so I again started the process of obtaining a visa that would allow me to join my bride. This time I didn't have to wait for a quota number, as I was married to an American citizen and could apply as a "First Preference Immigrant." The procedure should have been straightforward, but it wasn't. The first official I contacted told me he didn't "like the idea of helping refugees come to America unnecessarily," and he was no help at all. When I inquired to friends about him, I learned he had a reputation for being "unpleasant toward Jewish refugees." So I went straight up the ladder to the first secretary, the veteran China hand Arthur Ringwalt, who was running the embassy while the ambassador was out of town. Ringwalt, who loved the adornment of a bow tie, was a frequent visitor at the Legation Quarter's Commerce Club luncheons I had attended, along with teas at Dr. Grabau's.

During his young adulthood Ringwalt had spent several years in Europe studying music before returning to the United States when the Depression hit. He went to Washington DC to get into the foreign service and was accepted into the Department of State. In 1928 he was sent to Shanghai, to the so-called China Service. After getting married in Washington, he was assigned to Peking as third secretary in 1938. Ringwalt told me that when he was on his way to Peking, he and his wife had spent time in Budapest. There they met several Jews forced to wear the Star of David. The American consul was exhausted and described to the Ringwalts how difficult it was to go to work each day, turning away so many desperate Jews who were trying to get out. "These brave people refused to raise their arms and give the 'Heil Hitler,'" he told them. This was around the time that Chamberlain met with Hitler for appeasement.

Ringwalt turned out to be a friend. He suggested I get a sponsor in place with a relative I mentioned to him in America, William Ferdinand Breth. There would then be no question as to whether I could financially support myself.

Breth, a research chemist, was an L. Sonneborn Sons Oil Company vice president and a first cousin of my father. The same age as my dad, his mother had died at his birth, and my grandmother Marie had taken him in and raised him. When I was little, he was referred to as "Uncle Bill." Dad told me Uncle Bill was the first Zionist, "Jewish patriot," in the family; the second was Dad's oldest sister, Olga. As a chemist, Uncle Bill went to work in Mexico for a British petroleum company. He then went to work for L. Sonneborn Sons, an American company begun by some German Jews, dealing with specialty petroleum products.

The owner, Rudolf Sonneborn, was a well-known Zionist leader in the United States. When World War I broke out, Uncle Bill volunteered for the Jewish army in Palestine and ended up an officer in the British army under Gen. Sir Edmund Allenby. After World War I he visited Czechoslovakia, still wearing his decorated British army officer uniform. He split his time between New

York City and L. Sonneborn Sons' refinery in Petrolia, Pennsylvania, which he described in a letter as the "outback of nowhere." He wrote that he acknowledged that "from China you've experienced more outback than most."

Upon my request Uncle Bill placed two thousand dollars in my name in an account at the National City Bank of New York (slightly less than one year's average salary in America). Once Ringwalt helped me get started, the process moved with unusual speed because of the evacuation crisis. He knew the situation was grave, as Ringwalt had sent his wife, Mildred, and infant daughter back to the United States in October 1939.

Before I left Peking, Ringwalt, with his round spectacles resting on his patrician nose, offered another act of kindness. He warned Ruth and me of anti-Semitic feelings in America. He didn't want me to be surprised. He apologized, saying these sentiments were sometimes evident in the U.S. Congress, the armed forces, and even his own State Department. Ringwalt shared that a fear of Axis spies entering the United States had led to a reduced number of visas, and consuls general were instructed to prohibit entry to those they deemed politically unreliable. To make it even more difficult for some, with head bowed he told me the State Department supported Britain's policy, which had tightened refugee allotments to Palestine. (Six months after we left China, I learned that in June 1941 the U.S. State Department forbade granting a visa to anyone like me who had relatives in the Axis-occupied territory. As always, with contacts in high places, exceptions occurred.)

Before my visa was granted, I received a letter from a first cousin of my mother, Valerie Vodicka. She'd made it to America to be with her sister, Erna Mautner, in Chicago just before the war started. I'd written her and Erna months earlier, inquiring about possible opportunities there. The request preceded my quick courtship, so she had no idea my plans had changed. The letter from Camden, Maine, reinforced what seemed a not-so-latent anti-Semitic attitude in America:

Erna forwarded me your letter. I can imagine how you feel, and I would be happy if you could get here as soon as possible. Not that the conditions here are much better. There is a huge unemployment problem and strong anti-Semitic feelings. In the newspapers, you can read daily ads as: "Will hire Aryan" etc., signs on some houses read: "Will rent a flat, to Aryans only." I am not afraid of anything, and curiously waiting how it all ends. I don't see a bright future though.

Just as you, I considered myself a Czech first, Judaism was an inherited faith, which I was not interested in too much, but I would never deny.

After Sudeten, when almost everything would be blamed on Jews, I was deeply insulted. I finally understood the words of Theodor Herzl, who said that his Judaism awakened when he observed the French mob mentality, as they laughed, when Dreyfus's rank marks and buttons were ripped off, but they didn't laugh that a human has been degraded but because he was a Jew.

When I was pointing out in an argument how willingly Jewish people contributed to the state's security, my longtime friends told me: "It's only to save themselves, not because of the patriotism." I will tell you one thing: I came to a conclusion that the majority of people are narrow-minded, extra selfish, and ruthless. In the good days, they act as wolves with full stomachs towards the minority—they let them be. But alas if they are living in crisis, there are only a handful of respectable, intelligent, and unprejudiced people who make any serious change alone.

If someone asks about my nationality, I usually answer: I am a Jew, born in Bohemia. I would get christened only if someone threatened me that they will cut my head off if I don't obey. I don't mind being a Jew, but even at my age I would have to blush if they called me a christened Jew.

The Czech people in America have founded "National Coalition." I am not a member yet—I am still undecided. I went to a few meetings, but I don't feel that I belong there. I feel like I am between people who speak a different language. I know a few Jewish members, who contribute with huge amounts of money and are involved in everything, but I still have the impression that they are there only tolerated.

Please write again soon. I assure you that it doesn't bother us at all, if you need us to take care of some of your matters. If only we could do something that would bring the awaited outcome. Please take care and keep the faith.

Your Vala

Before year-end 1940 a holiday greeting letter arrived from my parents. It began as most did, with updates on relatives in my father's typed note, followed by my mother's handwritten lines. I was pleased to hear that Dad was reading Ruth's English letters to mom in Czech so all could become acquainted. When I wrote to tell my parents about my luck in finding Ruth, I mentioned that I gave her a pearl engagement ring but didn't add that the pearl cost a few cents. As happy as they were for my good fortune, my dad shared my mother's surprise and even a concern about what she assumed was my extravagance buying "Japanese" pearls for an engagement ring:

Dear Children,

You see what an advantage you have when you can view some nice films and see much new this way. That, we have not experienced for more than five quarters of a year. So you have again seen at least one acquaintance with whom you were leaving from here. Let's hope that your efforts managed to chase out those Dr. Weinstein's gallstones without surgery. Aren't you lucky, to win a whole five USA dollars! That isn't so staggering an amount, but for some good dinner it should have been sufficient; we can imagine how you made a night of it. Mom keeps racking her brain about how much such Japanese pearls would cost here, and so she surely will place a question with several jewelers in order to estimate how much you untied your purse strings for that wedding present. We wish our dear Ruth that she continues to have such luck with hunting for those pearls, and not only with this choice but also with all other life choices in front of my new daughter. So next time I will thank you in some good English. Of course I understand her letters well, and I impart their content to Mom.

. . . We are happy that our little shipment of sheet music was accepted by both of you with such gratitude, and I would have repeated it immediately had I already had the response to the letter mailed together with that parcel. I hope that you will write to me what would dear Ruth like from what I suggested, so that I could send some sheet music as her belated Christmas present. We thank her for her kind letter. We hope that you translate our letters to her, since they are naturally intended for both of you. I don't want to write in English today, till I learn how that first attempt at expressing emotions in English ended up sounding like, if it weren't a farce, since as I had already mentioned to you in my first such letter, "I will not lost the face." Nonetheless, we see that even you aren't certain about your stay and that you in the end turned for advice to America, from where they will be able to advise you well. We are therefore expecting your next news with great interest. You would certainly find a lot of friends there, and should you go through Frisco, stop by to see Epstein and give him my regards. He is behaving nicely to all those émigrés.

In one of the last letters, I also mentioned that we borrowed Rudla's record player. The machine plays nicely, and Rudla in part had nice records too, naturally mostly modern dance and only about two records with opera excerpts. I gave myself a great present for Christmas. I bought myself Smetana's quartet "From My Life," performed by a Czech quartet. You can imagine that I listen to it with passion and how often I play it. The same way you probably in turn listen to the beautiful melodies of Dvořák's Dances, Moldau and Fields and Groves. Only whether you manage to set the right pace for dear Ruth.

Well, I don't know what else to write to you. My brother Leo today reported to us that he also got that New Year greeting from you. Since Mother immediately put it with all the other trophies of yours, it escaped my accounting, and so I only remember it now. Thank you for it sincerely, and as I have already written to you, we wish you also a happy New Year and Merry Christmas.

Wholehearted greetings and kisses,

Yours, Dad

My dear Valdi!

I just came back from town, and so this pre-Christmas bustle in the streets reminded me of moments that we often spent together, how you always liked Prague before Christmas and those bargains. All is the same, only the Těsnohlídek's Christmas tree is missing. So I am often with you in spirit. You are surely celebrating a beautiful Christmas. You always wanted and liked the true Catholic Christmas, so now your wish came close to fulfillment. I am pleased that you so often think of me with presents, but believe me that I am no longer that vain. I have no other wishes just to see you once again.

In my mind kissing you and Ruth . . .

Curious about the missing Christmas tree, Ruth wanted more detail, so I tried to explain: "The Czech tradition of erecting a Christmas tree 'of the Republic' started as an expression of nationalism and statehood. It also was representative of social causes, associated with donation drives, and gained the name from Brno writer Rudolf Těsnohlídek. His favorite character, Eskimo Welzl, was known for his travels throughout the Arctic, from which he spun tall preposterous tales of his adventures. He became a beloved fellow countryman."

16. Valdik Holzer, MD, Peking, 1941. Passport photo.

"The same as someone I know?" she smirked.

We spent our first Christmas and New Year together in Peking dressed in new clothes—a Chinese tradition that ensures evil spirits will not recognize you. With all that was happening, when Ruth insisted on honoring this custom, I didn't argue. By the end of January I had obtained all the official papers required for leaving. As was common with foreigners in Peking, the *Peking Chronicle* and the *Peking and Tientsin Times* announced our departures. Before we went to Shanghai, we first boarded the ship ss *Peking Tsingtao Maru* for a quick trip to Japanese-occupied South Manchuria for a two-day stay at the Yamato Hotel in Dairen (Dalian)—a city with a tumultuous history of Chinese, British, Russian, and Japanese occupation. I was curious to see what was left of its mix of White Russian émigrés and Russian Jews who had escaped violent pogroms under Tsarist Russia. I knew one countryman who lived there whom I hoped to see, a "Škodavak," a Škoda company employee. As it turned out, he'd already left.

I'd been told in Peking that one of the reasons the Japanese won the Russo-Japanese War was the support they'd received from European Jews. These Jews, driven out of Russia by violent anti-Semitism, provided money to the Japanese effort while other European leaders refused. After they won, the Japanese hadn't forgotten who their supporters were, and perhaps it affected how they treated them throughout China, until they started cozying up to the Nazis.

On January 23 we set off down the China coast on the Japanese ship ss *Peking Tsingtao Maru* to Shanghai. On board was a large group of Jewish refugees from Germany who had crossed Russia on the Trans-Siberian Railroad to Vladivostok and from there by boat to Japan (the route my Uncle Leo had considered). As the passengers boarded, the Japanese had one of their immunization fits, insisting that all on board get a shot for smallpox. Some Germans panicked because they'd already been vaccinated, and they worried that a second vaccination would make them sick. In German I told the refugees not to worry, and I distributed small pieces of cotton with alcohol. I assured them they could avoid any problems by wiping their arms after being scratched by the Japanese needle. I was right except in one case: I was the only one who got sick.

In Shanghai we rented a small apartment in the French Concession while we waited for a ship to take us out. Most vessels were already booked solid. I got in touch with friends Rudla Rebhun, Pavel Kraus, and Frank and Vera Urbánek so I could introduce my new wife. Walter Schiller was fortunate to have already left for America. I did get to present Ruth to Leo Lilling, who was so kind and helpful during my trials in China. His congratulatory note struck me as amusing. The bachelor, with a long-standing beautiful Viennese girlfriend, Melitta Bliss, voiced his "great surprise" with the observation: "I never knew that such an enterprise could be undertaken so fast and painlessly."

During a visit to a Shanghai coffee shop, I was introduced by Rudla to a man who'd become a legend, Ignatius Timothy Trebitsch-Lincoln. He was a Hungarian Jewish opportunist whose changing roles and identities made my head spin as Rudla described what he'd heard about his acquaintance: "He issues warnings to warring powers and corresponds with the Dalai Lama, who is eight months old." At one time or another Rudla described Trebitsch-Lincoln as an Anglican priest, a Protestant missionary, a British member of Parliament, a German right-wing politician and possible Japanese spy, and a Buddhist monk in China. It was a time when eccentrics and the unexpected flourished in this old city. The man was always transferring his allegiances, and most in Shanghai knew he was a notorious impostor.

I visited the Czechoslovak Circle many times, learning the internal military organization was a serious affair, with real rifles and submachine guns. The unit spent several hours each day exercising on the racecourse grounds. They tried to talk me into joining them and going to Europe, but I was intent on accompanying Ruth to America.

The Chinese New Year celebration was under way with dancing lions, made up of two people in a lion costume and ten or more persons outfitted under a large snakelike dragon outfit weaving from side to side. The merriment felt fitting for our impending send-off, with the sounds of firecrackers and both of us dressed in bright colors.

At first Ruth was enchanted with the scene. Then things changed. With down-turned eyes, she glanced at me and offered a remembrance from her youth: "On the last Chinese New Year my family celebrated in China, when I was ten years old, Daddy told me I should never forget I was born in the land of lions and dragons. They represented strength and good luck, and Dad promised they'd follow me for the rest of my life. They followed me to America after the anti-Christian movement forced us to leave. I thought last year they were at my side, bringing me back to where I was born so I could teach. Now I'm not so sure about all this."

I couldn't think of a suitable response as I, too, was unsure why fate hadn't allowed her to stay. Then it came to me. "I'm sure of one thing. My *bashert* worked with your higher being to ensure we met and married. We must be patient. The rest will become evident." Her expression showed my comment had satisfied the moment.

On February 18 Ruth and I boarded the ss *President Coolidge*, an American luxury ocean liner being used as an evacuation ship. As we stood at the railing overlooking the harbor, tears rolled off Ruth's freckled cheeks and onto the deck. I heard her whisper goodbye, "Zài jiàn." I was thinking about how I'd made my way here alone but was leaving with the love of my life. As the ship's siren blew and steamed away from the harbor filled with boats, each glowing with a lantern, I took her hand and she raised it to her heart.

We sailed for San Francisco with thirty dollars between us, along with our mementos of China—a hand-carved chest, small bronze deer from four BC, and two antique lacquered red boxes with fanciful sword-fighting figures against a backdrop of mountains. In our big trunk, carefully wrapped in cloth, was the Victorian clock with hand-painted Chinese characters that I gave Ruth as a wedding gift. Once on board we were separated. She was sent to a cabin with seven other women and me to a cabin with nine men. As a result, we spent most of our time bundled up in warm clothes on the deck with some fleeing friends from the Peking Legation Quarter.

A few semiprivate cabins were available. They were reserved for special travelers, including a British vice-consul from Peking on his way to the United States. Welcomed by a personal visit of the chief steward, the vice-consul was accustomed to deluxe travel, not the accommodations on this American evacuation ship. As was customary on other large transoceanic liners, one evening the vice-consul placed his shoes outside his cabin, anticipating the staff would pick them up for polishing. In the morning he found them nailed to the deck. Annoyed, he shared the story with a group of us on deck but got little sympathy.

The boat stopped first in Kobe and Yokohama, Japan, spending one day in each port. The last major part of our relocation voyage from Hawaii to California offered up endless green ocean waves tumbling toward the future. Before we reached our destination, there was a ship's party. Luckily, we had the clothes we'd worn for Chinese New Year. Ruth felt this attire fit well into a vessel of people who were involved in life struggles much as in the ancient legend that birthed the Chinese tradition: "Each year there is a fight against a mythical beast called the 'Year,' an animal portrayed by an ox with a lion head that inhabits the sea. To overcome the beast and create a better 'new' year, a series of activities are launched that involve the color red, fire, and loud sounds because the beast fears these." Our party was indeed noisy.

Arriving in San Francisco on March 16, 1941, we had formalities to take care of before we could celebrate our arrival in America, the land I had dreamed of for some time. We stood in a long line before reaching a customs officer, who asked to confirm information from a column marked "Race or People." Above our names I noted others had identified as English, Russian, American, or Scandinavian. Beside Ruth's name was *American*. Beside my name someone had already scribbled *Slovak*. I told him that was incorrect, but before I could say "Czech" or "Bohemian," the man looked me over from my curly hair to my leather shoes. Without hesitation he crossed through *Slovak* and loudly and abruptly asked, "Hebrew?"

"All right," I meekly replied.

In a voice meant for all to hear as we walked away, Ruth spoke out: "A man should never have to lose his dignity because he loses his homeland, no matter what his heritage." (Later I learned I was one of 23,737 identified as "Hebrew" admitted to the United States between July 1, 1940, and June 30, 1941.)

Our first order of business during a brief stay in San Francisco was to cash a check from the small bank account Ruth maintained back in Virginia. Once again, an old friend of my father came to my assistance. Mr. Epstein, a schoolmate of my dad from Prague, was a wealthy banker in San Francisco. We had no trouble finding him in the telephone book. Happy to hear I'd landed safely in America, he cashed our check for the grand sum of twenty dollars. Although our conversation about Prague was dark, we tried to put a happy face on the future, talking about the day my parents would arrive in San Francisco for a visit.

While we were in port, we bought a small red, white, and blue American flag—the same colors as in the Czechoslovak flag—before reboarding the ship for our final leg. I'd reached the great melting pot, the country built by immigrants that encouraged newcomers to assimilate into the American culture. We agreed to save our biggest celebration for our final landing.

On March 18 we sailed into San Pedro Harbor, gateway to Los Angeles, where a large fleet of battleships was based. When I asked a shipmate what all these battleships were doing there, he told me they were due in a month to sail for Hawaii for annual exercises out of Pearl Harbor "to deter Japanese aggression." Exuberant about reaching the land of the free, Ruth and I celebrated our arrival in America with a bottle of champagne (without a single Brethren around to protest). That final fling left us with ten dollars. Confident that my "uncle" Bill Breth would help us get started on our new life with a loan, I gave it all to the cabin boy as a tip. I figured we might as well start anew from zero.

We were so pleased to have arrived. As we gathered our luggage, Ruth turned to me and, referring to my constant note-taking, declared: "Now you'll see the sentences you've written down have led to a significant new chapter." As I looked at the battered suitcase I'd first packed in Prague two years earlier, I couldn't resist proposing a chapter title: "What about something like 'Fairy-Tale Princess Brings Bohemian Boy to America'?"

Displeased I hadn't recognized the gravity of the moment, she gave me a steely-eyed reply: "You will see. You can live however you choose in America. I elect to be happy. I hope this will be your choice."

18

From Freedom to Infamy

March–December 1941

Ruth's uncle Henry Kroeger greeted us at the port, and we spent our first days in Los Angeles at his home. Henry was my new mother-in-law's eldest brother. Since both of us were stamp collectors, our initial conversations were mostly about that and were cordial. He had come to America from Hamburg, Germany, during World War I to avoid the kaiser's draft. He'd lost an arm in an industrial accident and wasn't able then to join anyone's army. Retired from his job as a security guard at Paramount Studios, he spent his days kibitzing with his pals from the Old Country.

At first Uncle Henry was pleasant enough by himself, but I didn't like his friends or the way he acted around them. I suspected that one wore a swastika armband under his street clothes so he'd be ready to salute if his Führer came marching around the corner. This old goat said terrible things about President Roosevelt, who had signed the Lend-Lease agreement to help Britain withstand the German onslaught by transferring arms and equipment vital to U.S. defense. The friends talked in German and didn't think I understood what they were saying.

His friend jabbered on and on about the glory of Germany under the Nazi regime: "Under Hitler we've seen the revival of Germany. It makes me angry some American Jews are boycotting German goods. We don't want another clash between Germany and America, so the president should keep his nose out of

European affairs." Uncle Henry knew my background and knew my family was living under Hitler's boot, but he never so much as interrupted his friend and often agreed with him. I ended up thinking of him as a first-class bastard, or shall I say, "second class."

I put in many hours walking the pavement those first few days, calling on various medical facilities that might need help. Each time I returned to the house, this windbag was still blowing strong. After three days my patience ran out as I heard him say to his friends, "I understand the boats coming from Hamburg are mostly people coming to the United States. What a darn shame that is."

Meeting a surprised look, I spoke to them in German. "There is a boat leaving New York every day for Germany and sometimes several ships. Most are half-empty and looking for passengers. Why don't you return and try that pleasant land?" Uncle Henry understood well the message in German. With a dropped jaw, he turned to Ruth, who also knew some German because it was her mother's first language. She cleared her throat and spoke loudly in English: "Yes. Several boats, each day." That ended the discussion, and it also ended our welcome. Happily, one day later I walked through the front door so buoyed by hope that I threw my hat in the air and announced, "I have a choice of two good jobs."

I took the first one—Seaside Memorial Hospital had offered me $150 a month. This was a decent salary for an immigrant physician's first job in America. Our finances and our lives also benefited from the spirit and friendship of my uncle Bill, who made us a generous loan of one thousand dollars with no interest and no repayment date, except "when it is convenient." The average yearly wage at that time in America was $1,750, so this large sum was a great help. (Until his death in 1957, Uncle Bill remained an important friend and relative in America.)

Now we had the funds to escape the unwelcoming atmosphere of Uncle Henry's house. I found a small apartment right next to the hospital in Long Beach. My demanding schedule came with the privilege of room and board, but the apartment meant my lovely wife would be close enough to allow us to share meals from time to time. Our four-room flat wasn't a Peking palace, but Ruth set to work making it resemble one—better, in fact!

Long Beach was a picturesque seaside city with a variety of palm trees lining the streets. Down by the beautiful beach was an amusement park that might have been great fun if I'd had time to go there with Ruth. But my job as house physician at Seaside Memorial Hospital was challenging because of the vast difference in administrative protocol from what I had experienced in European and Chinese hospitals. Seaside Memorial had around 250 beds and a separate 50-bed department for the coast guard. There were two other house physicians on staff, both women—Doctors Casey and Arvad. Each of us was on call every third day, which meant spending many hours in the laboratory, as any lab staff work had to be done at night by the house physician. To earn money and see more of me, Ruth got a job in the hospital's admission office, which added one hundred dollars to our monthly income.

I learned there was another Czech doctor living in Hollywood and looking for a hospital position, and I got in touch with him to help. His name was Rudy Lederer. I hadn't known him in Prague, but I did know Rudy by reputation, as he was a famous long-term student who spent ten years on the Charles University medical faculty before he got his degree, before the Nazis closed the school. Rudy had a famous brother, actor Francis Lederer, a Czech-born film star. Seriously handsome, Francis had starred in *Pandora's Box*, a silent film starring Louise Brooks made in Germany in 1928. Four years later he moved to Hollywood, where, ironically, although he was a Jew, like many other Jewish European refugees in the film business, he was often cast as a Nazi because of his accent.

My friendship with Rudy added excitement to our Southern California existence as he regularly got into some kind of trouble. He never dressed up for special occasions and mostly walked around in surgical scrubs. One day, wearing scrubs, he went to pick up his girlfriend, Helen, at a school where she taught. She was running late and did not come out of the building on time.

After a long wait Rudy got out of his car and started pacing the street dressed in his unusual outfit. He noticed a police patrol car pass him several times. When it stopped, the policemen asked him what he was doing. When he tried to explain in his typical frenzied manner and thick Czech accent that he was waiting for his girlfriend, they took him to the police station for further investigation. I tried to bail him out, but it required Francis Lederer's influence to get him released.

I worked long hours at the hospital during the week, and on weekends Ruth and I explored California. I surprised her with a Ford 60 automobile, the smallest Ford produced at that time. It was a black coupe with a rumble seat. We used to drive to the desert east of Los Angeles, through the mountains to Big Bear Lake, and into the desert to Palm Springs. We traveled as far north as Santa Barbara and as far south as San Diego. I loved to take pictures of every scene and mailed them to my folks and to our friends in China.

We'd been sending letters regularly to my parents but hadn't heard from them since our arrival, so I wasn't certain if they knew we'd gotten out of China until one of their letters reached us in May, after being forwarded several times. My father and I had taken to numbering our letters, so each knew if any became lost. As they had just received my letter saying we'd made it to California, they didn't know much and were concerned for us:

> We are sorry that you again have to run around chasing a new
> way of life. So far luck has been with you, and so I hope that
> this time, too, you may find something that will satisfy you;
> a year is not so long, and then you will be able to open your
> own medical practice and through that hopefully secure your
> lifestyle. In the meantime, you will have great financial worries.
> We've written about this to you many times and offered our
> help, but you have never fully responded. Recently we spoke
> to Ferdinand's sister, who told us she had a letter from him
> in which he mentions that he helped you somehow. We don't

know whether financially or only with morale. In this direction, something could be arranged. Is such a position in a hospital unpaid or maybe you do receive a small salary? Couldn't you turn to my acquaintance Epstein, who once offered you his services? Our telephone won't work because since March 1 we don't have one. Like others, we had to give it up. You would have to call us at the post office.

My mother then added her note:

Thank you and dear Ruth for your wholehearted wishes, which delighted me in no small way. Dad, too, distinguished himself. He bought a fountain pen and a pencil, in an exquisite Blues brand. Further, the postman delivered your delicacies like oranges, chocolates, and bonbons. And through his opening, Dad was gasping, saying—this is also from the boy. Your first letter from Los Angeles arrived, and you know how longingly we awaited it . . . I think that after China you will have to recuperate on that beautiful beach, which is not unknown here. When I mention "Long Beach" to anyone, everyone knows it "from the movies" . . . In my soul, I am with you when you are searching for a new way of life. Kissing you and Ruth.

Their calm and careful manner was the same—"All is well!" But my doubts were growing. I was surprised that American newspapers carried so little information about conditions in the occupied countries, although perhaps what they did report was more than enough to satisfy most of their readers, while I was much more interested in events abroad.

I liked nearly all the Americans I'd met in my short time in this country, and I found my new colleagues particularly useful and pleasant, but I was disappointed by the isolationist attitude I heard expressed even by educated people. At a dinner party I could barely contain myself when one doctor launched into his position: "President George Washington warned us about not getting involved in European wars." Fearing I might lose my temper, as she could see the raging tsunami below the surface of my cheeks, Ruth pinched my arm as the guy continued: "It's another case of us getting pulled into a decadent European conflict. Arms manufacturers are dragging America into a war where we should never be. If we stay out of their mess, these dictators will kill each other off."

Most seemed more concerned in whether the Yankees would capture another World Series than in whether the Germans would capture Belgrade. I knew from experience the world was a tiny place and that people here were fooling themselves if they assumed they could hide behind an ocean . . . or even two.

Part of my frustration came from the slowdown in the news from friends and relatives. The ones in Prague were obviously as cautious as my parents, so not much was being relayed to me by way of London and elsewhere, as they didn't get any insight either. I got a pretty good inkling of why this was occurring when I learned the Nazis had moved beyond confiscating radios from the Jews and were executing anyone in Prague caught listening in a group to any radio station not under German control or to any broadcasts of Czech exile groups. I also hadn't heard from Leo Lilling since we'd arrived in America. I was disappointed that he hadn't shown up at the dock in Shanghai, as I'd wanted to thank him personally for all his kindness. I got a letter from him in June, in which he explained that he'd come to the Customs Jetty at 9:00 p.m. with a flower bouquet to give us a fitting send-off but one of us got the time wrong, and we were gone by then. I wrote back but heard nothing more, which didn't surprise me considering the deteriorating conditions in China. A friend wrote in 1941 that Leo had married Melitta. I wondered whether Leo and Melitta would stick it out in China, but I never heard from him again. What became of this beautiful man remains a mystery.

On June 8, 1941, my seventy-nine-year-old grandmother, Marie Porges Holzer, wrote. I knew from my parents' letters that she'd spent the past two years with myriad illnesses, mostly brought on by stress. Travel was made especially difficult because of Nazi

17. Envelopes, 1941.

restrictions on all Jews. As I read her words, my heart ached because I knew my father rarely was able to visit his mother after the 1939 occupation. As was common for many older Czechs raised in the Austro-Hungarian Empire, Grandmother Marie wrote in an old German cursive handwriting known as "Kurrent," or "Kurrentschrift":

> My dearest,
>
> May you always have luck, as you have my dear Valdi, up to now. I was delighted by the last letter your dear father sent me in which he told me that you are doing well in your job and that you already bought a car . . . Your dear Father wrote you about my illness. Thank God, I am already doing fine.
>
> With best wishes and be dearly kissed from your loving Grandmother

Reading this short, simple letter brought a wave of tears to my eyes. Soon after my grandmother's letter, my dad wrote again, once again brushing aside my offer to help them leave:

From Freedom to Infamy

Your report about movie theaters is very nice. We, unfortunately, haven't known what a screen in a cinema looks like for a long time, let alone heard anything from a loudspeaker. All that we hear now is the gramophone, which we daily play in the evening after eight when we have to sit nicely home.

As far as our quota is concerned, we do not pay attention to it. It will not be so soon anyway, and then Mom is afraid of seasickness. So we ask you, dear Valdi, though we know you are kind and attentive and concerned about us, not to do or undertake anything until we call on you. In the meantime, you will receive your medical papers, it seems all is going quickly, then you will be able to visit us with dear Ruth, and then we can talk in peace about what can be done further. We thank you also for taking care of us, including insurance, but believe me it is not necessary, and we would surely cover the price for the journey and expenses as usual. We are pleased by your thoughtfulness, and it is a great solace for us that you care about us so much.

As 1941 progressed, the war going on elsewhere remained an enigma to Americans. Even Vice President Harry Truman was reported in the June 24, 1941, *New York Times* to be torn between Germany and Russia. Germany had attacked Russia, and America was unsure of what to do next. "If we see that Germany is winning we ought to help Russia and if Russia is winning we ought to help Germany, and that way let them kill as many as possible, although I don't want to see Hitler victorious under any circumstances. Neither thought anything of their pledged word."

As I read the headlines about German forces pushing their way into the USSR from the south and west, with a third force making its way from the north toward Leningrad, I was amazed that America still wasn't choosing sides. Despite warnings from Britain, Stalin had not prepared soon enough for this invasion. On BBC radio Winston Churchill condemned the action, saying the Russian invasion was "our danger and of danger to the United

States, just as the cause of any Russian fighting for his hearth and home is the case of free men and free peoples in every quarter of the globe."

Even with that call to action, America stood back. But all that was happening on the world scene didn't postpone the schedule of milestones in my life. Never offering a hint of any suffering, I knew how painful it was for my parents and me to be apart again for my birthday in July 1941. My parents' birthday message was heartbreaking:

> Valdi, the next month you will celebrate your thirtieth birthday. This is a milestone in everyone's life. You will celebrate it away from us so our thoughts will be with you . . . Ruth will certainly remember the day nicely and will, at least in part, make up to you for what we cannot do for you.
>
> Unfortunately, a bad fate forces us to spend several years of your life without you. You know how we loved being with you and that we now must miss what was the most beautiful thing in our life and, in fact, for so long the purpose of our lives. Only the hope that the day will come when we can hug you again gives us the strength to bear all the hardship that we must.

After I had gathered my composure, I read my mom's note:

> I read what your dad wrote, and it was as if he wrote my thoughts from my soul exactly. You know best what you mean to us and with such a festive day coming, I am always with you in my mind. I join the wish of your father and wish you lots of good luck and all the success in life for your next thirty years.
>
> We heard fourteen days ago that Dr. Eisner's parents and Dr. Wiener's mom left for the USA.

With kisses for you and your Chick.

Although I loved my work in Long Beach, I remained restless and did my best to make myself available for a more noble cause. Ruth and I felt our calling might be elsewhere and agreed China still held our promise. I offered my services to the American Red

Cross in Washington DC for assignment in the Far East. I wrote a letter detailing my experience and obvious qualifications, but I got a disappointing reply: "Only American physicians are being accepted now." I'd been through such rejections more times than I could count, but I still found my inability to volunteer my services frustrating. I had plenty of work to keep me busy and also had to concentrate on the task of improving my English in a hurry so colleagues at the hospital wouldn't laugh quite so hard at my accent. One had the nerve to tell me I sounded like the German actor Erich von Stroheim! I corrected him, saying, "No, I sound like Francis Lederer."

I worried nonstop about my parents but also appreciated that they hadn't lost their humor even as they were caught in the web of the Nazi regime. In late July they shared the news that gave me a reason to laugh even though it was about the most recent misfortune. It occurred in their newly settled apartment, where the Nazis had forced them to move. Inside the letter my dad enclosed an article:

I am copying a little article from the newspapers. It reads: "The long arm of the thief. On the balcony of his apartment in Slezská Street in Vinohrady, the owner of the apartment A.H. hung a short green man's fur coat with possum lining to air it out. Not even in his wildest dreams would it have occurred to him that his little fur coat, which he thought safe on the balcony being aired out, would disappear altogether. Nonetheless, that's what happened. Some scrounger with long arms stealthily snatched the fur coat from the balcony. The owner suffered a loss, as he announced to the police when he went to complain and request that the detectives look for both coat and thief."

As you see, our journalists have a sense of humor. The day of the event, I was cross at Mom for always cleaning and airing out clothes, but then I told myself, what's gone is gone, let's hope I am not going to Siberia. Here the frosts are not so bad; a good overcoat is good enough for me and I have one, so let's have it, it was God's will. A lesson not to air out things on the balcony. You take care over there. They could filch something the same way there. Otherwise, no one in the family has lost anything, and everyone's health is holding, except for Uncle Gustav, who is, poor thing, at his last gasp. So generally we can be content.

At the letter's end a handwritten note from my mother showed her own sense of humor.

You can imagine what has gone on with that fur coat. No one keeps airing things and cleaning so much as me, and so Dad allegedly has long expected and known that something would surely get lost. He waited thirty-two years and was proved right.

After reading my reply, Dad responded:

That you celebrated your big day so pompously was great to hear, we were pleased that you have so many friends. Well, but you wouldn't mind wolfing down some holiday delicacy of Mom's, would you? We have all our presents intended for you put aside and when we see each other one day, which we hope will not take long, they will be ceremoniously handed to you and there will be an opulent feast to celebrate all those foregone holidays.

It was not long afterward that Dad's notes began to show how claustrophobic their lives were becoming as their situation deteriorated:

We can see from your photographs of Southern California cactuses that you are content and how beautiful it must be there. Those cactuses have always been your hobby, and Mom almost anxiously guards every specimen that you once sent from Slovakia. When you will be taking those to America one day, it will be quite a transportation challenge.

Dear Mom still and constantly worries about all those flowers. In our apartment we don't have as much room as we used to, so she has to shift them constantly, searching for a sunny spot so they would thrive.

It was clear that this was a metaphor for their attempts to thrive as they and other Jews were forced to move to smaller or shared quarters. Soon another reminder of our separation arrived, due to "big waves":

> Now the fall storms will start on the ocean—you know how Mom travels only with difficulty. And me, it would be a trip like the one I experienced with you as a young boy, dear Valdi, when we went from Venice to Trieste, and you wanted to disembark in the middle of the sea. Let's leave it till when the sea calms down, and there won't be such big waves on it.
>
> If you firmly decide to stay in the United States one day, then we are ready to follow you as soon as possible so we could live together with you—because as we have written to you a number of times, it wouldn't be a life for us only to longingly await a letter and a visit once every few years.
>
> You must have read in your local newspaper about the strange symbol that we will wear on our chest in a week. We will soon know what general impression it will make. It is odd when we read all the time how racially different we are and because of this need to have that special badge so everyone can easily recognize us.

I'd not seen any news in the U.S. media that the Nazis had ordered Bohemian Jews to wear the Yellow Star of David pinned to the left front of their clothing. Dad assumed the world was watching, but sadly, I didn't think it was. Although my father termed the symbol "strange," he'd told me long ago about the use of badges and other articles of clothing as a way of identifying Jews. The practice was centuries old, but I never dreamed it would return from the Middle Ages. In what a few years earlier seemed such a cultured time, my parents were being forced to carry a mark I knew would bring my mother and him no good.

As my refugee friends and I agreed in our correspondence, Jews knew that even telling a joke about Hitler might lead to imprisonment or death. So my parents' letters didn't express any extreme viewpoints or disclose critical details. Mostly, Dad reported on daily life: "We live exactly the same life, from time to time a new edict comes out, making life more colorful and nervous, but that's what wartime brings, and we have to hope that one day this will be over and we will live our lives somewhere in calm and peace."

The most disturbing edicts dealt with the loss of rights—restrictions, as Jews, on jobs and education and then on where on a bus or tram they could sit or what hours they could go to the post office. They were denied attendance to cinemas and concerts or a simple walk along the Vltava River. Strict curfews were mentioned, and Dad couldn't even visit his ill mother in Benešov because travel was restricted. As part of the slow communications blackout, their telephone was disconnected and radio taken. In late 1941 Jews were ordered to surrender their bicycles and typewriters, which explained why Dad began to write letters by hand. Over time, as more letters arrived, I started to understand my parents' use of code words, such as *spa* for concentration camp. I recognized their attempt to create an illusion that "all is fine" so I wouldn't worry about them. It didn't work, but I did the same for them. I only shared the best photographs from my life.

Amid this disturbing news I felt guilty as Ruth and I took pleasure that summer in the gentle sea breezes during our weekend jaunts. September brought news that got my attention, though, as usual, the news probably meant nothing to most Americans. An administrator at the hospital handed me a *New York Times* with a story he thought I'd find interesting. The headline made me ill: "Czech State Gets Gestapo Master."

Hitler had installed his own security chief, a nasty fellow named Reinhard Heydrich, as the new "protector" of my former country. I paid close attention to any news I could find over the next weeks as the psychopathic Heydrich carried out a brutal campaign to eliminate even the mildest Czech opposition to the Nazi occupation while making life even more miserable for the Jews. He announced his intention to "Germanize the Czech vermin," but even before he got going on that, his murderous henchmen killed

Czech men, women, and children in large-scale public executions that were reported in the media. If there had existed any illusion that things might improve for my parents, it was gone.

My parents wrote nothing about this man because of the danger of writing about it. Before my father's September birthday, Mom expressed her own wish: "So Dad was not mistaken when he said: 'Next week a letter from Valdik will come. It's my birthday.' God permit that this is the last one without you. I don't have any other wishes but to see you again soon."

On October 22, 1941, less than a month after Heydrich took over, I got a cable from my parents in Prague announcing that they were ready to leave the country: "Go to the Travel Bureau Lubin Havana and get an entry visa and ship tickets for Ernst and Olga Holzer immediately."

I was already panic-stricken when I received a handwritten letter backing up the cable request. My parents hadn't received recent letters in a timely fashion or perhaps at all. My letters were censored, not only in Germany but in the United States.

Dear Children,

We don't have any messages from you this week, so we have been without a letter for the last three weeks. Just now, we would need your words. I told you in the last letter that transports are being sent, but we still are calm and haven't asked you to undertake anything for us. Meanwhile, many of our acquaintances decided to send a cable to their relatives overseas to ask them for help in emigrating.

As you know, I have turned down your many offers to help. However, given the present circumstances that confront us, with the advice of our many friends, and after much consideration, we decided to send you a telegraph. You undoubtedly received the cable, and we are waiting for your answer this week.

We don't want to burden you, and we hope that if you decide in our favor that your financial burden, however temporary, will be bearable for you. You will certainly also consider your obligations you took on for dear Ruth. We don't want your sacrifices to be at her expense.

We don't worry about making a living. In spite of my age, I feel strong enough to take any work. I don't have to write to you about your mom's vitality. As you know, she overcame hard time with her strong will, although she made the greatest sacrifices for us. We don't want to and will not owe you anything; we just need your immediate help so that we won't be sent away from here like I explained to you in detail last time.

Of our acquaintances, Dr. Langer and his wife and daughter have left on transports; further registered for transports are the Steiners, also old Fischer, and perhaps also my brother Leo with family Elsa and son Hanuš. That is all I wanted to write you about this matter . . .

Yesterday Franta Schoenbaum and his boy visited us. He would like to leave as well, but he faces obstacles that he won't be able to overcome easily. His boy, Honza, is a rascal, so we had fun with him.

This time I am not writing too much because I am not in the mood for it these days. I hope though that soon I will find my mental balance and will find the resolve for a long letter.

With warm greetings and kisses,

Your loving Father

And from my mother, finally an honest account:

My Dear Valdik,

You cannot even imagine how difficult it is to live here. My wish was not to see anyone of my friends depart. The Langers already had my farewell; the Kes family is already waiting for transport; cousin Hanička Steiner and her husband will stay yet because pregnant women are not sent in transports. She is expecting little Růžička in October. We often regret that we did not travel to join you. I admit that we were afraid to be a burden on you in a foreign country. We wish from the bottom of our hearts and souls to be united with you but will have to leave it to fate whether it decides that we should see each other again.

With kisses.

They instructed me to secure visas and passage to Cuba, which seemed open to receiving refugees. I was frightened and thrilled at the same time. I knew my parents wouldn't consider emigrating unless the situation had become dire, but I was excited by the prospect of having them join us in America. I contacted Uncle Bill, but his response was discouraging. He reminded me of the s s *St. Louis*, which sailed from Germany with more than nine hundred Jewish refugees in 1939. A few were allowed to disembark when the ship reached Cuba, and the United States refused to respond to passengers' pleas for asylum.

Bill was dealing with several such immigration requests from other relatives and warned that the red tape and cost were significant obstacles: "Cables like the one you mentioned came probably by the hundreds. I received three, two from my sisters and one from Franz Holzer, who probably must be a cousin of ours as he was born in Jeníkov, whom I met once in my life. They all ask the same thing—visas for Cuba."

Bill had generated a list of his closest relatives and narrowed it down to the twelve who most needed help. Bill's reply on October 29, 1941, offered little encouragement:

> The travel agency told me that it is not difficult to get a visa, but the sum they quoted took my breath away. First, the Cuban Government demands a $2,000 deposit per person, which is supposed to be refunded when the immigrant leaves the country. However, there is a Cuban bank that makes the deposit for you if you send them $150, which is, of course, not returned. Then next $250, the cost of the visas; $500 sustenance deposit; and $250 for the return trip ticket—altogether $1,050 per person. To this total must be added the cost of the steamship ticket

from Lisbon to Havana, which is at present $510 per person. Multiply this by twelve, and you can visualize what I am up against and why I cannot help cousins like Franz.

The bottom line was staggering, as was the cost of doing nothing:

If you want to rescue your parents, you will need immediately $2,100. You can use the thousand dollars I lent you and if you are absolutely unable to get the rest of the money, I will lend you some more, but please do not mention it when writing home because other relatives would swamp me with the same requests. It is hard to refuse; one feels like sentencing these people to deportation, God knows to where, yet my resources are limited. I am just a chemist, and all that I have is from saving from my salary. The issue is too big for one man to handle, yet it preys on my mind whenever I have to refuse.

Like a pin pierced deep in one's foot, I could feel the pain in Uncle Bill's words. I was determined to try, so I contacted several different consulate offices and agencies and began to speak at the hospital about my circumstance. I was introduced by another resident physician to a man named Gaspar Bilo Mendez, who worked as an orderly in surgery.

Mendez told me he used to be a police prefect in Panama City and that he was ousted from his office because of some political changes in his country. I could relate to that. He told me he was given refuge in America as payment for valuable services rendered by his father to the U.S. Navy. Mendez was a big talker, and I came to feel sure he had some valuable contacts in the Chilean consulate in Los Angeles. I asked Mendez whether it would be possible for me to secure a visa for my parents. He shrugged as if it was a silly question. "It will be an easy thing for my friend in the Chilean consulate to issue this visa or they would instruct the consulate in Berlin to do so." Mendez made it sound simple, "entirely a matter of personal favor," but it would cost money.

I gave him forty dollars to go to Los Angeles and contact his friend. Ruth helped me type up a "contract" for his services. I attached my parents' personal information and included a line: "Reason for leaving Germany: personal." As I had to work the day of the meeting, Rudy Lederer accompanied Mendez to Los Angeles, to meet with the other man he thought was a Chilean consulate representative. Rudy told me they were with someone for lunch who spoke no English and Mendez acted as interpreter. When Mendez returned, he confirmed all was set but that I would have to pay three hundred dollars as a deposit to the Chilean government to guarantee that my parents would not become public charges upon arrival in Chile. He promised the money would be refunded. [In 1941 three hundred dollars had the same buying power as fifty-two hundred dollars in 2018.]

I would have done anything to get my parents out of danger, so I borrowed the money and gave Mendez a cashier's check. After that Mendez avoided me and then disappeared. I learned from another physician that Mendez had defrauded her of one hundred dollars. Seaside Hospital staff told me Mendez paid a maternity bill for his "brother's wife" the day after I'd paid him. I contacted the Long Beach police, who seemed helpful but conceded they couldn't find Mr. Mendez. A letter followed from Manual Eduardo Hubner, consul general of Chile:

> The situation which you have now explained to me seems extremely important for in the first place it can clearly be seen that you have been the victim of fraud. Chilean visas are always priced between $1.70 and $10.00, never above or below those amounts. So as you can see the price you paid is outrageous.
>
> It is necessary that you send me as much information about Mr. Bilo Mendez as you possibly can and explain to me that connection he maintained with the Chilean Consulate. As soon as you can, please write to me giving me full details about Mr. Mendez. I shall do everything in my power to help you.

My dealings with Mendez brought my efforts to secure a visa to a halt. Before I could make another attempt, the Nazis ordered a stop to all emigration from the protectorate. The butcher Heydrich must have been behind it. We had no way of knowing why or what would happen to my parents. Once again, they wrote that they would be okay and there was no need to make any further fuss:

November 22, 1941

So far, five transports have left, so with them a few of my close acquaintances. Various messages have come from them, some of which calmed the nervous crowd. For the past three weeks, no transports have been sent, but there are rumors that they will be renewed at the end of this month. We are upset that, given our impression of the first measures, we didn't consider the matter more carefully and sent that telegram to you, Dr. Valdi. Today we would give much, much if we only could take it back. We could have avoided making your already hard position even harder and spared you all those sacrifices you had to make, the financial and physical ones, to obtain what we had asked you for so carelessly.

It is absolutely out of the question for us to live in a country where we would have to accept money for living, where we wouldn't be able to work and support ourselves.

As you advised me, I turned to Berlin but received no positive answer yet. Rules and regulations change often here . . . now older people are forbidden to leave, so anything you might send wouldn't help. I beg of you not to incur any more unnecessary financial costs and not to take any further steps and just to be satisfied with those you undertook already. You have done more than enough, and we hope the time will come when we can return everything to you to the last coin.

As soon as emigration from the country is opened again, we will let you know. Therefore, I beg of you once more, please do not take any more steps and do not spend any more money. That way we can all enjoy it all the better and merrier when times allow us to be reunited.

From Freedom to Infamy

I was devastated that I'd failed them. I couldn't even look at myself in the mirror. Ruth tried to comfort me, but for days I was in a dark place. It felt as if I was back in China being interrogated by the Japanese, but this time it was a suffocating room with no windows or door. I couldn't see any way out. How could I help my parents? While at Charles University, I'd read *Beyond Good and Evil*, by the famous German philosopher Friedrich Nietzsche, of all people. One of his maxims echoed in my head: "He who fights with monsters should look to it that he does not become a monster. And when you gaze long into an abyss the abyss gazes into you."

I was falling down this bottomless shaft when Ruth, in her wisdom, pulled me up. She interpreted the language of my emotions and helped me realize I could keep my head above water even though it was up to my nose and getting deeper. "If you don't do this, you will never be able to help your parents," she said. Then, on December 5, to remind me of the futility of not just my efforts but of others caught in the Nazis' deceptive web, I received a letter from Uncle Bill:

> My brother Hugo's request added five persons to my list, which amounts to seventeen. I obtained the seventeen visas promptly and in a few days I was able to cable them the numbers as given to me by the Cuban Consul in Berlin. A few days later I received the following cable: "Klein Stein Jula Abgereist Lederers Ausreise Unbestimmt Werden Bekanntgeben Masareks Visum Fehlt Sendet Lederer Masarek Schiffskarten—Hapag."
>
> First I rejoiced, thinking that "Abgereist" means that they have departed for Cuba, but people who know more about these things told me that it means that they were sent to Poland. I cabled back. But though this cable was sent on November 24, I haven't received any answer. I am afraid that every one of them was deported.
>
> In the Czech Colony in New York there is a rumor that nobody is allowed to leave for America and the Nazis never

intended to release our relatives and the only reason why they made them send the cables was to make us waste our money. Thus, we cannot do anything but wait and hope for the best.

In an earlier letter Dad reported the Langer family was taken away on a Nazi transport. This was my friend Milena, Bála's wife and children and her parents. Uncle Bill's report seemed to confirm this. I felt helpless on this ladder of many rungs. There was nothing left for me to do but go on with my work. I had to make morning hospital rounds on December 7, but once I finished, Ruth and I planned to drive south to the hills near San Juan Capistrano for a picnic. My final stop on my rounds was a single room on the third floor to the left of the elevator. The patient was a permanent hospital resident, a nurse who was a paraplegic with a fracture of her second lumbar vertebra. She used to prop the door of her room wide open so she could see the action down the hallway. The invalid nurse knew everything that was happening on that floor, and sometimes the young doctors would drop by and have coffee with her to learn the latest gossip.

When I visited that day before noon, she fixed me a cup, a thick, dark brew that reminded me of the Turkish coffee we drank at the Café Mánes. Jazz music was coming from the radio as we talked, when the program was interrupted by a bulletin announcing the Japanese attack on Pearl Harbor! The Andrews Sisters resumed singing "Boogie Woogie Bugle Boy," but our conversation came to a halt. We stared at the radio until the network flashed another bulletin and then returned to music. This was how I learned America was being pulled into war, in a series of short, frantic bulletins. It was as if the news was so startling it made the radio stutter.

As reality sank in, I realized I should be home with my wife. I rushed to the apartment, where Ruth was packing a picnic basket. I told her about the attack and turned on our radio, but there was no more news. We had already allowed the Japanese to interrupt our honeymoon, but we were determined not to let them ruin our picnic. So we loaded the car and set off for the hills. Near our

From Freedom to Infamy

parked car, we spread our tablecloth on a grassy pinnacle overlooking the blue Pacific and spent the afternoon listening to music
coming from the car radio, interrupted by more bulletins, until the
news took over completely. At one point Ruth turned her gaze
from the ocean to me. "What will happen?" she said. "There is no
longer any place in this entire world where it is peaceful."

I had no answer. It appeared there was no safe harbor anywhere.

I could sense from the slightly higher-than-normal pitch and
an unusual number of misspoken words that even these professional reporters and announcers were rattled by the day's events. It
sounded as though America's entire Pacific fleet was out of action.
The ships that had greeted us on arrival in San Pedro Harbor
were likely among those destroyed, along with many lives. What
could stop the Imperial Japanese Navy from sailing straight on
to California? Or stop the Japanese air force from hop-skipping
to California? It became apparent I wasn't the only one speculating about this when the local announcer broke in at about three
o'clock with an advisory for all civilians to return to their homes.
Los Angeles had ordered a complete blackout, meaning no lights
in homes or along the streets. Even car headlights had to be turned
off, so it was vital to get inside before dark. The forty-mile drive
took three hours in bumper-to-bumper traffic. We were all stuck
in the same mess, and we all knew why, but people honked their
horns anyway out of frustration and fear.

As we walked through our apartment door, with high resolve
Ruth encouraged me to leave: "Go where you are needed most.
This is not a time to sit and think about safety. This is the time
to serve those in need." I agreed my place was in the emergency
room and left Ruth home in the dark and walked over to the hospital. With each step my heart thumped so hard behind my rib
cage that I felt my chest move. I wasn't sure I'd done the right
thing, leaving her behind.

Over time all the other doctors and staff showed up too. We
treated one accident victim after another, as panicked drivers with
no headlights collided. We all worked through the night, sleep-

ing as best we could between cases. Among my hardest-working colleagues that evening, and any other night, were three American physicians of Japanese descent who came to the hospital to help. When daylight arrived, several police officers appeared and asked for them. The doctors were taken down to the station and forced to register as "aliens," even though they had been born in America and were American citizens.

I was a stateless refugee from the German-occupied territory, so I could hardly help them, but this episode angered me. I thought of my parents and friends who were distrusted and mistreated—aliens in their own country. How could such a thing happen in America? This question came back to me when Eleanor Roosevelt expressed concern about the "security threat" posed by California's population of Japanese Americans. (Ultimately, more than 120,000 citizens of Japanese ancestry were taken from their homes and held in internment camps behind barbed-wire fences and guard towers for the rest of the war.)

The day my colleagues were taken to the police station, an elderly Japanese lady brought her little granddaughter into the emergency room. The child was about three years old and had stuck a piece of carrot up her nose. I was teasing the little girl and playing with her when the nurse brought in some forceps to pull the carrot out. When the old lady saw the instrument, she grabbed the little girl and rushed from the hospital saying that she wouldn't let her granddaughter be tortured. The poor woman must have thought that we were trying to retaliate for Pearl Harbor!

On December 8 the United States and Britain declared war on Japan. On December 11 Germany and Italy declared war on the United States. U.S. participation was no longer in doubt and a declaration of war followed. Around twenty-five hundred Americans were killed, over one thousand injured, two hundred airplanes destroyed, and the U.S. Pacific Fleet crippled. Although the Brits continued referring to the conflict as "the War," Roosevelt publicly put a label on it as the "Second World War."

With America at war with Germany, my parents were considered to be behind enemy lines, which made direct communication impossible. The single connection remaining was through the International Committee of the Red Cross. I was informed it would establish a message service for civilians cut off by the war as it had elsewhere in the world.

19

A New Life in a New World

January 1942–May 1945

J apan followed up its sneak attack by landing troops in the Philippines, which was American territory. After Germany had declared war on the United States in support of its Asian ally, I felt complete confidence that the right side would win as I witnessed a surge of patriotism and determination sweep the country. The morning after that first assault, crowds of young people lined up outside army recruiting offices as if the sergeants were handing out free tickets to a Benny Goodman concert. Seeing them recalled my frustrated attempts to enlist in the army—in a variety of armies. Now that America had joined the fight, it might be worth another try. As always, there were complications.

The United States had instituted the draft even before Pearl Harbor, and I was required to register when we settled in Long Beach. With my accent and relatives living behind enemy lines, I anticipated a cold reception from the draft board—so I never got around to it. Despite my concern for the consequences of that inaction, I contacted Draft Board 275 in Long Beach to inquire about my status—and as usual, I did not get a satisfactory answer. Even though the United States was at war, the government wasn't interested in an alien as a military physician. I was informed I'd be drafted as a private sometime in the future, but for now that honor was reserved for American citizens. The draft board's advice was to enlist as a medical officer in my country's army. The Czechoslovak army in exile was recruiting from the British Commonwealth, but even that army had too many chiefs and not enough braves, so all the officers in the reserve had to resign their commissions and start as buck privates. For that privilege I'd have to go to Canada to join up and then be shipped to Britain.

I didn't want to do that but was determined to serve in some capacity as a military physician. I decided to go to Washington DC, the center of things military, and find out exactly what my U.S. military status was. The bureaucracy in Los Angeles wasn't providing much helpful information—Washington was the headquarters. And by going there, I would finally meet Ruth's family, who lived nearby. They had wanted to see us since we'd arrived, and Ruth was more than ready. So we resigned our positions at Seaside Memorial Hospital and bought a small trailer for the Ford for fifty dollars.

With the United States no longer neutral and communications with my parents impossible, I couldn't tell them we were leaving California. I had nothing to sustain me except blind hope, and even that vanished with Uncle Bill's next letter, which arrived before we left on our trip: "I do not know whether you have received any news from Bohemia, but I am afraid that everything we did for our people there was fruitless. I am of the opinion that the cables which our relatives have sent us were inspired by the Nazis, who want to put the American Jews to considerable expense, the Nazis not having the slightest inclination to release their victims."

We packed our belongings and headed east on January 15, 1942. Unlike so many of my earlier journeys, this was a splendid trip—a fantastic opportunity to see America before the restrictions of wartime gas rationing and tire shortages made travel far more difficult. We spent our first night in Las Vegas, where there were slot machines at each service station but no casinos at the time. We drove on to see the Grand Canyon and to Oklahoma City, Kansas City, and into Terre Haute, Indiana, where we stopped when it started raining. There were not many motels then, but there were a few private guesthouses that would accommodate travelers for the night.

In all it took us about five days to cross the country with our little Ford and trailer. I kept notes for the day I'd get to tell my parents all about the trip. The drive through America was a lot less harrowing than my drives across Shansi Province, but I admit to experiencing a twinge as we approached the quiet town of McConnellsburg, Pennsylvania. On the map it was little more than a rest stop halfway between Philadelphia and Pittsburgh, but the way my stomach was doing flips, you'd think I was approaching the Forbidden City for an audience with the emperor. Actually, that would have been much less imposing. McConnellsburg was the home of Horace and Emma Lequear, Ruth's parents, and I was about to meet them for the first time. I guess I felt the same jitters any prospective son-in-law feels under such circumstances, except I was long past being "prospective" at this point. My wife had offered me assurance that her folks would love me as much as she did, but I still felt the need to see a welcoming smile as I trudged with our luggage onto the front porch of their little house on First Street and came face to face with my father-in-law.

I didn't see a smile of any sort. Reverend Lequear looked solemn in his black, crisply pressed suit, but I may have been reading into his upright preacher's posture. He was a distinguished man, a good six feet tall with graying red hair that suited him well and blue eyes that softened his features. He extended his right hand without saying a word, and I shook it before realizing he was reaching for a suitcase. We both realized my mistake at the same time, but instead of correcting me, he returned my handshake with a firm grip and then broke into the broad smile I'd been hoping for. From that moment on I knew we'd be friends.

At first Emma appeared as stern as her husband did, looking the preacher's wife in a modest housedress, her long hair pinned up in a bun. She was thin, which I mistook for frail until I saw her bustling about as she put the final touches on an all-American feast that would have graced any Thanksgiving table. More than once she apologized for the house's appearance, which was immaculate and tidy. "We're still settling in," she said, although they'd been in

A New Life in a New World

the house for more than a year since Horace had accepted a post as pastor of St. Paul's Reformed Church, about two blocks away. I understood that my mother-in-law was offering a polite explanation for the family's simple circumstances of sturdy but sparse furnishings in a home that wasn't much bigger than our apartment.

Their limited budget had to stretch along with their limited space to accommodate Ruth's sister, Rachel, who was paralyzed from the waist down as the result of an automobile accident. Ruth's youngest brother, Hank, lived there too, as he was still in high school and quite a baseball player. Thank goodness her other brother, George, was away at college, or we'd have had to sleep in the car. Yet neither of my wonderful in-laws gave any hint of complaint about their burdens. To the contrary, as we chatted that night, they both shared the joy that sprang from a lifetime of service and dedication. As they recounted their experiences for Ruth and me, I was struck by the uncanny resemblance between their story and ours: two people from exceedingly different places and cultures who had found each other in China.

Horace was descended from a family that traced its American roots back before the Revolution. The earliest ancestor, Jan L'Esquyer (with last name often misspelled), arrived in 1658 on the ship *Bruynvis* (Brownfish) in New Amsterdam (now New York). One of Jan's sons went to New Jersey, and over time Horace's ancestors settled throughout Hunterdon County, New Jersey, and Bucks County, Pennsylvania, where he was born. Before he went to China in 1907, he was a Salem Reformed Church member in Doylestown, Pennsylvania.

Emma (née Kroeger) was born in Germany, and in 1893, as a ten-year-old girl, immigrated to America. Each followed a different path to the Protestant mission center of Yochow (now Yueyang) in Hunan Province. Horace was a respected teacher in the boys school there when, in 1911, Emma arrived to become a nurse at Yochow Hospital. As Horace offered their history, Emma made sure I knew the moment in time of her calling: "When studying to be a nurse, one day while sitting on a garden bench, I heard a voice say to me, 'China, China, China.' I knew it was the voice of the Lord."

Like his daughter Ruth, Horace was a strong, independent person, who loved adventure and thrived on challenge. He'd spent his career rooting for the underdog and cared deeply about the underprivileged. As part of Horace's missionary work, serving as the mission business manager, he'd organized relief in three major famines. Emma, the trained nurse, had already mastered English well enough to teach it to local students while learning Chinese. Love drew them into its whirlwind the night Horace and Emma met, upon her arrival at the mission.

As Emma listened to Horace describe their meeting, she spoke up: "I know the Lord called me to China and his grace was enough for me. But the way to the Lord is a winding path, and in my path he placed Horace. Sometimes the way the Lord leadeth is a mystery. We took our time to get to know each other and to make sure others in the ministry approved. We waited a year and half to marry."

Like Ruth and me, they experienced a rude intrusion on their honeymoon, except instead of artillery shells, theirs was interrupted by the arrival of mumps and measles. Horace contracted both, but he'd married his own nurse! With his health in order, the honeymoon resumed in full vigor because they had four children by the time they were forced to sail to America during the anti-imperialism uprising of 1926.

I felt a moment of perhaps undeserved pride when Horace shared some history I didn't know about Shansi Province: "You were brave to go to the Brethren Hospital there. The greatest loss of missionaries during the Boxer Rebellion happened there. Fifteen members of what they called the Oberlin Band, Christian missionaries from Oberlin College in Ohio, were executed. I heard that men, women, and children were executed by order of the provincial government, probably many of which still live there. It is reported that after the missionaries were murdered, soldiers robbed them, but sympathetic local villagers buried them." Horace recalled standing beside a minister in their missionary compound "in the path of the warlord armies" when his friend was shot dead by the leader of a roving band.

I was relieved to discover we had so much in common to talk about and so many languages in which to discuss it all. We conversed in English, but we had a good bit of fun in Chinese, while Emma and I shared a few amusing observations in German.

"Did you encounter in Pingting the custom of Chinese foot binding?"

When I replied I had seen it, she described her efforts to end the practice: "It was a matter of conscience versus a sin against God. Before Ruth was born, I worked in the remote areas near the mission where foot binding lingered after it was outlawed."

The one time we discussed Judaism was when we spoke of my grandmother and my parents and many others who were being persecuted under the Nazi regime. They abhorred hatred of any kind. Horace and Emma expressed their hopes that someday they would meet my parents and this brutality would be behind us.

I felt at home with my new family and would have been happy to stay longer, but my sense of service forced us to move along to Washington. Already the frantic preparations for the war effort had factories that previously made vacuum cleaners retrofitted to make machine guns. After a two-hour drive we reached Washington DC, and I went directly to Gen. Lewis Blaine Hershey's headquarters. Hershey was President Roosevelt's Selective Service director, and I insisted on speaking to him in person. I must have been pretty persuasive because he agreed, although it didn't do much good. The general confirmed that I would not be called to military service anytime soon because I was not a citizen—and I was technically still a reserve officer in the Czechoslovak army.

There remained the question of a proper medical license. Although the hospital in Long Beach had accepted my credentials, and others would continue to do so, the federal government did not, and most states would not allow me to take their licensing exams without further study in an American medical school.

Because of this, I was not eligible for duty as a physician with the army, navy, or Public Health Service, including the Veterans Administration. Hershey was impressed that I'd come to meet with him personally and told me the need for skilled physicians in America to fill in for those joining the military would continue to grow. As a graduate of a foreign medical school, my only hope, he suggested, was to enroll with the Surgeon General's Bureau of Procurement and Assignment, a wartime agency partnered with the American Medical Association (AMA) that matched medical personnel with military needs.

We returned to McConnellsburg and stayed with Horace and Emma for two months before I found a new position in New York City. On April 28, 1942, I became a resident physician at the West Side Hospital and Dispensary in Manhattan. Ruth found a job at the Presbyterian Medical Center. We spent the spring and summer sharing a small townhouse in Forest Hills with my Czech friend Karel and his wife, Katka. By then Karel, believing his name Schoenbaum was "too German," had chosen a new last name out of the phonebook and was legally renamed K. Charles Sheldon. Although he held two Ph.D. degrees, upon his arrival in New York he took what work he could get; his first job was selling underwear at Macy's. (He became the head of the Czech desk at Voice of America.)

What a wonderful reunion this was, a chance to converse in Czech and reminisce! Before our forced separation three years earlier, we'd shared a long history from our Benešov birthplace to Mánes. We talked about his two brothers, Honza and Franta, along with Franta's wife, Andula, and young son, Honza—all trapped behind in Bohemia. His sister, Anka, with husband, Kamil Neuman, had reached New York, where Kamil was able to reestablish a medical practice. Karel and I were frustrated with our inability to communicate directly with anyone back home as they were considered behind enemy lines. I still corresponded with some Czech friends scattered around the world, but they were also cut off from the source of our concern.

Our general concern significantly increased when the Czech community in New York City was stunned by news reports that a state of civil emergency had been proclaimed in Bohemia and Moravia on May 27, 1942. On that morning an assassination attempt happened on the streets of Prague on the life of Reinhard Heydrich, the infamous Nazi "protector." Details were sketchy, but we all supposed there would be retribution of some kind. Soon we heard the Germans had destroyed Lidice, a small Czech Catholic village outside Prague, because they suspected that some former Lidice residents might have helped with the attack on Heydrich. I felt sure my parents knew about the massacre. Beyond that, even with Karel's contacts, we were unable to learn much more except the attack had involved Czech paratroopers trained in Great Britain.

Within a week the world learned that Heydrich had died from his wounds at Bulovka Hospital, where I'd done my university medical training and where my good friend Vladimir Wagner worked. I wondered what Vláďa knew. It was a good thing the world was rid of this brutal man, but I was haunted by the innocent Czech lives lost in the Nazi payback.

That summer I learned of a new position that would add to my experience and that I hoped would bring me a step closer to full licensing in America. We moved once again, this time to the Midwest, to Lafayette, Indiana, where in August 1942 I became a surgical resident at Lafayette Home Hospital. The hospital name came about in the late 1800s because it started in a house where the community made sure the homeless and destitute were cared for. It was called "The Home for the Friendless." By the time Ruth and I arrived, the hospital had many supporters, and we found the management and the community to be welcoming. Along with my residency I took part-time work in industrial medicine with the Arnett-Crockett Clinic.

While in Lafayette, in the mail I received American Red Cross envelopes three times that included the allowed official correspondence from my parents. Limited to twenty-five words, the one-page German Red Cross forms were relayed via neutral Geneva but were required to pass through the hands of German censors on the way. This International Red Cross process was slow but popular, as it was the lone means of contact with so many people. By the war's end the Red Cross had relayed thirty million messages—three of them from my parents, Arnošt and Olga. The first, dated February 24, 1942, carried a stamp at the form's top and was addressed to our Long Beach address: "We are healthy and confirm your letter of November 23, 1941. With the best wishes for Chick's birthday and . . . to you, from Mother!"

The referred letter was one I wrote after their alarming request in October 1941 to leave Bohemia. My letter was written two weeks before the Japanese attack on Pearl Harbor.

Unlike all the earlier letters signed "Táta," Czech for "Dad," this form was signed with my father's full name, *Arnošt* Germanized to *Ernst* Holzer. At the time it was written, Ruth and I had left California to visit her family before continuing to Washington DC. The Red Cross delayed delivery was four months.

The message from Prague hadn't reached us when Dad wrote a second time, on March 13, 1942; it reached us in July 1942: "Dear children! We hope that you are healthy, which we can also convey from our side. Hopefully, we will soon get good news from you. Our most sincere greetings and kisses, Ernst Holzer."

Elsewhere in a world engulfed by war, in August 1942 the Czechoslovak government-in-exile achieved an important step toward the nation's restoration, should the war be won. British commitments made nearly four years earlier in the Munich Agreement were formally annulled and reported worldwide. One month later Gen. Charles de Gaulle, in his role as the French National Committee representative in London, declared the Munich Agreement invalid from the beginning. The action came late for me and my friends, who were forcibly scattered around the world. It did give me a glimmer of hope for a return to my homeland if, after the Nazis had been done in, there was anything left of it.

While scanning newspapers to see if I could find out what my parents' circumstance might be, I read two articles that made me wish I hadn't. One reported that on November 24, 1942, an American Jewish leader, Rabbi Stephen Wise, president of the World Jewish Congress, held a press conference in New York City to announce news of the Nazis' "extermination campaign." On December 17 the United States, Britain, and ten other allied governments made this news official, feeling confident in the evidence to reveal their knowledge of the Nazi plan to systemically kill all of Europe's Jews publicly. They released a formal declaration confirming and condemning Hitler's extermination policy toward the Jews.

It was a moment when I wondered if civilization would stand or fall. During my helter-skelter days of the Japanese soldiers clashing outside my Pingting window with the guerrilla civil fighting armies of China, I'd been so focused on my misery, I hadn't taken the time to conjure what might be the worst outcome for my parents and relatives. I came face-to-face with a reality that I could never have imagined. Again, Ruth worked to change my depressed outlook with her belief that good would triumph over evil.

As General Hershey predicted, the war created a shortage of physicians. At Home Hospital I worked sixteen-hour days, and often six-day weeks, while also performing preemployment physicals to earn extra money. This was my routine in March 1943, when I got word the procurement service, the wartime military agency partnered with the American Medical Association that matched medical personnel with military needs, had turned up an intriguing possibility with British-owned Balfour Guthrie Company, Ltd. The company was managing South American oil fields to supply fuel to Allied forces.

By 1943 the entire production of crude oil coming from the company's field in Los Lobitos, Peru, was going into the war effort. The oil field maintained Lobitos Hospital to care for its ten thousand workers. Usually there were two American surgeons on staff, but the assistant surgeon had just resigned. The company was eager to fill the position, but the U.S. State Department was in no hurry to issue a passport to this alien doctor without a license. Once again, I had no choice but to wait.

As the wait continued, I received another Red Cross note from my father dated March 26, 1942: "We have been without your news for a long time and hope that all our messages reached you. Otherwise everything the same . . . Wholeheartedly greeting and kissing you." The message had originated from the German Red Cross, was sent to the International Red Cross, and then was passed on to the American Red Cross. It bounced from my last known address in California to New York and finally to Indiana, the Lafayette Red Cross, where it was postmarked October 18, 1943. I received it a year and a half after it was written. When I saw the last postmark on the envelope, my heart split open. It was exactly two years after my parents' ill-fated desperate request for a Cuban visa, hoping the island nation of Cuba would welcome them with a visa. The thought triggered my depression again as I fought back an unrealized dream of them disembarking at the port of Los Angeles with a joyful reunion for me and their first meeting with Ruth.

I still held hope they were alive, but with news from Europe of atrocities against Jews, I could not put my worries away in a safe place. No other notes were arriving, and I could only hope I'd be reunited with my parents. It was up to an uncertain "fate," as my mother described in her last handwritten note: "We wish from the bottom of our hearts and souls to be united with you, but we will have to leave it to fate to decide that we should see each other again." I was still waiting for any news from my parents when a breakthrough occurred, the one that ensured I would never have to seek any special exception to alien status. On April 27, 1944, in the county of Tippecanoe, Indiana, I received my certificate of naturalization. As Oswald Alois Holzer, I became a United States citizen. By then Ruth was in her third trimester of pregnancy. The accomplishments, citizenship, and natural pregnancy meant there would soon be three American citizens living in our small Lafayette home.

With swollen pride and belly, Ruth watched me swear allegiance and receive a small Stars and Stripes flag. The picture on my sanctioning document shows a somber, overworked man with uncharacteristic bags under his eyes. Bad photograph aside, I was an official citizen of the Land of Opportunity, where anything seemed possible if you took the initiative to succeed.

Afterward, while celebrating, as we sat in our tiny garden drinking Ruth's freshly brewed tea, I expressed my feelings as the newest American in Indiana: "For so long, I felt as though I'd been drowning and all of a sudden someone saved me. I'm free to speak my mind. I will probably do this in English, but if I want, I can use Czech, something my ancestors were forbidden to do for hundreds of years in their own native land. I will fulfill the promise of this nation."

Ruth's face lit up as she saw my commitment. "No one saved you," she said. "You did this yourself. You earned this astonishing gift as generations of immigrants before you who have come here full of hope for a brighter future. This is the promise of citizenship. You are no longer second class; you are an American able to enjoy equal rights and human dignity. But with the benefits of free speech, voting, and protection from deportation, you must contribute to your new nation. You can't be an observer but must be an active participant in civic life. This is the price of your new citizenship." Following what sounded reminiscent of a speech from my immigration officer, she stood up and then paused to make sure I gave her my full attention until she was finished. She did this so well. "I suspect that as you start afresh, you will never lose sight of what will always be your homeland. I've never lost sight of China, where I breathed my first breath on the shore of Dongting Lake. China's people and places are always in my heart. Never hide your pride in who you are or where you came from. I hope you will find the real bequest of being American—not just tolerance but full acceptance. We exist equally before the law—free to be ourselves."

This was an exhilarating time. The Allies liberated Rome in early June, and two days later our troops charged onto the beaches of Normandy. At last they could drive the Germans out of France and chase them back across the Rhine. The war wasn't yet over, but I knew I'd been right about its outcome. I was even more thrilled on June 26, when Ruth gave birth to our first child, Thomas Lequear Holzer—the first Holzer born outside Bohemia. We called him "Tommy."

Now I was not only an American; I was the father of an American. Ruth chose his middle name, Lequear, to honor a family that traced its American history to the 1600s, with a long line of Thomases in the lineage that Horace had described. I wanted Thomas to honor the name of Tomáš Masaryk, the first president of Czechoslovakia. The reference wasn't clear to our American friends. Most people assumed we named our son after Republican presidential candidate Thomas Dewey because Tommy was born on the opening day of the Republican National Convention.

All that remained to complete my rebirth as an American was to be able to contribute my medical training to the war effort. Nothing stood in my way except the hospital where I worked. The management found me so valuable, especially at a time when many other doctors were already in the military, that they wrote to the Selective Service System and requested a draft deferment on my behalf. Their prevailing wisdom was that I'd need a complete year of study at an American medical school to be fully licensed, so right now I could be nothing more than a run-of-the-mill private anyway and they needed my help. But I hoped otherwise.

I made my case to hospital management and the draft authorities, and both agreed the Los Lobitos position was the best way for me to serve my new country and military. I was assigned to the "Civilian and Industrial Use" category of physician procurement. My new status as an American allowed me to obtain the required paperwork. I was reclassified by the Local Draft Board #275, Los Angeles County, in Long Beach, from 2A to 1A. I received from George Dewey in Washington my release based on the request of the Indiana chairman of the Procurement and Assignment Service for Physicians. When I read his request to Dewey, I became emotional, and I realized I could at last serve in a meaningful way.

"Doctor Oswald Holzer, Home Hospital, Lafayette, released to accept the essential position. Clearance for him is urged in view of faithful service to date and of his repeated efforts to enter service in Armed Forces as Commissioned officer. Home Hospital also supports us." By winter's end our little family was on the move again.

Blond and blue-eyed Tommy was five months old when we left Indiana for our newest adventure. It was January 1945. We traveled to New York City, where we boarded the Silver Meteor express train for a twenty-four-hour ride to Miami. As we sat in a compartment getting ready for lunch, a group of fifty uniformed Italian war prisoners marched through to the dining car. Before their U.S. prisoner of war incarceration, they appeared to have been paratroopers as they were attired in well-worn uniforms of stone-colored camouflage fabric with dark apple green and brown. As they passed my seat, I heard one whistling "Rosamunda—Roll Out the Barrel." A passenger near us speculated they'd been captured in North Africa and "lost the war because of too many second tenors."

Their guard saw to it that these prisoners were fed before the passengers, which didn't sit well with me when I thought of their support of Hitler. I recalled the Italians held near Benešov during World War I. Mostly, I was irritated that they were being treated so well. My wife and son deserved to eat first, but I behaved myself.

We spent three days in Miami enjoying the beach and flew by Pan Am Clipper to Colombia. On the way we stopped in Havana, Cuba, and then made an unscheduled layover in Kingston, Jamaica. The clipper was grounded because, at our final destination in Colombia along the Magdalena River, extensive flooding mixed with tree logs made a river landing impossible. Although I held an American passport, the immigration authorities in Kingston interrogated me as if I were a German once they realized I'd been born in the old Austro-Hungarian Empire. This experience turned out to be pleasant because as long as the questioning continued, the sympathetic stewardesses kept bringing me unlimited Planter's Punch made with limes, nutmeg, and rich, dark rum.

After more delays, with stops in Cali and Barranquilla, we reached Peru in a DC-3, and I began my assignment as assistant surgeon for Lobitos Oilfields, Ltd., in a modern hospital. I worked an easy and routine schedule from nine in the morning until four each afternoon. We lived on the Lobitos oil field in a clean two-bedroom house right on the beach and didn't even mind the regular earthquakes—about five each week, usually late in the afternoon. Ruth spent her days with young Tommy, and in the evenings we enjoyed the tropics. Lobitos was a town developed at the end of the nineteenth century for the petroleum industry. A Scottish firm based in Santiago de Chile had led the development, but by the time I arrived, it was a public company, of which a subsidiary of Standard Oil of New Jersey owned half. Not only did the fields produce oil; the town had a deepwater port for large ships to transport the oil to refineries. Ocean cruise liners visited the port, and it was reported that the prince of Wales and Prince George of England had docked on their way to the World Expo in Buenos Aires, Argentina, fourteen years before we arrived.

Because of its history, the town and surrounding area developed into a British and American colony that leased land from the Peruvian government. We made friends with other international staff—British, American, Peruvian, and Columbian—all on assignment to help end the war with an Allied win.

Working conditions in the oil fields were often hazardous as men drilled well sites thousands of feet into the earth next to the older producing fields. Others ran production rigs under steamy conditions. The oil wells pumped, and the refineries worked at full capacity. The results gave us doctors something to do. Ships loaded with vitally needed fuel steamed across the Pacific daily. It was gratifying to realize that my work was at last a service to the Allies as they completed the last strokes in erasing the Nazis from the map of Europe. Hitler's final, frantic gamble failed as the Americans and British beat back his army at the Battle of the Bulge. By late April the Russian Red Army marched into Berlin.

I had two regrets during that thrilling spring. I was sorry when President Roosevelt died a few weeks before Germany surrendered. He deserved to see it through. My other regret was that the coward Hitler managed to shoot himself in the head before he could be captured and forced to answer to humanity for his crimes. None of this kept us from celebrating on May 8 as our new president, Harry Truman, declared Victory in Europe Day. I wondered what my parents knew and where they were.

I learned via the radio that the liberation of Prague had begun three days before May 8 with an attempt by the Czech resistance to end the German occupation. The uprising started with armed resistance fighters, ethnic Czech residents of Prague, who took back radio buildings and broadcast a call to the Czech nation to rise up and build barricades in Prague. The Czechs tore down or painted over the German-language road and store signs and attacked any German they saw. They erected hundreds of obstacles and surrounded German garrisons throughout Prague. The rebellion lasted for more than three days, ending with a cease-fire on May 9, the day the Russian Red Army arrived. Around seventeen Czechs and a thousand German soldiers had been killed by then. The American Third Army under the command of Gen. George S. Patton was in Czechoslovakia near Plzeň (Pilsen) and could have liberated Prague, but a political arrangement was made so that this highly symbolic act could be carried out by the Russians.

The war wasn't over, as the Japanese refused to accept their situation. American troops had liberated the Philippines and swept the Japanese off island after island across the Pacific. Now we were on their doorstep, in Okinawa, and the Imperial Army fought wildly for each inch of ground. While our weary troops in Europe toasted victory, they knew they could soon be headed to the Pacific to invade Japan. If the Battle of Okinawa was any preview, an invasion of the Japanese mainland would be the most brutal battle of the war.

I got my transfer of duty from the company in July and was reassigned to Ecuador as a surgeon for Anglo-Ecuadorian Oil-fields, Ltd. Subject to the performance of my duties, according to my contract, I was to be paid "four hundred dollars in U.S. currency per month, along with suitable board and lodging save and except laundry and other like personal expenses." The contract called for withholding 5 percent of my salary each month prior to consideration after a year whether I would affiliate as a "subscriber to the Institute of Social Welfare in Ecuador." I was familiar with that type of system, as it was devised for Mexico during the early 1940s by a famous Czech mathematician and actuarial expert, Emil Schoenbaum, who, as a Jew, had sought safe harbor in Ecuador. Emil was an uncle to my good friends Karel and Franta Schoenbaum and a friend of my father.

By the time we set out for Ecuador, Ruth was six months pregnant with our second child, due in October 1945. We drove in a station wagon along the coast to Lima, Peru. In the desert between the Andes and the Pacific Ocean, trucks had left enough trails in the sand that we could follow their route. As we covered the desolate area, clouds of dust rose behind us as short paved sections of road barely existed in the valleys and most driving was on hard sand.

From Lima we boarded a Norwegian freighter to Guayaquil. It was a pleasant three-day trip, as there were six other passengers on board, and we sat at the captain's table for all our meals. Next we took a narrow-gauge railroad from Guayaquil to La Libertad. There the oil company's car picked us up and took us to the Campamento Minero de Ancón oil field in Ecuador. The oil fields were located in the Santa Elena Province, near what originally was born as an oil camp called then the "parish Ancon." The British had drilled their first oil well there the year I was born, 1911. Workers came from all over the country, as the oil helped the British during World War I, and then the company stayed on afterward. The level of activity in Ancon had grown to host first-run movies at a theater that showcased films before they even arrived in Quito or Guayaquil.

The oil fields were near Salinas, where America had a presence pertinent to the war. During its prime there were twenty thousand U.S. soldiers at Salinas Army Airfield, fifty thousand in Talara Army Airfield, Peru, and twenty thousand on the

Galapagos Islands, along with the land iguanas. These three air bases were primary for the defense of the South American coast and Panama Canal against Axis powers submarines. In 1945 there were some two hundred men at each base, mostly maintenance crew.

We settled in a house high on a cliff overlooking the ocean named for peace, the Pacific, (*mír* in Czech) and started our new household. The oil company arranged for a young Ecuadorian woman named Maria to help Ruth at home, and over time little Tommy became bilingual. Our house, provided by the business, was about four miles from Salinas's airbase, which we frequently visited. We enjoyed the casual nature of the officers' club, where no one wore formal military attire with insignia but usually sported shorts and casual shirts.

We were eating in the officers' club on August 6, 1945, when word arrived of the atom bomb dropped on Hiroshima. Most people weren't sure how to react, as news reports were slow to provide much detail. It was apparent there was an enormous loss of Japanese lives by this bomb that had been, to that point in time, unknown to us. Leaning over our table, an officer friend whispered, "In one fell swoop, it looks like this long war might be ending." I was ready.

The next day, as we sat in the club again, we saw the Ecuadorian commanding general, dressed in his fancy uniform and in the company of his staff, marching toward us. When the delegation arrived, everybody jumped up and buttoned their casual shirts to appear more presentable. The ranking American officer, a major, dressed in shorts and shirt without any insignia, greeted the general. After niceties were exchanged and drinks offered, the general asked the major what he knew about the atomic bomb. Nobody knew at the time that the United States's *Enola Gay* airplane had dropped the first atomic bomb used in warfare on the city of Hiroshima. Ruth and I sat nearby, listening to learn more.

Hearing no real answers, the general stood up and spoke with a booming voice: "I am officially requesting the United States give one or two bombs to the Ecuadorians to drop on Peru." Ruth and I tried not to laugh. When the general and the major looked our way, we decided it was time to leave the club.

Peru and Ecuador were technically allies. But in 1941 the Peruvians and Ecuadorians declared war against each other. The skirmish was caused by a coastal town in northern Peru and southern Ecuador that changed hands frequently because of imprecise mapping left over from Spanish Colonial times. After World War I the United States had all kinds of surplus equipment, along with a yacht it had borrowed from the Vanderbilt family and used for coastguard duty. They changed the color of it and painted it battleship gray. They put a few naval guns on top of it and painted the shiny brass railings and the mahogany railing on the deck. After the war they tried to give it back to the Vanderbilt's, but the family didn't like the changes, so the U.S. government considered it surplus and gave it to Ecuador. They brought it to Guayaquil and anchored it in the Guayas River. It became the Ecuadoran navy flagship. It sat in the river, and sailors periodically scrubbed the deck and shined the metals. They changed it from an oil-burning ship to a wood-burning ship. They threw logs under the boilers to get it ready for the next war with Peru.

When the 1941 war broke out, they were going to shell the Peruvian coast from the ship. They put a few more logs under the boilers. When the steam pressure came up, they tried to move it, and it wouldn't budge. For years they'd thrown the ashes from the boat overboard, and it was sitting in its own ashes. They tried to move it, but the bottom stayed in the ashes. The hull was rusted all the way through, and the top went down in the deeper water. This was the end of the Ecuadoran navy, and the battle ended. I'm not sure how accurate this action story was, but the major who answered the Ecuadoran general's question about the bomb had told me this tale a few weeks earlier over a few drinks at the officers' club. His purpose of telling me the story was because the 1941 Peruvian army had used a battalion of Czechoslovak manufactured tanks, as he described it, in "the longest-running armed conflict in the Western Hemisphere." It appeared from the general's question the skirmish was still considered unresolved.

Shortly after the atomic bomb request episode, and following the second bomb dropped on Nagasaki, we celebrated v-j Day at the club in Salinas. There was a vivacious and noisy party at the officers' club and another celebration with riotous laughter at the oil fields. It was about then that most base activities in Salinas were deactivated.

At the time no one knew the extent of the bomb's effects on civilians. No one questioned it or the second bomb dropped on Nagasaki three days later, when, on August 14, 1945, President Truman proclaimed Victory over Japan Day. Those brave American troops in Europe and across the Pacific were able to celebrate instead of heading into another battle in which thousands, perhaps millions, would have perished. (How fortunate we are that those days in August 1945 remain our singular experience of nuclear war.)

In 1945 electronic communication hadn't advanced far. No twenty-four-hour news channels reported stories of the millions of displaced citizens wandering throughout Europe and the world. I got much of my news from grainy black-and-white weekly newsreels at the air base theater. That's where I saw General Eisenhower's soldiers free the remaining emaciated concentration camp victims, human beings with vacant eyes dressed in striped uniforms, sitting stunned in the stench of surrounding dead bodies, dumbfounded that they had survived. I saw on the film soldiers setting fires, destroying those horrific places where countless humans had been gassed, shot, or starved. Showcasing Germany's organized carnage, corpses of people burned alive in furnaces filled the screen. The film did not deliver the stench of death, but it must have been overwhelming. Appalling as it was, the truth was at last being told as people all over the world saw those newsreels. "A man hardened by the blood and shock of war seems appalled by these unbelievable sights" was how the narrator described Eisenhower. With tears filling her eyes, Ruth pulled at my arm to get me to leave. "I'm afraid you'll see someone you know," she whispered. But I couldn't move. I needed to know what happened after I left my homeland. Despite my anguish over my parents' disappearance since their last letter to me in late 1941, I stayed until I couldn't stand to watch anymore.

Through all we'd experienced, I never stopped thinking and worrying about my family and my friends back home. So I carried on even as we all learned more about what had happened. Long before we saw those ghastly newsreel images, the international press had reported that Hitler was exterminating human beings by any means possible. I remember one evening in Indiana, when Ruth and I sat by the radio in our living room as President Roosevelt spoke about his hopes for a better world after the war. He warned that the criminals in Germany and Japan responsible for the slaughter of civilians would be punished not only because they deserved it but as a warning to others that these crimes must not be repeated. Then he revealed something that stopped me from breathing. He disclosed that the Nazis were carrying out the "wholesale, systematic murder of the Jews of Europe," and he called it "one of the blackest crimes of all history." I squeezed my beloved wife's hand, and I'm afraid I pressed harder than I should have, but she did not make a peep. She knew what I was thinking.

Even after the fighting stopped, there was little information from abroad concerning the millions of missing persons. Horrifying images, however, were all around us—from bloody battles to the stunning liberation of the concentration camps. Uncle Bill wrote: "We can only hope that possibly sometime later some of our dear ones who are missing will show up, but the prospects are not encouraging."

We were still in Ecuador in early fall 1945, when I received a letter from Aunt Válda Mařík sharing what she knew about the outcome of most of my extended family.

20

The Letter That Changed Everything

August 1945

As the Second World War came to a close in the reborn Czechoslovakia, the complicated transition period from war to peace began. The people of western Czechoslovakia, those whose lives weren't cut down, had lived under Nazi tyranny the longest of any in occupied Europe. I wished I could have been in the Sudetenland region when they greeted U.S. general George Patton Jr.'s Third Army. Patton's soldiers put an end to the misery I'd first witnessed in late 1938 as a Czechoslovak soldier.

Newscasts in Ecuador informed me of chaotic conditions. Images of German soldiers retreating on foot, bicycle, and horseback gave me hope. Retribution soon began, with Czechoslovakia indiscriminately expelling ethnic German populations. I felt irresolvable anger for what the Germans had done, so when I heard of the brutal treatment of the persons who'd endorsed such horrific actions on us, I felt little remorse.

What I wanted most was news from home, even details of the tragic face of war. The day the first letter arrived was a day like most, the end of a workday signaled by a siren screeching through the humid air. Alerted by the sound, the few remaining workers streamed through the oil field gates on their way home after a shift. The need to produce oil in support of the American war effort had at last ended, making my days numbered there as the chief surgeon for the Anglo-Ecuadorian Oilfields.

As I walked to my car, I imagined my Ruth and her lightly

freckled arms resting on her pregnant belly waiting at home for my return. Her red hair blew in the breeze as she called out from the porch, like she did each day, "Time to go, Maria." With a second child due to enter the war-ravaged world in two months, we both appreciated Maria's help, the caregiver and maid provided by Anglo-Ecuadorian Oilfields, Ltd.

While I drove home, I thought about our long journey together, starting in Peking, where we fell in love and married. It continued to Shanghai; Long Beach, California; New York City; Indiana; the Lobitos Oilfields in Peru; and now Ecuador, where our love grew stronger each day.

After I parked the car and walked the narrow shell path to the house, I heard the screen door slam as Maria came out of the tiny house overlooking the Pacific Ocean. Unnoticed, I stopped to watch as she held my blond son, fourteen-month-old Tommy, on her sturdy hip. Their skin colors contrasted sharply, like the swirl of chocolate in a yellow cake mix. Tommy squealed with joy as Ruth took him in her arms and perched him on her protruding middle.

"Maria, my sweet, you can go home. Valdik will be back any minute." With the setting sun reflecting in her steel-blue eyes, Ruth paused, gathering her limited Spanish. "I can't wait to show him the letter from Czechoslovakia."

My heart raced as I saw Ruth gaze at the turquoise of the ocean. Then, abruptly turning to Maria, she flashed her luminous toothy smile as she gave the Ecuadorian woman a warm goodbye hug.

"Mañana, mi Tomás," Maria said, squeezing little Tommy's ample cheeks before disappearing in the other direction down a path laden with giant pink hibiscus blossoms.

As they entered the house, Tommy grinned and, to Ruth's delight, at full volume repeated "*mañana.*" Not wanting them to know I'd been watching, I waited awhile before I opened the rickety screen door and greeted them with my usual, "I'm home!"

I reached for Ruth and folded her into my arms, and she kissed my dark curls and cheek. Each time she touched me, sparks flowed like electricity through my blood. At the sight of my pipe smoke swirling around his mother, Tommy reached up to be held. I leaned down, tickling the boy's bare tummy until he gave way to a giggly pile on the spotless plank floor.

Ruth took out the envelope from her pocket, showing me the familiar handwriting of my Aunt Válda. I felt my stomach lurch. With words meant to soothe, Ruth looked deep into my eyes. Being near her made my senses come alive. "I know you're afraid, but this may be the answer you've been waiting for. No matter what the news is, I'm here for you."

She placed the letter in my hand along with a finely carved jade letter opener, a memento of our time in Peking. "Why don't you go out on the porch and read it? We'll stay inside so that you can have some quiet."

My chest hammered with anxiety as I walked out, took a deep breath of air infused with the light smell of the salt spray, and then sat on a bleached wicker chair facing the wild waves of the Pacific. My eyes went back and forth from the vast space stretching into the horizon to the envelope. Dark clouds were building over the ocean with a threat of a looming storm. A few times my index finger slid little by little across Aunt Válda's name, written above the return address. I waited several minutes before slicing the envelope open. It held five handwritten pages from Aunt Válda and a sealed envelope with my father Arnošt's recognizable script: *Můj drahý Valdíku* (My dear Valdik). Seeing dad's writing made my heart beat fiercely.

Aunt Válda's envelope bore a newly issued Czechoslovak stamp; my father's envelope was tan and plain, without any stamps or marks. I'm not sure why, but I chose to read Aunt Válda's letter first. The last time I'd seen my aunt, her husband, Jaroslav, and their two sons, Jiří and Pavel, was in May 1939 at their home in Neveklov, days before I'd escaped to China. I'd walked the entire way from Prague along winding roads, through spruce forests, and across potato fields. When she realized I was there to say goodbye, she'd fed me a sumptuous meal, a memory that stayed with me everywhere I'd gone over the following years.

With eyes beginning to mist, I read Válda's words aloud, welcoming the longed-for sound of my native Czech.

August 5, 1945

Dear Valdik!

I was tremendously happy when dear Hanicka wrote about how well you are doing and that you are already even a father of a one-year-old sonny. It seems unbelievable when I realize that this makes me a Grand Aunt already. I am looking forward that you will send, on the first occasion possible, photos. I already know your dear wife a little bit from a picture, but some newer pictures would please me very much. As soon as I have pictures of our boys, I too will send them to you. I and Jaroslav prefer not to let ourselves be immortalized. The war has taken a number of years off our lives, and the sorrows did not contribute to our beauty. But nothing can be done. Even if one worried to death, one couldn't change the reality, and so one cannot but to reconcile with fate. I imagined the end of the war would be completely different. Even though I was trembling for the lives of my loved ones, I nevertheless never allowed myself to think that something could happen to them. I am using the first opportunity to report some news about us, which you probably must be awaiting with great anticipation . . . I want to brief you shortly on what transpired here in those six years of war . . .

Your parents left in April of 1942 for the Theresienstadt [Terezín] ghetto, but shortly thereafter they were deported to no one knows where. We received a single card from them, from their journey to the east. They went to the transport bravely. Unfortunately, I couldn't even say goodbye to them since by that time Hitler already banned us from traveling, but I heard this from several acquaintances. Your father was allegedly in a good mood. Maybe that's why I was deluding myself that surely nothing could happen to him, a man of such life experience, and both he and your mother would succeed in escaping. This fixed idea accompanies me constantly, and I can't stop hoping that they will contact us from somewhere far away.

Uncle Rudi and Aunt Olga were in Theresienstadt until October of last year, when they wrote to me last. Aunt Olga allegedly still looked well then, Uncle Rudi had been sick for a long time, supposedly he had angina pectoris in an advanced stage, and I was thus worried for him. Your Uncle Leo left Theresienstadt on September 25 of last year, alone. He held such a position there that no one would believe that he too would be transported. He was the chief of housing. Supposedly, he was content with his employment, looked well but in the end must have been leaving in a terrible mental state. My heart is bleeding when I remember all that he must have gone through. There, your cousin Hanuš got pneumonia, inflammation of pleura in April of last year but was able to survive . . .

Grandmother, the poor thing, died after a three-month stay in Theresienstadt, but that you surely know. I mourned her a long time, but when I learned about the suffering of old people in Terezín, I wished her that peace. Should I get the urn that was buried in T., I will have it transferred to Benešov. It is uncertain since one of the Nazi beasts took it upon himself to empty all the ashes into River Labe before the end of the war. It would be a miracle if the urn remained untouched . . .

The Nazis took over ninety villages around here for military training ground. We were given such a short notice that we couldn't even find a place to deposit everything. We were moving—almost pauperized and with no recompense since I am a Jewess—here to Božkov by Mnichovice. To top it all up, Jaroslav was in July 1944, last year, called up to labor, respectively, internment camp in Tvoršovice and me, two months later, to Hagibor a similar establishment. There I spent eleven weeks, and then I was transferred to the Jewish hospital, where I allowed myself to be operated on. I resolved to have the surgery only in order to escape further deportation. The surgery went well, but several days later the wound started to fester and my life was in danger. In the meantime Jirka was gone too, he was, together with other half-bloods, dragged away to Upper Silesia, and when the front approached, they were transferred to Harz. Poor Pavel, he was alone the whole time. He was kicked out of school because he could only attend school up to the age of fourteen, and then he went for an apprenticeship in a grocery in Mnichovice, just to tuck himself away somewhere from the Nazis . . . Believe me, I had not even hoped that we would all meet up again, but then on the eighth of May that happy day came, and we met together again. Dear Jaroslav came back broken, both mentally and physically, and is slowly recovering at home. Jirka is good; he is much stronger and looks great. Pavel has become a lanky fellow, as tall as Jaroslav. I haven't changed much . . . Until the end of the war, we had no inkling whatsoever what those Nazi beasts had been doing with our people, and all in all, if the rescue had not come yet, we all had been predetermined to perish by the same means.

I'd had no idea my grandmother Marie had perished nor about the transports of any of the others. I continued reading reports of what my aunt had learned about various relatives while yearning for more about my parents. It was still a mystery to me how she'd received the letter she'd enclosed from my father. At last I saw the reference I'd been waiting for.

Before his departure for the transport, your Daddy left an envelope with us. Written on it was: "Open only if I do not return." Jaroslav did not want to allow me to open the envelope, but a few weeks ago I did so anyway. Inside there was a letter for you and another one for your mother, which naturally I left unopened. I'm sending your father's letter to you. Enclosed in his envelope there was a list of your parents' things and where they are stored away. Almost everything is with some Miss Nenadálová, daughter of the janitor of the apartment house where they last lived. I didn't know her at all but still sought her out and told her that you wish that I gradually send you the things and therefore I have to take them. She was making all kinds of excuses . . .

I cared nothing about "things," so I stopped reading my aunt's letter. Taking care not to disturb the seal with my father's cursive handwriting with the three Czech words in blue ink: *Můj drahý Valdíku* (My dear Valdik), I gently sliced the top of the second envelope to remove a single sheet of paper dated April 21, 1942. Clearing my throat, I read aloud the first words I'd received from my father in more than three years:

My dear boy!

Today we are leaving for an assembly point so that in three or four days we can follow the fate of those unfortunate people who have been, since last October, gradually chased out of their homes and sent to concentration camps, robbed of everything they had. This happened to us as well, and we had to leave the ground floor and its furnishings, the flat that had always been such a cozy home to us.

Carrying only the necessary clothes, we are setting out on a journey, not knowing the day of our return or when and where we might be united again. I am not certain whether I will get to see you again, so I decided to write these lines as my goodbye to you.

I deeply regret that I wasn't able to know Ruth and your family life. I wish both of you much, much happiness.

I had a lot of failures in my life. However, I have tried, when possible, to spare you from my shortcomings and help you to become a doctor, a profession you always sought. You have always been a good boy, and we are proud of you. I wish for you to find full satisfaction in your profession. I also wish that your profession of curing doesn't just become a source of wealth for you but that you yourself become a benefactor to the suffering humanity.

Should my dear wife, your mother, be left without me, I implore you to remember the great sacrifices she always made for you and to take care of her the way she deserves. She has a small pension that she herself earned and secured, thus her means of living. She will never be a burden to you. I myself don't have much property; everything is communal. Therefore, I don't want you to ask for your property share from your mother during her life. In case we don't see each other, everything will go to you. Uncle Jaroslav Mařík of Neveklov or Cousin Robert Fischer should give you a detailed list of the property. You then can decide how to liquidate the inheritance. I have one more wish in that respect. If, after all the expenses, you are left with at least 30,000 Czech crowns, please pay my brother-in-law, Rudolph Winternitz, or his descendants, the sum of 30,000. For everything he has done for me, I would like to pay my debt to him at this moment. If you can, please fulfill my wishes.

With warm kisses and greetings, I bid you both, you and Ruth, a farewell. I remain,

Your loving Dad

While I read my father's words, aloud I could hear his deep, calming voice coming from the downturned corners of his lips. Even in the face of what might have been an unknown fate to some, I knew when Dad, the old World War I soldier, wrote this, he envisioned the worst prospect laid before him. He would not survive. And then, when he and my mother went to the transport, my protective Dad put on his happy, all-will-be-fine face that he'd tried to maintain throughout his "journey" while I was on mine.

Once I stopped reading, the sound of his disembodied voice vanished, and my pulse raced. The images I'd seen of Eisenhower's soldiers walking past emaciated corpses in abandoned concentration camps flooded my mind. Overcome with surging nausea, I tried to recall his voice by reading the first lines, but all I heard was my own.

I thought about how Aunt Válda stated he'd also written a letter to my mother and wondered if I should have hope for her. Dad believed he faced death, but surely, this gentle woman did not. At once the images from the newsreels of female corpses flooded my mind. All I could think of was the sound I'd heard one midnight long ago as a child—my mother's brittle sobs, when my father was missing, lost in the tide of battle in World War I.

As my hand wiped away a tear that crept down my cheek, I sensed a frightful disconnection between how I felt and thought. I'd found the answer I so desperately needed but feared.

I returned to his final wish—"that your profession of curing doesn't just become a source of wealth for you but that you yourself become a benefactor to the suffering humanity"—and read and reread it several times. These were the words of my decent and principled father. No one else in the face of sure death except my irreproachable, self-sacrificing dad, would choose to sit down to write an altruistic wish for the suffering humanity—those who would remain on this earth long after he was gone. His soothing voice, whispered in my ear, once again spoke my name. It was Dad's wish for the kind of man I should become.

21

Dealing with the Outcome

1945–1952

Awash in the unimaginable, I might never have left the porch had it not been for Tommy's cries beckoning me back into the house. It jarred me to the reality: I was half a world away from my devastated homeland and had no doubt my parents were dead. They'd never met Ruth and didn't even know they had a grandson. I wasn't sure I could face Ruth.

Since we'd first met, she worked to convince me that good is stronger than evil. With complete faith, she believed that good could obliterate evil. She would say, "Knowledge helps in times of such great oppression." I'd held onto her thin thread, clinging to hope for a conclusion that was not to be. For six years I'd lived a life terribly excited by fear, assuring myself that some all-powerful God would take care of the people I loved. As it turned out, my life became cruel. Six years was a long time to have been away from my parents, and now I was an orphan and a displaced person. My fear of no home to return to was real. Terrified of what lay ahead, my life at thirty-four seemed pointless.

As she'd done from the first moment I was drawn in by the otherworldly light around her face, Ruth did not disappoint. Without words she comforted me with constant expressions of love. Affectionate hugs, thick coffee, and phonograph music, featuring Dvořák and Smetana, both jolly and melancholic, filled our small house. To that she added her steady hand touch on my hunched shoulders. While I couldn't face returning to work, she took Tommy for long walks to give me privacy, time I desperately needed. They'd return with hibiscus flowers that she placed within my sight. After a few days, while Tommy was taking a nap, she augmented her silent presence with gentle insight in an attempt to help me look forward.

"After the war our choices need to address a new world order—a challenge for how to move on," she said. "We can't choose what haunts us. I see what the message is for our lives today. The choice that matters is how we deal with the outcome, whether we overcome or succumb to the situation endured."

With a quivering chin, she took a deep breath and sat beside me on the couch. She held my hand as the rapid tapping of rain punctuated her words: "What might have happened or not happened will never be known. Do we dwell on what can go wrong or think of what can possibly go wrong? In the end, as your father asked of you, we should choose to serve humanity with our talents. Together we can create a meaningful future."

Always gracious, her strong presence kept me stable as I processed an existence I'd never expected and for which I felt immense guilt. Word by word she was a bridge, not a goal. I had to find my own way out of the abyss. There was no immediate remedy. I think she knew rage follows grief, and I was entering the storm.

In the aftermath the days exploded with a mixture of emotions. Flopping around like a pigeon that hit a window, the fleetingness of life consumed me. With no appetite and difficulty sleeping, I tried to cope with my guilt-ridden anger by remaining silent but could not stop the questions. Could I have done more? Was there a chance to rescue them before the brutality escalated? I considered myself a criminal, praying for forgiveness, horrified for the part I might have played. I thought of how my parents must have felt—unsure if they would survive. In the end Hitler knew no mercy. That realization must have hung over them like a black cloud. I received the letter more than three years after they were murdered—deliberately exterminated, gassed or shot in a field. Why had I not sensed their death sentence unfolding? Why was I spared?

I took long solitary walks, yelling and screaming in grief along the isolated beach. On gray-white sand that resembled chalk, I lay facing the sky and looked at the gateway to infinity and wondered if my parents could see me. In my weakened emotional state, I wondered if I walked into the water where the current would take me. One day as I left the beach, I was attacked by a thorn bush, which tangled around me. As I wrestled myself free, I cried out at the untamed waves, "Am I being punished?"

The depravity of what my parents had suffered cut through my soul like a razor. I questioned the purpose of life and the meaning of death and why, if there was a God, he was unwilling and unable to prevent evil? When I did sleep, vivid dreams of my parents created immense anxiety, with my throat closing and having difficulty breathing. When I began to completely withdraw from my family, Ruth placed our squirming little son in my arms. In Tommy I saw the gleam of my mother's eyes and knew I had to keep my parents' memory alive.

I read and reread the letters stored in antique Chinese boxes—my father and mother's words, handwritten five years earlier: "*As soon as emigration from the country is opened again, we will let you know. Therefore, I beg of you once more, please do not take any more steps and do not spend any more money. That way we can all enjoy it all the better and merrier when times allow us to be reunited*"; "*I admit that we were afraid to be a burden on you in a foreign country. We wish from the bottom of our hearts and souls to be united with you, but we will have to leave it to fate.*"

It was the last time they were able to correspond, just weeks before they were deemed a threat to the United States, living in "enemy territory." I thought about how my parents were born and died under tyranny, the last more maniacal than the first. Dragged off to a bloody first world war Dad hadn't chosen, he and my mother were murdered in a second world war for the crime of being Jewish. Continuously running a jerky hand through my hair, I questioned how this could have happened. Could fate have dictated such a cruel plan? Or did it turn out this way because of my ineptitude to save them?

Dealing with the Outcome

As I second-guessed aloud the options in China that had come before me, desperate to find answers, Ruth intently listened. Supporting my arm, she tried to convince me my behavior wasn't something that needed reexamining: "You did the best you could with the information and resources you had at hand. You didn't have the advantage of hindsight and had no way of knowing what would happen next. You're a good human, a wonderful son, who tried your best."

Sitting, then standing, then sitting again, she finally told me that we must accept this horrific outcome as a "warning sign with a purpose": "We are forewarned of evil and will watch for it with both eyes. We'll be an army of two, looking for ways to create a better place wherever we choose to live. We will live not with indifference but will make a difference with love, empathy, and compassion." After taking a deep breath, she went on: "I feel blessed that this can be our choice. Your father's wish recognized your greatest strength. Your medicine bag can be your touchstone. You will do more than cure. You will care."

As I read and reread my father's soul-crushing letter, it became apparent his wish held the answer to quelling my misery. I had to look outside myself.

Within weeks of reading my father Arnošt's last letter, our daughter Patricia was born in the nearby rural parish, Ancon. Honoring a grandmother Patricia would never meet, she was bestowed the middle name Orlík. The name was an appropriate choice as she inherited my mother Olga's artistic talents and temperament.

It wasn't long until our conversations turned to the topic of joining forces in China—Ruth as teacher, returning to her mission field; me as physician, the head of a charity hospital battling contagious diseases and protecting the health of the suffering masses. There seemed no greater need, the largest country on earth reeling from war damage and a society that needed economic advancements to recover. Our interest coincided with a need to return to civilian life, and another consideration was to return to Czechoslovakia. Ruth was supportive of whatever I chose.

Presenting both options to my Aunt Válda, she responded with her concerns: "I read with much surprise your note that you plan to move to Czechoslovakia. I should be happy to have you here. I feel like your mother after our family shrunk so terribly, but I do not want to hide that I am afraid that you might encounter here many inconveniences in this postwar period. I presume that you live in full happiness, and I should suffer if you do not feel comfortable here."

She was right. There was no guarantee that we people who'd been displaced weren't going to have a repeat of the cycle of upheaval. It was too early to return to my homeland, a land where my parents no longer would greet me and Ruth, as they had hoped for in so many letters.

One morning when I awoke, the first words from Ruth's lips felt like an elixir: "The secret of life is the power of hope. What does your intuition say to you today?" An hour later I started corresponding with the United Nations Relief and Rehabilitation Administration (UNRRA) about opportunities in China. UNRRA was the world's first operational international relief organization. Founded in 1943 by forty-four countries, led by the United States, it operated in Europe and Asia, working to repair the world. In Europe, in the aftermath of Nazi persecution, forced labor, German and Allied bombing, and the Holocaust, the agency was trying to piece back the lives of over ten million displaced persons. UNRRA's largest undertaking was to help China recover from the crippling effects of eight years of war. I wanted to be a part of that effort. After some preliminary interviews through the mail, our family of four returned to the United States, settling in until my UNRRA selection with Ruth's parents, living in Rimersburg, Pennsylvania.

To gain UNRRA admittance, I was required to have a personal interview in New York City with the director of UNRRA, the former mayor of New York, Fiorello La Guardia. He had studied my file; when I came in, he asked me if I spoke Czech. When my answer was affirmative, he started talking to me in the Czech language.

He had picked up several languages while soliciting votes from different national minorities in the city of New York. The whole interview took about five minutes, as there was another bunch of interviewees waiting behind me. In April 1946 I was advised that my appointment as general surgeon with UNRRA had been approved. I was appointed to China Field Operations, with my assignments to depend upon the need at the time. To get ready, I attended a course for personnel going to China. This was mostly to learn basic Chinese history and information about the present political situation. After UNRRA learned I had lived in China for a couple of years, I became an instructor.

Once in China, the agency said I'd be named to specific locations by the chief medical officer and warned me that "work would be difficult and the supplies and equipment would be limited." I already knew this would be the case and couldn't wait to return. We decided Ruth would stay at Horace and Emma's house with Tommy and Patty during my anticipated yearlong assignment.

My return to China was under different conditions than my first arrival by ship, with a flight out of Washington in a chartered DC-4. We next flew out of Riverside, California, on an army transport plane via Hawaii to the Far East. It was my willing choice to return to China, as the Japanese forces were no longer the primary antagonist. Without the Japanese at the end of the Sino-Japanese War, there no longer was a need for an "anti-Japanese United Front" between the Communists loyalists to Mao Tse-tung and the Kuomintang regime led by Chiang Kai-shek. The collaboration broke down, and civil war seemed to resume in full force.

As World War II ended, U.S. general George C. Marshall negotiated a truce between the two, but ailments at the base of Chinese society were too significant to ignore. The peasants bore the heaviest burdens of the war. Because of extreme poverty and hardship, the Communists' popularity among the peasantry was gaining ground. Without the presence of Japanese forces, new to the strife were increasing waves of labor strikes in big cities by the Chinese working class. While America hoped for a democratized

China, it faced persistent class eruptions and civil war until one side or the other took control.

My UNRRA work was chiefly in Peking and the North Anhwei (Anhui) Province in east-central China. I organized surgical service at the Peiping Municipal Hospital and was an instructor in a general survey at Pei Ta University. I served as consulting surgeon for the National Health Administration at Wuhu General Hospital, Wuhu, Anhwei Province. While I was in China, I sought out information about people I'd encountered during my first sojourn.

The indestructible Max Engel was still in Peking, and this time he was making a living selling Chinese antique carpets. I bought four rugs from him and inquired where they came from. He changed the subject. They were probably stolen somewhere in the Forbidden City or who knows where. I made an inquiry about Professor Grabau, which led me to believe that he had died of ill health after internment in a Japanese camp. I went to see the man who'd printed our wedding invitations, Mr. Hundhausen, who was still living on his island. When I arrived there, I was shocked. The whole estate was in terrific disorder. There were Chinese running all over the place. His print shop was changed into a dormitory, with about twenty Chinese living there and cooking right in the middle of his office. Sometime before my arrival, he had had a stroke. He had right-handed paralysis and great difficulty talking, but he recognized me. One day, while I was sitting in a rickshaw returning to the language school, a traffic policeman stopped the rickshaw. He rushed over to me. He recognized me, as he used to be a houseboy in the language school before the war, and inquired about the "caring missionary Ruth."

I learned that my friend Arthur Ringwalt, the kind diplomat, had returned to the United States in 1941, before the U.S. war with Japan broke out. He'd been lucky to have scheduled a leave home, figuring the war was coming. I was told that while he was in Washington DC, his taxi driver had turned the radio on to a concert and he heard that the Japanese had attacked our fleet in Pearl Harbor. Arthur was back in China at an American embassy, operating out of a cave at Chungking, but our paths never again crossed.

Another assistant in the Peking U.S. Legation hadn't been so lucky, with his leave scheduled for January 1941. He ended up being interned by the Japanese. The manager of our Western Hills honeymoon hotel in Patachu had been cooperating with the Japanese. When the Chinese returned to Peking in 1945, he was arrested and shot. This kind of retribution against those considered traitors was commonplace.

I stayed in Wuhu close to a year and heard allegations of massive misappropriations of our aid by the Kuomintang and Chinese Nationalists. It was obvious how difficult UNRRA's task had become in the agency's largest single country effort. The man who'd hired me, La Guardia, resigned from UNRRA at the end of 1946. A newspaper quotation before he left troubled me: "Human beings cannot be placed in a deep freezer of indifference, awaiting debates of diplomats and decisions of politicians. This stockpile of human misery cannot be abandoned after UNRRA ceases."

After my work in the interior, I returned to Peking for reassignment, then flew to Shanghai via Tsingtao on December 30, 1946. I stayed overnight because there wasn't a connection to Shanghai. I was supposed to leave on a noon flight but was delayed in the UNRRA office. That plane crashed into a mountain outside Tsingtao on takeoff; everyone was killed. I boarded another plane transporting a marine band from Tsingtao to the French Club in Shanghai for New Year's Eve. Instead of the passengers being joyous, it was a white-knuckle crowd.

By January 1947 the United Nations was cutting back on relief personnel in China and started sending people home. At the end of World War II, our U.S. troops had been heroes to the people of China. Then America added many thousands of troops to occupy and protect the China coast. Many Chinese people became unhappy with this arrangement, and the sentiment changed. Reports suggested those forces supported the Nationalist side with air reconnaissance and transport, which caused further unrest in the turmoil of civil war. Our relief effort was viewed with suspicion, as so many previous foreign initiatives in China had been. UNRRA ceased operations in China in 1947. The civil war led to the collapse of the Nationalist regime and the Communist takeover in 1949, forming the People's Republic of China.

My Shanghai "reassignment" turned out to be "go home." To return, I was offered a flight to San Francisco from Shanghai a number of times, but by then the army transport planes were in pretty bad shape. Quite a few didn't make it across the Pacific. One day on the street in Shanghai, I met my old UNRRA friend Dr. Lester Schultz. He told me he was returning to the States on a boat as an attendant with a U.S. Army colonel who exhibited some psychotic tendencies after drinking too much in China. Schultz was setting up a team of attendants to go with the colonel, so I became an attendant for his trip across the Pacific.

It was a long trip on the USS *Breckenridge* back to Pennsylvania by way of Japan and Hawaii, but I was at last reunited with my family in May 1947. Even before I left Shanghai, I knew that Ruth's and my dream of returning to China was unlikely.

At the end of my UNRRA service, I received a letter and certificate from Mr. Lowell Rooks, director general of the UNRRA, that I believe was written with my father's wish in mind. It was dated May 13, 1947.

Dear Dr. Holzer,

Because of the termination of UNRRA's activities, you are leaving the services of the Administration. You have been a part of the large army of employees whose efforts have allowed UNRRA to pioneer in the field of international agencies, proving beyond any question of doubt the feasibly of the United Nations to operate in concert. You have helped to avert starvation for millions, to restore their health and to give them courage to meet their problems. Your efforts have helped the war-torn nation to make an appreciable start on needed rehabilitation of their national economy which, unfortunately, will require years to complete.

Dealing with the Outcome

For your loyalty and your devotion to the task of helping others help themselves, I personally, am most grateful. I am sure I speak for the unnamed millions who you benefitted by your labors.

I sincerely trust the future may bring you happiness and an opportunity to continue to serve in some capacity making fullest use of your experience.

The certificate that accompanied the letter carried a stroke of serendipity as it mentioned "great work of relieving the suffering and saving lives."

Ruth and I came to accept that our life would be in America. Exactly where was uncertain. After some scouting, I turned up an ideal situation in a seaside suburb of New York City called Bay Shore, Long Island. An elderly physician named George King had a private hospital there and an opening for an associate. I signed on, and we were soon on the move again. We bought our first house ten miles away, in Sayville, with two bedrooms and a full basement on a large lot. It was a block from a beach club, so we became members.

It was sometime during this early period of rebuilding my life that I began to consider myself agnostic. Any small amount of religious conviction I'd had was shattered. In no way did I waiver in my support of Ruth's deep faith—her Christian-based love and compassion for others. We agreed our children were to follow her spiritual lead on our shared commitment to nurture good human beings. My mother always told me that Judaism focuses more on actions than on beliefs. Ruth and I wanted our children to lead an ethical life on the basis of reason and humanity.

On occasion I speculated about whether Ruth's higher being who'd brought us together might also be mine. "It's the eternal question," Ruth supposed, as she gently reminded me that she believed we are all God's children. We discussed what we knew were the organized spiritual practices, beliefs, and worldviews of various religions. We agreed there were great commonalities based on moral values and compassion for others. We knew people who didn't follow any organized religion who lived laudable, compassionate, and just lives.

We were living on Long Island when a letter dated January 17, 1948, arrived from Justin Bennett of the U.S. Department of Justice, Immigration, and Naturalization Service:

> It has been ascertained from the files of the Long Beach Police Department that in January 1942 you filed a complaint with the Bunco Detail against one Gasper Bilo Mendez, a Panamanian, who was then employed as a janitor at the Seaside Memorial Hospital, alleging that he had swindled you out of the sum of $300 in October 1941 in connection with a proposed plan to effect the removal of your parents from Czechoslovakia to Chile through the assistance of an alleged personal friend of Mendez then in the Chilean consular or diplomatic service.
>
> Through roundabout inquiry your wife's uncle, Henry Kroeger, was contacted by mail and your address obtained from him.
>
> Mendez, who has been found an unlawful resident of the United States and subject to expulsion, has applied for suspension of deportation on the basis of having a United States citizen wife and two U.S.-born children, and in connection with such application he is required to establish that he has been a person of good moral character for the past five years. If he knowingly and willfully defrauded you this office would like to have the particulars, which you might specify in an affidavit executed before a Notary Public.

Seven years had passed since I'd fallen for the fraudulent stories of Bilo Mendez. Six years had passed since the murder of my parents by the Nazis. In a letter written to Mr. Bennett in January 1942, Ruth and I went to work as we recounted exactly what had transpired in the fraud. Forty-four ghosts stood beside me as I considered the response.

With Ruth's help, encouraging me to feel my suppressed emotions but not let them take control, I showed no bitterness in my words. I stated my case beyond the loss of money: "The saddest part is that my parents perished in a concentration camp. Whether or not they could at that time have been aided through any channel by me is open to question, of course."

In a world that had denied my family justice and after being "knowingly and willfully defrauded" at a moment of life and death, the concluding paragraph was written without malice: "Though it is not my wish to harm the apparently innocent family involved, by the witness that I have recorded for you, I hope that it may assist you in your efforts to deal with the case justly." To this day I do not know the resolution of the Bilo Mendez case. Ruth assured me there would be justice in the next world.

Like each job, the one in Long Island had its pros and cons. As time went on, there were too many cons, as I seldom got interesting cases but usually got the longest and least desirable shifts. The 1947 winter weather also was rough. Snow blanketed the Northeast, one day burying Long Island under twenty-six inches of snow in sixteen hours. One time I couldn't make it home from the hospital for four days. The severe winter weather was blamed for some eighty deaths.

I started to feel discouraged by the pace of my advancement in America—frustrated enough to at least think about returning to Czechoslovakia. Ruth and I talked about the possibility, but we got no further than that before the Communist Party took political power there in February 1948, after they'd forced the other coalition parties out of the government. Rigged elections followed in May to validate the Communist takeover. Beneš resigned, and his former foreign minister, Jan Masaryk, the son of former president Tomáš Masaryk, died suspiciously. The private business sector was nationalized, and all Czechoslovak life was subject to central control. Thousands suffered harsh treatment or ended up being executed. The free press ceased to exist, and once again an intolerant ideology of a single-party state ruled my homeland. A very small fraction of Czechoslovakia's pre-World War II Jewish community existed and for them, anti-Semitic attitudes continued. The shadow of the Soviet Union and Stalin's dictates placed Czechoslovakia behind closed borders described as the "Iron Curtain."

That ended all thoughts of returning to Bohemia, but it didn't make me any less eager to move on from New York. Then one day I saw an ad in the *Journal of the American Medical Association* (JAMA) that the State Hospital in Chattahoochee, Florida, was looking for a personnel physician. I wrote to the medical director, Dr. William Rogers, and sent him my curriculum vitae. In return he called and requested I present myself in person so he could see how I looked. In June 1948 I drove down some twelve hundred miles to Chattahoochee and met Dr. Rogers and the staff of the Florida State Hospital. Right from the beginning, we hit it right, and Rogers and I became lifelong friends. He talked me into staying, so I didn't even return to Long Island until we made our move. I called Ruth on the telephone, and we decided she could stay there with Tommy and Patty through the summer and enjoy themselves. I took the position of a staff personnel physician at the state hospital and drove my family back when they were ready for Florida sunshine.

The Florida State Hospital was the only mental institution in the state. At that time the hospital had about eight thousand patients and eighteen hundred employees. I was responsible for preemployment physical examinations and keeping the employees in good shape. I was not supposed to have anything to do with the mental patients, but my office was right across the hall from the emergency room for the whole hospital, and I didn't have enough work to keep me busy. So I took on more assignments with the patients, including orthopedic surgery, where I worked with Dr. Eugene Jewett of Winter Park as he perfected the Jewett hip nail, which revolutionized the treatment of hip fractures. Gene and his physician wife, Ruth, became our good friends. I became involved in many interesting cases and new challenges, including work in two big prison camps across the river, in Jackson County. But all that is a story by itself.

The most significant event after our arrival in Florida occurred

18. Tom, Joanie, and Pat Holzer, Melbourne Beach, Florida, ca. 1952.

on December 15, 1948, when our third child was born in Chattahoochee. That month she was the one person admitted by birth
to the mental hospital. We named her Barbara Joan Holzer, nick-
named Joanie. Announcing the event, Ruth described in a letter to
her parents our new baby as "a blue eyed little Blondie, although
her hair has a sheen of red-gold through it. The nurses are all in
love with her and I am afraid I shall have some un-spoiling to do
if I don't get her out soon from the hospital."

At last our family was complete. After working at Chattahoochee for three years, I took over the practice of a retiring doctor in nearby Chipley, Florida, where I remained for a year. As fate
was again due to intervene, through a friend's reference we learned
of a critical need for physicians in burgeoning Brevard County on
Florida's east coast. The idea was to start an independent medical practice in Melbourne, Florida, so in the summer of 1952 I

became the seventh doctor on the Brevard Hospital staff. (Being a "foreign-trained doctor," I was required to wait a year before I could be accepted into the Brevard County Medical Society.)

As a family physician dedicating myself to the pursuit of healing others, I mostly restored lives and welcomed new ones into the world. Our family of five settled on a nearby palmetto-covered barrier island in a cozy Melbourne Beach house one block from the ocean—our only enemy the ubiquitous mosquito. A busybody neighbor, with raised eyebrow when she detected my accent, made sure to tell me German U-boats had sunk a merchant ship off the nearby shore in early 1942. After Ruth clarified my accent was Czech, the old woman proceeded to tell us the rumor that the first European, explorer Juan Ponce de León, set foot in Florida farther south down the island in 1513.

The first night in our house Ruth told me this was where we were meant to be. Blazing pink hibiscus welcomed us home. You could watch fishermen lay out the morning's catch from the brackish, saltwater Indian River or greet rocket scientists on the palm-lined shell streets that glistened in the sunlight, while a few miles to the north America's space age was beginning.

It was a perfect landing place for my escape. Hope seemed eternal in my gifted life.

Epilogue

I ask not for a lighter burden but for broader shoulders.

—Jewish proverb

This story is not over. Fate wrote me—his loving youngest daughter—into Valdik's narrative as a supporting character. From my reconstruction of the scenes of my father's life, it is clear that Valdik took his father's last wish to heart and breathed life into it. Dad never readdressed the choices he had made and didn't let guilt drag him down.

My father devoted his life to being "a benefactor to the suffering humanity," and his retirement was no exception—it was busier and more productive than the prime of most people's careers. After he closed his medical practice in 1974, he established a student health program at Florida Institute of Technology and volunteered for ten years as the director and "Campus Doc," accepting no compensation. With my mother he endowed a chair in genetics research, donated funds for the Holzer Student Health Center, and helped begin their botanical gardens.

While he was busy practicing medicine, Dad served in leadership roles on multiple community boards, including for the chamber of commerce, mental health, and senior housing. He became a fellow in the International College for Surgeons. His myriad

19. Dr. Valdik Holzer with nurse Sue Barge and patient, Florida Institute of Technology, Melbourne, ca. 1982. With permission, Florida Institute of Technology, Melbourne.

awards included one from the Brevard County Medical Society for "performing exemplary service to medicine in the Brevard community." Much of that devoted service was pro bono for the most vulnerable in our community—the poor, the frail, and the elderly. Dad understood the socioeconomic aspects of disease and sought out the poor and gave them free medical care. For all this warmheartedness, I greatly admired my dad. Yet growing up, I knew little of what propelled him to channel emotions into such a positive outcome. Then, at age forty-five, things changed.

During a 1993 visit to my parents at their condo, I overstepped the bounds of our special father-daughter rapport. Like nearly everyone else in America, I'd read about a new Steven Spielberg film called *Schindler's List*, an epic historical drama about a Sudeten German businessman who helped save many of his Jewish factory workers from the Holocaust. Oskar Schindler was an ethnic

German and Catholic who came from Svitavy, in Moravia. Schindler served in the Czechoslovak army, attaining in 1938 the rank of lance corporal in the reserves. Perhaps my father had met him in the army. I thought my father could identify with the film's theme and hoped that seeing it might encourage him to talk about his family's experience, so I invited him to go to the movie with me.

I saw the pain in his eighty-two-year-old face and those eyes that had seen so many things. At a snail's pace he rose from his seat across the dining table from my mother and me. When he reached his full height, with a pale and troubled gaze he spoke in a deep voice, with its still-resonate Czech accent: "No. I will not go with you. It is not a movie that I intend to see . . . ever!"

The memory of my white-haired father, his gray eyes welled with tears, will remain with me always. I felt an overwhelming sorrow and realized I should say nothing more. In that moment my childhood bond was transformed into a grown-up one, and I began to discover my real father. That evening we sat together— just the two of us—as he pried from his heart the memories of the most painful time in his life. I stayed by his side as he used his old Voss typewriter to slowly record the names of the forty-four relatives who had perished in the Holocaust. He also painstakingly listed the names of those who had survived and spent the war in Nazi slave labor camps.

I've called it "Valdik's List" ever since.

Name after name appeared before my eyes in black letters. I was stunned. I knew my father had lost family in the Holocaust, but I'd never understood the scope or the details. These were secrets he'd guarded for a half-century. He might never have shared them if I hadn't been foolish enough to ask if he wanted to see a movie that featured a scene in which ash of the incinerated dead falls like snow from the sky.

As he typed, Dad created a code to explain relationships: *A* for an aunt, *O* for an uncle, *GA* for great-aunt, and so on. With the surnames grouped together, it became clear the victims had disappeared from his father's and mother's families in equal numbers. If he believed he knew how and where someone had died, he wrote the name of the concentration camp—*TZ* for Terezín or *A* for Auschwitz—and added the year of death, almost always 1942. (From 2008 research I learned that on his list my father only had the place of death wrong for two people—his own parents. He thought they had perished at Auschwitz, but it's likely they perished at Sobibor).

On Valdik's List, next to the names of some of the aunts or uncles, like Arthur Porges, he added a notation such as "Family of 4, A," indicating the entire family was murdered at Auschwitz. For survivors, such as his Aunt Valerie "Válda" Mařík and several cousins, he wrote what he knew of their circumstances. Under the heading "3rd Generation" he added his own name: "Oswald Holzer left Prague May 21, 1939, for China & USA."

My father never revealed how he had gathered all this information or how he felt about this incredible tragedy. We didn't speak; he typed with two fingers as I watched and swallowed tears. When he finished the list, he penciled in a few Czech diacritics on appropriate letters as if an ultimate sign of respect.

That was as far as my father could go with his meticulous list because he was scarred by the past, his double life, in a way that I had never known or could have then comprehended. Say this aloud: "Forty-four of my relatives were murdered. My grandpa, my grandma, my great-grandma, great-aunts, great-uncles, cousins. . . ." Imagine how that feels. Most of us have no idea.

Whenever I imagine typing a list of forty-four of my closest relatives who were murdered, I believe I can never conjure the depth of emotion he kept buried inside. How can we relate to this? I have no doubt that many in Syria or Sudan have kept their lists of relatives who were murdered as well as people in Rwanda, Armenia, Cambodia, and Bosnia. Why so much senseless death? I can't answer that, but I can learn from my father's actions and my grandfather's request and do my part to help generations to come—through education and inspiration—not merely to care but to act. We must choose peace and compassion for "suffering humanity" if we want to end prejudice and stop hate.

O = Uncle   GO = Grand

MARIE HOLZER (G.m.) TZ 42 +TZ Pneumonia (age 86)   TZ- Terezin
  ERNEST HOLZER F.TZ 42 + A-(age 57)   80   A- Aushwitz
   OLGA HOLZER M.TZ 42 + A-(age 54)
   RUDOLPH WINTERNITZ TZ 42 + A- 42 (O)
   OLGA WINTERNITZ(HOLZER) TZ 42 + A.42 (A)
   MARIK JAROSLAV, 41 Slave lab.Germany (survived) (O)
   VALERIE MARIK,evicted from Neveklov 41,survived in Prague (A)
 : LEO HOLZER,TZ 42 last day of war in transport aut of the camp. (O)
   ELSA HOLZER,TZ 42 Survived' (A)

3rd Gen.: OSWALD HOLZER,Left Prague may 21 39 for China & USA
          HANA WINTERNITZ (BELL)in England in school in 39
          GEORGE MARIK,41 Slave labor,Germany (Survived)
          PAVEL MARIK,in hiding in Prague with his mother (Survived)
          HANUSH HOLZER,TZ 42,(survived)

          GUSTAV STEINER,TZ-42 +A 42 (O)
          ERNA STEINER,TZ 42 A+ 42   (A)
            LILLY STEINER,TZ 42 + A 42
            HANA STEINER (---)TZ 42 A+ 42 1 year old baby + A 42
          KARLA FISCHER TZ 42 A +42   (A)
            ROBERT FISCHER,hiding in the bohemian country
                       during the war with the underground(survived)
            ROBERT FISCHER,Emegrated to England(survived)
          KANTOR EDWARDTZ 42,A+ 42   (O)
          KANTOR BERTA TZ 42,A+ 42   (A)
          KANTOR JOE TZ 42,A+ 42
          KANTOR EDITH (---) TZ 42.A +42
          KANTOR ?   TZ 42 A +42
      OHRENSTEIN OTA TZ 42 A+ 42   Mother Ema Holzer + 37
      OHRENSTEIN FRANC . Belsen & Dachau (survived & returned)
      OHRENSTEIN HEDVA 42 TZ A= 42
      FURTH JAKUB (FERDINAND) TZ 42 A+42
      FURTH REGINA TZ 42 A+42 (GA)
      FURTH JOSEPH TZ 42 A+42 (Family of 4)
      FURTH ERNEST 39 Belsen + ?(Family of 3)T 42 A+42
      PORGES GUSTAV TZ 42 A+42
      PORGES JULIE TZ 42 Survived
      PORGES ARTHUR TZ 42 A+42 (Family of 4)
      PORGES OTTO TZ 42 A+42
      PORGES(KLEIN)OLGA TZ 42 A+42 (Family of 4)
      HOLZER RUDOLF & WIFE (Ruzkolhotice)TZ 42 A+42
      HOLZER ROBERT & WIFE (?) TZ 42 A+42
      HOLZER ERNEST (Jenikov) TZ 42 A+42

20. "Valdik's List" of family members who perished in the Holocaust or
escaped; created 1993, coinciding with movie premiere of *Schindler's List*.

After my parents' deaths and the discovery of the letters, as I
spent years doing research, I began to absorb the reality that my
grandparents—my flesh and blood—had disappeared from this
world as the result of a developed plan for human extermination

on a scale beyond comprehension. Did their lives begin with that as their *fate*? I pondered this idea, trying to reach a place where any of it made sense.

Little from my long-ago high school history classes helped me understand how the Holocaust could happen in supposedly civilized twentieth-century Europe, much less what sort of people could carry out such an atrocity. One of these people, Reinhard Heydrich, especially haunted me. I felt compelled to learn all I could about him, but nothing I uncovered even hinted at the answer to the most puzzling question: How could any human being be so inhuman?

Some historians recognize Heydrich as second to Heinrich Himmler in importance within the Nazi leadership after Hitler. From 1934 Heydrich commanded the secret state police, the Gestapo. In 1938 he took control of ss actions against the Jews. He directed the ss mobile killing squads—the Einsatzgruppen—that herded Jews into ghettos or forests and massacred them. When the Nazi government claimed that Kristallnacht was a spontaneous uprising of German citizens, evidence showed that Reinhard Heydrich, then a general in the ss and chief of the Reich's Main Security office was involved just before that "spontaneity." On November 9, 1938, Heydrich sent a telegram to various ss members stating that "demonstrations against the Jews are to be expected in all parts of the Reich during the coming nights, November 9/10." The subsequent violent action against Jews was publicized and caused worldwide alarm, but there was little response. I couldn't help but think about this in the context of the recent global suppression of protests and attacks on human rights and the free press.

When Hitler placed Heydrich in charge of the protectorate, he declared martial law while proceeding with a plot to annihilate resistance in the Czech Lands. He earned the nickname the "Butcher of Prague" for his brutality. As Hitler and Himmler, along with other Nazis, plotted the downfall of Europe's Jewish population, they turned to Heydrich to take on a growing role at the January 1942 Wannsee Conference, which Heydrich chaired in a beautiful lakeside suburb near Berlin.

The functionality of how to deal with what Hitler described as the "Final Solution to the Jewish Problem" was a primary reason for the meeting. Lt. Col. Adolf Eichmann, Heydrich's assistant, took notes for the fifteen men who attended, representatives of the German government and military branches who would need to deal with the practical matters. Most of the fifteen men held doctorates. The Heydrich-led discussion included details for what had begun as coerced Jewish emigration and confinement in city ghettos to mobile killing squads and a growing program of their forced removal into concentration camps. Decisions were made prior to the meeting. The intent was to inform the various lines of Nazi bureaucracy of their coordination responsibilities. One element discussed was the opening of three death camps, Treblinka, Belzec, and Sobibor, solely to exterminate people.

In my history classes I learned the names of Himmler, Göring, and Eichmann, all part of Hitler's inner circle. But in Florida during the 1960s there wasn't much time spent in class on this subject, and we were taught about three concentration camps: Auschwitz, Dachau, and Buchenwald. I'd never heard of Sobibor until 2008 through research at the United States Holocaust Memorial Museum. I checked the transcripts from my father's 1989 interviews to see if Dad had offered any insight into Heydrich and his colleagues.

Heydrich's name was indeed there, in a taped account of my father's 1963 trip back to his homeland, where he heard much about what had happened to friends and relatives during the war. One of the 1963 storytellers, his good friend Dr. Vladimír "Vláďa" Wagner, was a classmate from Charles University Medical School. Vláďa was an assistant professor and chief of pathology throughout the war at one of the university hospitals. My father said Vláďa, a non-Jew, worked in a hospital called Bulovka in Prague.

Dad recounted the story of Heydrich's death at the time he served as a Reich protector for the Protectorate of Bohemia and Moravia.

I had already learned this much from reading about him in several sources, including a 2002 special purpose publication from the Ministry of Defense of the Czech Republic: *Assassination, Operation Anthropoid, 1941–42*. Heydrich was fearless but arrogant, described by Hitler as "the man with the iron heart." He liked to ride in an open-top green Mercedes without an armed escort, believing he so frightened the Czechs that no one dared attack him; he was wrong. Two agents, one Czech, one Slovak, trained in Britain—Jan Kubiš and Josef Gabčík—parachuted into the protectorate and lay in wait as Heydrich's car rounded a corner on May 27, 1942.

As the vehicle braked into the curve, Gabčík jumped in front of the car and pointed a machine gun at Heydrich. The weapon failed. In a split second Kubiš pulled a special bomb from his briefcase. Equipped with a sensitive impact fuse, the hand grenade was planned to maximize its effect around the target without harming the attacker with shrapnel. The bomb missed the target, exploding above the running board in front of the right rear fender. It ripped out the right door and punctured the vehicle's body embedding shrapnel into Heydrich. Although wounded, Heydrich managed to draw his pistol, shooting back at the assassins before he collapsed in the street. They escaped.

The attack occurred near Bulovka Hospital, where Vláďa Wagner worked. Heydrich was taken there and attended by Czech physicians, while a Nazi doctor was summoned from Berlin, likely on Hitler's orders. Heydrich appeared to be recovering, when his condition deteriorated and he died on June 4. By most accounts his death was the result of an infection caused by horsehair upholstery fragments that were driven deep into his wounds by the explosion.

This is where Vláďa's account takes a surprising turn. When Heydrich was brought in, according to Vláďa, he was not critically injured but was bleeding profusely and needed transfusions. The Czechs in the hospital wanted to get rid of him before the Nazi doctor arrived. So, according to Vláďa, they tampered with the blood transfusion, perhaps hastening his death.

Vláďa noted that throughout the war Czechs were forced to

donate blood to treat wounded German soldiers. He claimed he and other Czech doctors developed techniques to disguise blood types, making the blood extracted under duress useless and occasionally fatal. Dad recognized why Czechs didn't want to help the Germans, but as a physician sworn to help all patients, he balked at sabotaging the blood supply. Vláďa's reply: "Well, it was total war."

With a refreshed memory of this story and its significance, I began studying various sources to learn more about the official version of Heydrich's death. Beyond the consideration that he had died from a post-injury infection, there was speculation by one expert that blood tampering may have played a factor.

I could not find any scholarly confirmation of Vláďa's story about Heydrich's death, but I did uncover one intensely personal coincidence. On the same day, May 27, 1942, that Heydrich was attacked, a group of Bohemian Jews, possibly including Arnošt and Olga, were transported first from Terezín to Lublin, Poland, then on to the Heydrich-inspired Sobibor death camp, where they were gassed or shot. The strange timing seemed to me a small piece of justice in an otherwise horrendous story. I hoped he suffered.

As much as they hated Heydrich and the Nazis, some Czechs blamed the resistance for instigating the terror by carrying out the assassination. When the countrywide Nazi butchery ended, more than sixteen hundred Czechs in the small villages of Lidice and Ležáky were executed in revenge. The brutality was named "Heydrichiáda."

It's no wonder Vláďa and his compatriots remained quiet about their exploits even after the war. I have neither reason to doubt the story he told my father nor suspicion that he'd be less than honest with his old friend. We'll never be certain of what happened because the hospital records are incomplete or destroyed and all the witnesses are deceased.

As with so many discoveries I've made along my journey, another powerful connection between my father and the monster Heydrich came about through a chain of events that began when I found a pair of old riding britches stored among my mother's linens. They

were made of heavy gray cotton with blue-and-red-striped pip-
ing and patched with worn suede. Attached to the belt line were
blue suspenders held in place by slightly rusted clips and tiny buttons. I recognized the pants; they were from my father's story of
his escape from his Czechoslovak army regiment, which I had
recorded in 1989: "I was dressed in an army uniform, but I had
my riding britches and boots. The color of these riding britches
was a standard gray, so anybody who was riding a horse could
have had a pair just like this. All I needed to get out of the army
was to replace my military jacket and get a shirt with a necktie."

As I unfolded these remarkable pants that had kept my father
safe, I could hear his voice telling me about outsmarting the Wehrmacht guard at the gate as he read to him in German from his
own order to inspect the meat supply, then sneaking past the Nazi
ss on the Brno train back to Prague in late March 1939.

As I rifled through unidentified black-and-white photographs,
I found one of my smiling father wearing his Czechoslovak army
uniform and the gray pants like the ones I possessed. He stood with
his hands in his blossomed pockets, his gun holstered and fastened
to the belt. My breath left me as the photo dropped to the floor.
On the back was my father's distinctive handwriting: "November 17
by Krina on the riverbank of Tisza River." The photo was taken in
1938, four months before Nazi troops marched into snowy Prague.

I clipped the picture to the pants' suspenders, next to its tiny
buttons, and continued sorting through the letters. After a couple
of months working day in and day out, I'd become overwhelmed
by the vast quantity and emotional impact of my research. The
more I grasped what had happened in my father's world during
that time, the more overwhelmed I became and the less sure I
was of how to proceed.

Before I received the translated letters, in 2008, I could tell by
the few written in English that the collection was full of beauty
and adventure but also loneliness, confusion, and grief. It was a
rugged world for me to live in day after day. I began to fear that
the project of organizing, translating, and preserving the letters

was more than I could handle. A friend suggested that it might help if I stood in my father's escape pants and experience their power. At first it seemed a strange suggestion, but I was desperate, so one morning I walked into my writing room and did just that. Alone, I took off all but my underwear and put on the pants my father had worn when he escaped the situation that would have most surely ended in his demise.

As the suspenders hung on my shoulders supporting the heavy cotton bloused pant legs, I noticed there was an old yellowed tissue in one pocket. I held it in amazement. I rubbed the gray fabric thinking they had once served my father well and played a fateful part in my own existence. I felt certain I was chosen to inherit the responsibility of sharing the voices from the letters with the world. It was as if some higher being had whispered a spell to me to speak for these people—my father and his parents, aunts and uncles and cousins, best friends, classmates, drinking buddies, and acquaintances—without fear of consequences. From then on my connection to the pants guided me on my journey to understand my father's young life and what it meant.

In late 2009 I found perhaps the eeriest link between my family and Reinhard Heydrich. While examining the pants for the umpteenth time, I noticed Czech words engraved on the three small brass buttons circling the edge of the waistband. With my magnifying glass, I jotted down the letters. My Czech American assistant, Kathy Bowman, translated the words. On one button: *Zakázková práce*, which meant "custom work" or "specially ordered." On the second: *Ferd. Chára Pardubice*. Kathy recognized Pardubice as a Czech town about one hundred miles east of Prague and speculated that *Ferd.* might stand for the name Ferdinand. We assumed "specially ordered" meant the pants had been fashioned for the army.

I Googled the town name, and the search engine revealed a University of Pardubice. I sent an email message and photographs of the buttons to its library link with my question: "Did Pardubice have a button-making plant there before the war?" Responding in English the next day, the university librarian Jana Ivanegová wrote: "There has never been a button factory in the town of Pardubice. But there used to be a riding battalion. Therefore, the riding britches appeared. Ferdinand Chára was a known military tailor, born April 20, 1892, in the village of Zdechovice (approximately fifteen km far from Pardubice). This man was executed in 1942 in Pardubice by Nazis for his cooperation with Alfred Bartoš, group Silver A commander. This group helped to organize the attempt on Heydrich's life."

Incredibly, the buttons that held up the pants that gave my father his freedom were made by a brave man who had assisted in the most famous and heroic act of Czech resistance, the assassination of Heydrich. This courageous tailor gave his own life to end the life of the Butcher of Prague, the man who had viciously engineered the death of my grandparents and millions of other innocent people. I so wished I could tell my father about the news the precious buttons had held all these years, waiting to be part of the vast mosaic I was assembling.

We shall not cease from exploration, and the end of all our exploring will be to arrive where we started and know the place for the first time.

—T. S. Eliot

My grandparents Arnošt and Olga mentioned "Providence" several times in letters to my dad, and it has played a repeated role in my experience. Springing from Latin roots, *Providence* is defined in the *Merriam-Webster Online Dictionary* this way: "(1a) divine guidance and care; (1b) God conceived as the power sustaining and guiding human destiny."

I remain at a loss to explain why the "guided human destiny" for my grandparents and so many others, about six million Jews and five million non-Jews, had led to an unimaginable outcome of barbaric slaughter in the Holocaust. But I have come to believe that Providence led me to tell a story that allows them to be alive once again for remembrance and universal learning.

Because my parents departed this earth without a word about what lay hidden in those Chinese boxes, I will never fully understand why they joined forces to keep the collection of letters, photographs, and personal mementos secret. I can speculate that my mother's complicit role was because she recognized that if my father brought them out to discuss, he might have been forced to answer questions he never wanted to face with his adult children. My mother protected my dad as his parents had protected him long ago. The Holocaust was the most formative event of his life. Because these items were the remaining tangible representation of loved ones left behind and mostly lost forever, it was beyond consideration that my father would have thrown them away.

My dad knew the letters would bring closure to a story he could never bring himself to tell or write. These and a resilient character are the greatest offerings he gave me beyond his own stories and moral integrity. Until I read the letters, I had no idea there were questions to which I needed answers. These primary sources provided remains from people, places, and events that occurred and testimonials to reconstruct aspects of daily life. These paper people of my writing room became my companions. Going into their pain, akin to having open-heart surgery without anesthesia, helped me move to the other side of it. As T. S. Eliot said, "I know the place." I now recognize the learning opportunities that should be offered beyond the four walls of my writing room and my responsibility to this cause of working toward compassion and peace, not hatred and war.

Words cannot protect us from harsh realities—lives shattered, or worse, by atrocities and war—but when I read them, I am with my parents, then and now. Their lives were filled with sorrow and joy, and they consciously chose to live with the light, not darkness. The finest bequest they left their children was the lens they provided to look at the world—a hopeful vision that illuminates the oneness of the human family.

My grandfather Arnošt left behind the legacy of how we should live within that family, each doing our best to help humanity. Seek something that matters; it's what's inside of us. I am so proud of how my father lived out my grandfather's wish.

Rest easy in deserving peace, my dear Valdik. Amen.

21. Valdik and Ruth Holzer, Indialantic, Florida, 1968.

ACKNOWLEDGMENTS

When I was old enough to wonder, I could have asked my father a lot more questions about his past. But I imagine even if my dad had brought forward the four hundred letters he'd hidden away and spun the narrative in his own manner, without me reading each letter the complete story may never have been told. Dad would have whitewashed the painful content as he once again attempted to protect his family and perhaps his own sanity and soul.

It is with a great sense of gratitude I first acknowledge my father for his role in *My Dear Boy* and its companion book, *Adventurers against Their Will: Extraordinary World War II Stories of Survival, Escape, and Connection—Unlike Any Others*. By not revealing the Holzer collection before your death, the full truth became available to hear in its unvarnished version. In this manner we learn firsthand from the actual human circumstance as it unfolded. Dad, you made it so I couldn't get your stories out of my head. Then you passed the baton to me for my turn at recounting your dazzling legacy. I suspect you knew precisely what would happen. Thanks, Dad. I hope the stories told make people live differently—fighting for what some may foolishly describe as the impossible, identifying peaceful solutions, and creating a world in which people treat each other with respect and dignity.

Because of Mom's guidance, I was prepared for this gargan-

22. Joanie Holzer Schirm and cousin Tomáš Mařík at author's great-grandfather Alois Holzer's grave marker honoring family members who perished in Holocaust. Jewish cemetery, Benešov, Czech Republic, 2009.

tuan task. She was never one to shy away from taking on a meaningful cause. When she did, she always carried it out with grace and sincerity. She once wrote: "The talents and character we carry with us are the tools that build our lives, step by step. Old Man Luck plays a part for sure, but the realization of our goals comes from real effort and work." As I worked hard to put the pieces together to the puzzle I'd found in the letters, I never lost sight of my mother's abiding faith in a higher being.

My parents engendered empathy in me for contemporary social justice issues and protection of human rights. In their learning-rich environment they instilled in me the love of people, travel, photography, adventure, history, and reading (even if mostly news and tabloid magazines). They ensured I'd incorporate these loves into the last worthy assignment of my life, creating a more profound, emotional relationship with history. I now realize stories can ignite readers from what was to what can be, allowing us to build a bridge to a better world.

For a decade, through the magic of the letters, I lived in the 1930s and 1940s sepia-toned world. I got to know my grandparents, who'd vanished from the earth via murderous Nazi hands. Knowing turned to loving—and then mourning. I was introduced to some three hundred people I'd never met before, most of whom were deceased. I traveled with each of them, carrying heavy baggage, as they maneuvered an unfair world of hatred. I experienced vicarious suffering as well as love.

In my previous professional career I'd never been a *real* author— just a periodic article writer for technical journals or occasional mouth-off as a community activist in *Orlando Sentinel* opinion columns. I discovered writing can be a lonely business. Worse yet, the revolution in modern book publishing unfolded before my eyes in everyday breaking news stories. Brick-and-mortar bookstores closed, and large publishing companies gobbled up smaller houses. The trending welcome mat seemed chiefly extended to already-famous authors or celebrities, while electronic book formats matured and gained popularity. Not only did I have to earn a home-schooled M FA in creative writing and self-awarded honorary doctoral degrees in world, Jewish, Chinese, and Czech history; I had to become educated about the new publishing world. Every day was a real-life test to see if I could get all the pieces to fall together so they fit. History, culture, human nature, language, writing, and publishing all became lobe-shaped protrusions seeking their own spots in the jigsaw of my life.

Now I know what it feels like to be an insecure author of not one but three books meant to be read by strangers, not just family and close friends. Thankfully, I have many supporters who coached and coaxed me on to reach the point where I stopped fiddling with the final draft and let the words speak for themselves. I engaged experts in their fields, further ensuring that phrases spoke intelligently. These patient people have been mentors, counselors, knowledge wells, manuscript readers, and promoters. In autumn 2013, four months after the publication of my first book, I received confirmation that I was on the right track. *Adventurers against Their Will* won first place in Biography Nonfiction (as well as first place for Best Ebook Trailer) in the 2013 Global Ebook Awards. Further confirmation came in 2014, when the book was published in Czech, my dad's native tongue, and a lesson plan was published in German by the International Tracing Service (ITS). The Florida Department of Education's "Just Read, Florida!" promotion of the book as "recommended reading" reinforced the unbreakable interconnection of literature and history, necessary disciplines in Holocaust education. In 2016 it was included in the prestigious book *Essentials of Holocaust Education*, edited by Samuel Totten and Stephen Feinberg, under the chapter "Incorporating Literature into a Study of the Holocaust."

My most heartfelt thank-you is reserved for my family. My husband, Roger Neiswender, has been at my side every step of the way. He's given me encouragement, sage wisdom, and love when I needed it most. He never lost faith in or patience with me. He is my guiding light.

My daughter, Kelly Schirm Lafferman, and her two children, Ty and Ava, who live a bicycle ride away, were unrelenting cheerleaders. My son, Derick Schirm, offered constant "you are up to the task" reassurance and shared hours of conversation equating current world events to this era. My brother, Tom, and sister, Pat, patiently answered my questions about what they remember from our childhoods and loving parents. Visiting from California, Tom was the first hot-off-the-press galley proofreader of *Adventurers against Their Will*. Nieces and nephews Mark, Scott, Holly, and Beth encouraged me as they wondered if their aunt would ever finish.

Cousin Tomáš Mařík and my extended family in the Czech Lands made this excursion into a world far from mine seem as if it were next door and made me feel I belonged. My father's first cousin Jiří Mařík was Tomáš's beloved father; Valdik and Jiří's bond was active and devoted. The letters I found from Jiří to my father, written while Jiří and his family were trapped behind the Soviet Iron Curtain, show the depth of that relationship as my father offered to host young Tomáš in America for his education. The response is heartbreaking as the family realized if they sent him to America, he might never return. It was typical of the difficult choices of that era. As travel restraints softened in the 1980s (some five years before the Velvet Revolution), my father hosted Jiří for a whirlwind trip across America. That experience is worthy of a subsequent book, a story of a gentleman who spent his entire life behind the wall of totalitarianism, finally experiencing what the world of freedom felt like in America. Jiří died in 1989, six months before his own country reestablished democracy.

Tomáš represents the best of the Czech people, with his tenacity, humor, and kindness. He captured our hearts as he drove Roger and me on the route my father traveled in 1937–39 and to Sobibor death camp to honor my grandparents, Tomáš's great-uncle and aunt. Together we stood at the Benešov grave marker of our shared paternal great-grandparents, Alois and Marie Holzer, and where some of my dad's cremated ashes were interred. Tomáš and I will forever have a friendship bond, well beyond blood, like that shared by our fathers. I sincerely thank Tomáš and all my Czech cousins for their open-arms welcome.

Like family is Kathy Bowman (née Pinkas). This Czech American young woman arrived in my life as she completed an MBA and yearned to work a little on the side. The "side" turned out to be forty-hour workweeks at my home, helping me piece together the puzzle at hand. She served as a crucial assistant for anything needed to get this gargantuan job done and became my friend. While I completed my first book, Kathy gave birth to her son, Adam, a lucky little boy who is learning fluent Czech in addition to his native English. During the writing of *My Dear Boy*, she and her husband, John, brought daughter Anna into our world. Kathy, you are the best!

The expert translation and editorial superstars ensured my work had the clarity and factual correctness it deserved. Primary translators and Czech history mentors included Mirek Katzl and Lukáš Přibyl. Both talented professionals, they are well versed in the history of the Czech Lands. Formerly the Czech Centre director in Tel Aviv, Lukáš's award-winning documentary series, *Forgotten Transports*, brought forward images of what several of the letter writers had suffered at Terezín. I will never forget the stories revealed in these three unique films. Amid images of Holocaust atrocities (many never seen before), Lukáš showcased the tenacious human spirit as he highlighted courageous and ingenious survivors. I only wished Arnošt and Olga had been a story of survival. A unique volunteer translator, the late Gerhard "Jerry" Bochner, a Czech American Holocaust survivor, holds a place forever in my heart. Jerry helped me at the beginning deliver voices from Czech to English. He kindly shared his language skills plus his own incredible story in a memoir appropriately titled "Surviving the Holocaust with Chutzpah."

Early developmental edits came from Doug Kalajian and Linda Carbone. Without their resourceful culling, the reader might never have waded through the chronicle to find the pearls.

Alice Peck, editor for *Adventurers against Their Will*, also served as primary editor for *My Dear Boy*. A veteran who helps authors maneuver the maze of storytelling and modern publishing, she is wise, caring, and thorough. Alice knew from her first encounter with the material how essential it was to get the story told. Working together on three books written over eight years, we've had many occasions to celebrate—and shed more than a few tears. Without Alice I don't know where I'd be.

To my literary agent, Steve Harris, I am forever thankful for his sincere recognition that the story held by *My Dear Boy* deserved to be shared. His enthusiast professional approach and kind heart made seeking a publishing house an experience I will always cherish.

To Michlean "Miki" Amir of the United States Holocaust Memorial Museum (USHMM), a massive thank-you for being an enduring friend and expert. She arrived in my life in 2008 as I did my first in-depth research at that incredible facility. Miki, who shares an even more immediate Czech heritage, became my steadfast ally to get this story of struggle and triumph told.

To Rollins College history professor Yusheng Yao, I owe a debt of gratitude for being a first reader of draft manuscripts for early versions of *My Dear Boy*. His shared wisdom about China and the Chinese people warmed my heart. Yusheng's review of *My Dear Boy* was for readability, accuracy, and the addition of pinyin names to Chinese cities. His research interest is twentieth-century Chinese history, especially the issue of modernity and cultural identity. I will never forget our philosophical discussion about what sustained my father during the worst time of his life.

My dear friend, first reader Barbara (née LaCapra) Kercher, provided unimaginable hours of listening and reading time. Her insight into the emotional toll that an effort like this takes, developing as she observed my mood swings, allowed me to be myself with no mask required. Her moral support will never be forgotten.

Another early reader and lifetime friend, Amy Sewell Rickman, read the draft manuscript in two and half days. She gave me her "I love it" thumbs up—life's full circle with her childhood familiarity of my parents.

Others who helped along the way with knowledge, clarification, or advice include Bill Younglove; P. R. "Rick" Pinard, Ph.D.; Petr Šraier; Jacob Labendz; Linda Vlasak; Peter Black; Margit Meissner; Owain Bell; Pam Kancher; Mitchell Bloomer; and many more.

In addition to the terrific resources available at the USHMM, I want to thank other organizations that assisted my research. The Jewish Museum in Prague, archives at Charles University and Benešov, memorials at Terezín and Sobibor, the YIVO Institute of Jewish Research in New York City, the Holocaust Memorial Resource and Education Center of Florida, and Yad Vashem in Jerusalem all participated. Associations that played a critical part in research, as well as moral support, include the American Friends of the Czech Republic (AFOCR), the Czechoslovak Genealogical Society International (CGSI), the National Czech and Slovak Museum and Library in Cedar Rapids, and the Jewish Genealogical Society

23. Valdik Holzer, Melbourne, Florida, 1967.

of Greater Orlando (JGSGO). Search engines like Google and websites Ancestry.com and Geni.com brought forward helpful information. Facebook, LinkedIn, and Twitter helped spread the modern words. They enriched my knowledge of the time period, culture, and people that live in my books. I remain very thankful to organizations that dedicate their efforts to ensure accurate information is available to us all—a task not so simple in this age of online malfeasance.

Acknowledgments

Finally, a big thank-you for bringing *My Dear Boy* to published life goes to Potomac Books' talented publishing team at the University of Nebraska Press. Tom Swanson, Joeth Zucco, Rosemary Sekora, and Anna Weir led the way. Elizabeth Gratch provided copyediting and an observation that will stay with me forever. "So many books make clear how meaningful every life is, but this one ripples outward, across time and space, amplifying human life and the power of writing and observing—and caring so much."

My father's story gave me permission to dream of a book that could share an against-all-odds-story that will live on as one that teaches us humanity. From the moment of my discovery of my grandfather Arnošt's altruistic last wish, my life mission became clear: illuminate his message on how to achieve a more humane world.

Imagine a world where we take loving care of one another. It is possible. It's up to you to follow through with what you've learned.

INDEX